The IDEA MAGAZINE FOR TEACHERS® MAILBOX®

2007–2008 YEARBOOK

HOLY REDEEMER CATHOLIC SCHOOL
127 N. ROSA PARKS WAY
PORTLAND, OR 97217

The Education Center, Inc.
Greensboro, North Carolina

The Mailbox® 2007–2008 Kindergarten–Grade 1 Yearbook

Managing Editor, *The Mailbox* Magazine: Amy Erickson

Editorial Team: Becky S. Andrews, Diane Badden, Kimberley Bruck, Karen A. Brudnak, Kitty Campbell, Jenny Chapman, Kathy Coop, Pam Crane, Lynette Dickerson, Lynn Drolet, Sarah Foreman, Margaret Freed (COVER ARTIST), Tazmen Hansen, Marsha Heim, Lori Z. Henry, Dorothy C. McKinney, Sharon Murphy, Jennifer Nunn, Tina Petersen, Mark Rainey, Greg D. Rieves, Kelly Robertson, Hope Rodgers, Eliseo De Jesus Santos II, Rebecca Saunders, Donna K. Teal, Joshua Thomas, Zane Williard

ISBN10 1-56234-855-8
ISBN13 978-156234-855-7
ISSN 1088-5528

Printed in the United States of America.

The Education Center, Inc.
P.O. Box 9753
Greensboro, NC 27429-0753

Look for *The Mailbox*® *2008–2009 Kindergarten–Grade 1 Yearbook* in the summer of 2009. The Education Center, Inc., is the publisher of *The Mailbox*®, *Teacher's Helper*®, *The Mailbox*® BOOKBAG®, and *Learning*® magazines, as well as other fine products. Look for these wherever quality teacher materials are sold, call 1-800-714-7991, or visit www.themailbox.com.

Contents

Math Units

Science and Social Studies Units

Teacher Resource Units

Thematic Units

Arts & Crafts

Arts & Crafts

Bright Blossom

Showcase several of these sunflowers on a hallway wall to create a giant-size welcome. Or use the project to launch a sunflower unit. **For an easier version,** fold the petals and leaves in advance. (You can stack them and fold several at once.)

Materials for one sunflower:

student photo (optional)
4" brown circle
eight 2½" x 7" yellow construction
  paper petals
four 2" x 5" green construction
  paper leaves

green crepe paper streamer
brown marker or crayon
glue
clear tape

Steps:

1. Draw brown dots on the brown circle. Then glue a student photo to the circle if desired.
2. Fold the petals and leaves in half lengthwise and then unfold them.
3. Glue the petals to the back of the brown circle.
4. Twist the streamer to make a stem. Then tape one end of it to the back of the blossom.
5. Glue pairs of leaves together and then use tape and glue to attach the leaves to the stem.

Elizabeth M. Kirby
Paul Bank Elementary
Homer, AK

Paper Tree Sculpture

With this clever idea, no cutting is needed to transform a paper bag into a three-dimensional tree! For easy management, work with small groups of students to complete the project.

To make a tree, begin with a flat brown paper lunch bag. Make several tears from the top of the bag to the middle of the bag. Then open the bag and stand it on a flat surface. Next, hold the middle of the bag with two hands. Twist the bag a few times to form a trunk. Then flatten the bottom of the bag to form a base for the tree. To make branches, gently separate the torn strips and then twist each of them tightly. If desired, tear pieces of green tissue paper to make leaves and crumple pieces of red tissue paper to make apples. Then glue the leaves and apples to the branches.

Joy A. Kindoll
Winn Primary School
Carrollton, KY

"Beary" Simple

Whether you use this idea to complement a favorite bear book or to reinforce the letter *B,* it's sure to prompt lots of smiles! To make one bear, stuff a medium brown paper lunch bag with newspaper. Fold over the top two inches of the bag and then staple the bag closed. Next, cut out a brown bear head, two brown arms, and two brown feet (patterns on page 17). Draw a face on the bear. Cut two inner ears from pink construction paper and glue them in place. Glue the head to the top of the bag. Glue the arms to the back of the bag and the feet to the bottom of the bag as shown. Cut two small ovals from black construction paper and glue them to the paws. Draw details on the feet as shown. Finally, glue a 3½" x 5" brown oval to the bear's belly.

Dick Freeman
Benson Hill Elementary
Renton, WA

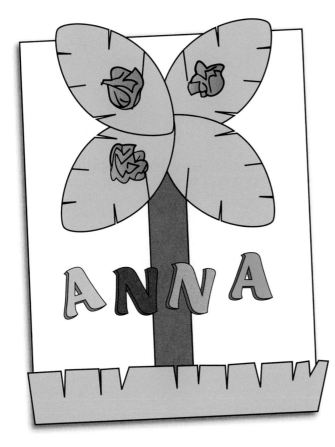

Snip, Snip, Crumple!

This follow-up to *Chicka Chicka Boom Boom* by Bill Martin Jr. and John Archambault is perfect for the beginning of the school year. To make one project, glue a brown paper tree trunk to a vertical sheet of paper. Fringe-cut the edges of four large leaves and then bend the resulting tabs forward. Glue the leaves to the top of the trunk, leaving the edges free. Crumple three or four squares that have been cut from a brown paper lunch bag and roll them into balls to make coconuts. Glue the coconuts to the tree. Next, make cuts along one long edge of a green crepe paper streamer to make grass. Glue the grass to the bottom of the paper, keeping the cut edge free. To personalize the project, arrange self-adhesive craft foam letters on the paper or stamp the appropriate letters using alphabet stamps and colorful ink.

Arts & Crafts

Fine-Feathered Friend

Stand a flock of these cute owls on a shelf or table for an eye-catching fall display.

Materials for one owl:
construction paper copy of the owl patterns on page 18
paper lunch bag
newspaper
craft feathers
yellow and orange paper scraps
stapler
scissors
black marker or crayon
glue

Steps:
1. Stuff the bag with crumpled newspaper.
2. Fold the top corners of the bag inward as shown. Then fold over the top of the bag. Staple it closed.
3. Cut out the patterns. Cut two eyes from yellow paper and a beak from orange paper.
4. Draw a pupil on each eye. Then glue the eyes and beak in place.
5. Glue the body to the bag. Glue a few feathers to the body.
6. Cut two feet from yellow paper. Glue them in place.
7. Glue the wings to the bag and then bend them forward.

Veronica McElroy
Deposit Elementary
Deposit, NY

Step 2

Jumbled Pumpkins

Give students practice tracing and cutting with this project fresh off the vine! In advance, cut out a copy of the pumpkin pattern on page 18 and an enlargement of the pattern that is about 7" x 9". To make one project, trace the small pumpkin several times on a horizontal 9" x 12" sheet of white paper, positioning the pumpkin at various angles. Color each tracing and draw faces on the pumpkins if desired. Next, turn the paper over, being careful to position it right-side up. Trace the enlarged pumpkin on the back of the paper and then cut out the tracing. Glue the cutout to a larger piece of orange paper. Then trim the paper, leaving a narrow border. Repeat the gluing and trimming process with a larger piece of black paper to frame the one-of-a-kind pumpkin artwork.

Valerie Wood Smith
Morgantown, PA

web wonder

To "spin" a glistening web, cut several slits around the edge of an eight-inch black poster board circle. Tape one end of a length of string to the back of the circle. Next, pull the string through a slit and to the front of the circle. Then poke the string through a different slit and pull it to the back of the circle. Continue making a web as described until a desired effect is achieved. Then tape the loose end of the string to the back of the project. (Trim the string if needed.) To make a spider, glue together two one-inch black pom-poms. Then glue lengths of yarn to one pom-pom so that they resemble legs. After you glue the spider to the web, embellish the web with silver or iridescent glitter glue.

Keely Peasner
Wilkeson, WA

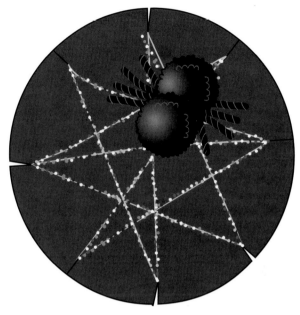

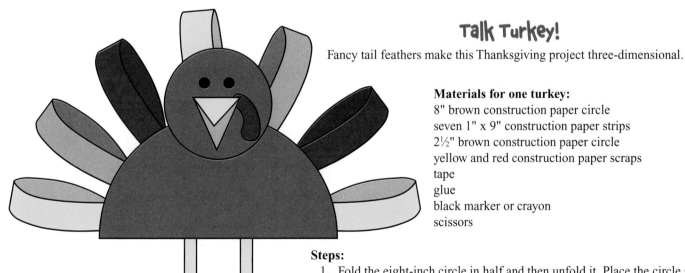

Talk Turkey!

Fancy tail feathers make this Thanksgiving project three-dimensional.

Materials for one turkey:
8" brown construction paper circle
seven 1" x 9" construction paper strips
2½" brown construction paper circle
yellow and red construction paper scraps
tape
glue
black marker or crayon
scissors

Steps:
1. Fold the eight-inch circle in half and then unfold it. Place the circle so the fold line is horizontal.
2. Fold each paper strip in half without creasing it. Tape the ends of each strip to the top half of the circle so that the strip extends beyond the top of the circle.
3. Glue the circle closed.
4. Draw two eyes on the 2½-inch circle. Fold a small piece of yellow paper in half and then cut a triangle along the fold. Glue the resulting beak in place.
5. Cut a wattle and two legs from paper scraps. Glue them to the turkey. Cut two triangles and then glue them to the legs to make feet.

adapted from an idea by Dawn Best
Dunkerton Elementary, Dunkerton, IA

Arts & Crafts

Triangular Tree

Not only is this adorable project simple, but it is also a perfect gift! To make one, glue three jumbo craft sticks together to form a triangle. Allow the glue to dry. Then paint the sticks green. After the paint dries, glue a brown craft foam rectangle to the bottom of the tree to make a trunk. Then choose an option below.

To make an ornament, tie a length of gold cord to the project to make a hanger. Crumple a piece of yellow tissue paper and then glue it to the top of the tree. Use a hole puncher to make circles of various colors. Then glue the circles to the tree.

To make a frame, cut a piece of paper the same size and shape as the tree. Glue a photo to it. Glue the paper to the back of the tree so the photo shows in the opening. Adhere magnetic tape to the back of the project.

Rachelle Price
Belle Alexander School
Kewanee, IL

Roly-Poly Pal

What better way to welcome winter than with this self-standing snowpal?

Materials for one snowpal:
three 3" x 7" strips of white paper
5" x 6" construction paper or tagboard rectangle
construction paper scraps
clear tape
stapler
scissors
glue
cotton balls

Steps:
1. Form each strip of white paper into a cylinder and secure it with tape.
2. Staple the cylinders to one another to make a snowpal.
3. Staple the bottom cylinder to the 5" x 6" rectangle.
4. Cut facial features and arms from construction paper and then glue them to the snowpal.
5. Complete the snowpal with desired construction paper details.
6. Stretch out a few cotton balls and glue them around the snowpal.

Jo Fryer
Kildeer Countryside School
Long Grove, IL

Branching Out

Making this unique greeting card reinforces seriation skills. To begin, arrange seven different-size green construction paper semicircles in a row from the largest to the smallest. Then fold over the straight edge of each semicircle to make a tab for gluing. Next, glue a brown rectangle (tree trunk) near the bottom of a vertical red paper rectangle. Glue the largest semicircle at the top of the trunk. Then glue the remaining semicircles in descending order, as shown, to make a tree. Cut a star from yellow paper and glue it at the top of the tree. Next, fold a sheet of white paper in half to make a card. Inside, write a holiday message or staple a holiday letter. Then glue the tree to the front of the card.

For an easier version, instead of using graduated semicircles, use green paper strips of different lengths. Glue the strips directly to the red paper without folding them.

Tenille Weaver
Holly Springs Elementary
Canton, GA

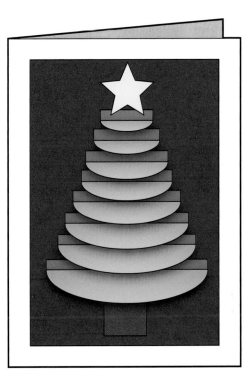

Pleasing Penguin

No patterns are needed to make this stately fellow!

Materials for one penguin project:
2" orange circle
4" x 9" white rectangle
2½" x 6" white rectangle
4" x 9" black rectangle
9" x 12" blue paper
orange scrap paper
glue
2 hole reinforcers
scissors
cotton swab
shallow container of white paint

Steps:
1. To make the background, tear one long side of the 4" x 9" white rectangle. Glue the rectangle at the bottom of the blue paper so the straight edges are aligned.
2. Glue the smaller white rectangle to the black rectangle as shown.
3. Adhere the hole reinforcers near the top of the black rectangle.
4. Cut a triangle from orange scrap paper to make a beak. Glue it in place.
5. Glue the resulting penguin to the background.
6. Cut the orange circle in half to make feet. Glue the feet in place.
7. Use the cotton swab to make paint prints (snowflakes) on the background.

Heartwarming Card

Deliver a Valentine's Day message with this adorable mouse! To prepare, cut a large heart from a vertical 9" x 12" sheet of tagboard to make a tracer. For each student, cut two three-inch hearts from red paper and two smaller hearts from pink paper.

To make one card, fold a 12" x 18" sheet of red paper in half and then position it with the fold on the left. Trace the tagboard heart, aligning its left side with the fold, and then cut out the tracing. Next, write a holiday message in the card or write the message on a large blank index card and then glue it in the mouse card. To complete the card, draw two eyes above the point of the heart. Glue a pom-pom or a piece of crumpled tissue paper on the point to make a nose. Fold two red hearts and two pink hearts in half and then unfold them. Glue each pink heart on a separate red heart. Then glue the resulting ears in place.

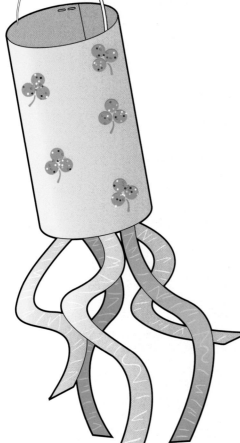

Shiny Shamrocks

To make a windsock, position a 9" x 12" sheet of yellow paper horizontally. Dip a fingertip in green paint and make prints in groups of three so they resemble shamrocks. Then sprinkle gold glitter on the wet paint. After the paint dries, shake off any excess glitter and use a green marker to draw a stem on each shamrock. Next, turn the paper over, making sure the shamrocks are right side up. Tape or glue six 12-inch lengths of green and yellow crepe paper streamers along the bottom edge of the paper so the colors alternate. Then roll the paper into a cylinder with the streamers to the inside. Staple the overlapping edges together. To make a hanger, tape a length of string to the inside of the cylinder on opposite sides.

Janet Boyce
Cokato, MN

Hippity, Hop!
This bunny is made mainly with two white circles!

Materials for one bunny:

two 8" white circles	crayons, including pink
small pink pom-pom	glue
white curling ribbon	black marker
cotton swab	shallow container of paint
scissors	for decorating the bow tie

Steps:

1. Draw two ears on one circle, as shown, and then cut them out. Save the scrap paper.
2. Color the inner ears pink and then glue the ears to the intact circle. Gently curl the tips of the ears forward.
3. Use the marker to draw two eyes and a mouth. Glue the pom-pom to the face to make a nose.
4. To make whiskers, glue lengths of curling ribbon to the face on either side of the nose.
5. Fold the scrap paper in half and cut a bow tie on the fold as shown.
6. Unfold the bow tie. Color it. Then dip a cotton swab in paint and make paint prints on the bow tie. Allow the paint to dry.
7. Glue the bow tie to the bunny.

Step 1

Step 5

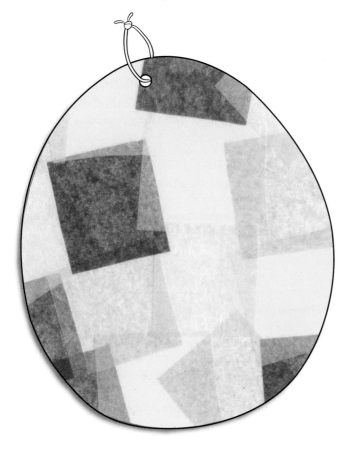

"Eggs-traordinary" Suncatcher
For this Easter project, remove the backing from an eight-inch square of clear Con-Tact covering. Place the Con-Tact covering sticky side up. Then place rectangular pieces of pastel tissue paper all over the covering, allowing the tissue paper to overlap. Next, remove the backing from a different eight-inch square of Con-Tact covering. Place the covering on the project sticky side down. Press the covering firmly to seal the edges. Next, trace a seven-inch tagboard egg on the project and then cut out the tracing. Punch a hole in the top of the decorated egg, tie a length of thread through the hole, and then display the egg in a window.

Lenny D. Grozier
Endicott, NY

Arts & Crafts

Splendid Spring Mobile

Materials for one mobile:
copy of the butterfly wing and body patterns on page 153
construction paper copy of the spiral pattern on page 19
9" x 12" construction paper (wings)
2½" x 9" black construction paper rectangle
construction paper scraps, markers, or crayons
scissors
glue
stapler

Steps:

1. Cut out the butterfly patterns. Fold the 9" x 12" construction paper in half. Trace the wing pattern on the fold as shown. Cut out the tracing and then unfold it.
2. Trace the body pattern on the black rectangle, cut it out, and glue it to the wings. Decorate the wings.
3. Cut out the spiral pattern. Staple the pointy end of the spiral to the bottom of the butterfly.
4. Suspend the completed mobile.

Diane L. Tondreau-Flohr
Kent City Elementary
Kent City, MI

Step 1

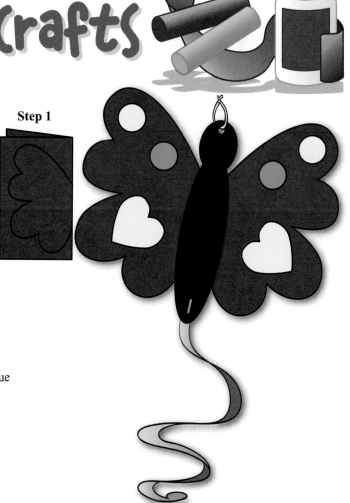

Flowers for Mom

This Mother's Day gift includes thoughtful offers to help at home! The recipient picks a flower to invite the gift-giver to help with the corresponding chore.

Materials for one gift:
several construction paper tulips (patterns on page 19)
7" x 8" vase cutout
several 1" x 12" green paper strips, each programmed with a chore
12" x 18" construction paper
crayons or markers
glue

Steps:

1. Use crayons or markers to decorate the vase.
2. Turn the vase facedown. Squeeze a line of glue along the sides and bottom. Glue the vase to the 12" x 18" paper, keeping the top edge of the vase free.
3. Glue a tulip to one end of each paper strip. Then tuck the flowers in the vase.
4. Write a Mother's Day message on the project.

Laurie M. Sykes, Boyce Elementary, Ionia, MI

14

Arts & Crafts

Painted Posies

The grass for this project is made with crepe paper streamers. It's a time-saving alternative to cutting paper strips!

Materials for one painting:
empty plastic thread spools
two 12" green crepe paper streamers
9" x 12" white paper
blue crayon without a wrapper
shallow containers of paint
green marker
scissors
glue

Steps:
1. Use the crayon to do a rubbing all over the paper.
2. To make blossoms, make paint prints with the spools. Allow the paint to dry.
3. Draw stems and leaves.
4. Snip one long side of each streamer. Glue the streamers at the bottom of the paper so they overlap and the cut sides are free.

Amanda Renchin, Kid Zone, Lakeville, MN

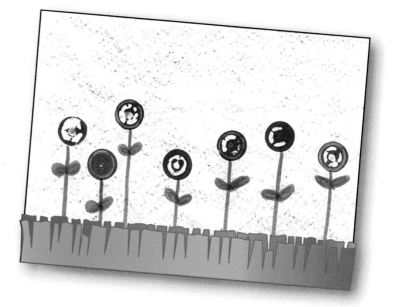

Metallic Masterpiece

For best results, arrange for children to complete this project over two days.

Materials for one butterfly:
copy of the butterfly mat on page 20
5½" x 8½" cardboard rectangle wrapped with aluminum foil
tape
blue pen
permanent markers, including black

Steps:
1. Lightly tape the butterfly mat to the prepared cardboard rectangle. Carefully trace the butterfly with a blue pen, pressing firmly.
2. Remove the butterfly mat. Use a black marker to trace the butterfly image on the foil.
3. Color the butterfly with markers.

Diane L. Tondreau-Flohr, Kent City Elementary, Kent City, MI

15

Pond Pal

To keep the plate from curling as it dries, allow the tissue paper to extend past the edge of the plate.

Materials for one project:
green copy of the turtle head and shell patterns on page 20
white paper plate
small pieces of blue and pink tissue paper
green paper scraps
waxed paper

white glue thinned with water
paintbrush
scissors
shallow container of green paint
glue
black marker

Steps:
1. Put the plate upside down on the waxed paper. Use the paintbrush and glue mixture to adhere blue tissue paper all over the plate. Allow the tissue paper to dry overnight. Trim the excess tissue.
2. Cut out the patterns. Use green paint to make fingerprints on the shell. Let the paint dry.
3. Glue the head to the shell and draw two eyes. Cut four feet and a tail from green paper. Glue them to the shell and then glue the turtle to the plate.
4. Cut green lily pads and glue them to the plate. Pinch the pink tissue paper squares to make flowers and then glue them near the lily pads.

Lori L. Scott, Central Point, OR

"Hand-Some" Flag

For a simple, eye-catching display, showcase several of these flags with the poem below.

Materials for one flag:
silver adhesive stars
construction paper for the painting and for backing it
washable red, white, and blue paint in shallow containers
paintbrush
glue

Steps:
1. Brush blue paint on the thumb and palm of one hand. Brush red and white paint on alternating fingers as shown.
2. Make a handprint on a piece of construction paper. Let it dry.
3. Put adhesive stars on the blue paint print.
4. Glue the painting on different-colored paper to frame it.

When it's time for the pledge to start,
I put my right hand over my heart.
I promise to honor the red, white, and blue,
And to America I will always be true.

adapted from an idea by Beth Howard
Red Arrow Elementary
Hartford, MI

16

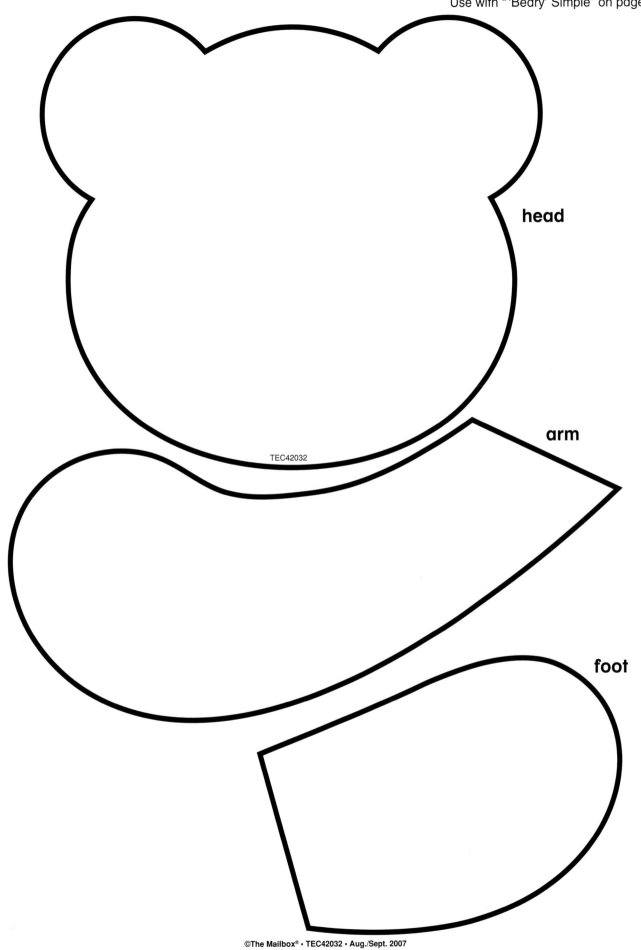

head

arm

foot

TEC42032

Owl Body and Wing Patterns

Use with "Fine-Feathered Friend" on page 8.

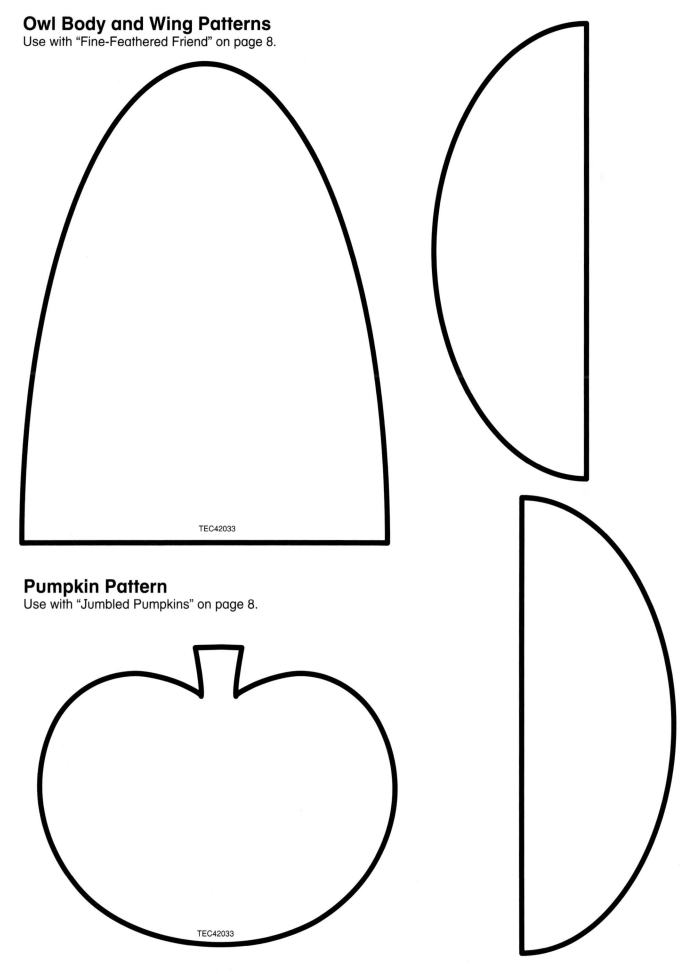

TEC42033

Pumpkin Pattern

Use with "Jumbled Pumpkins" on page 8.

TEC42033

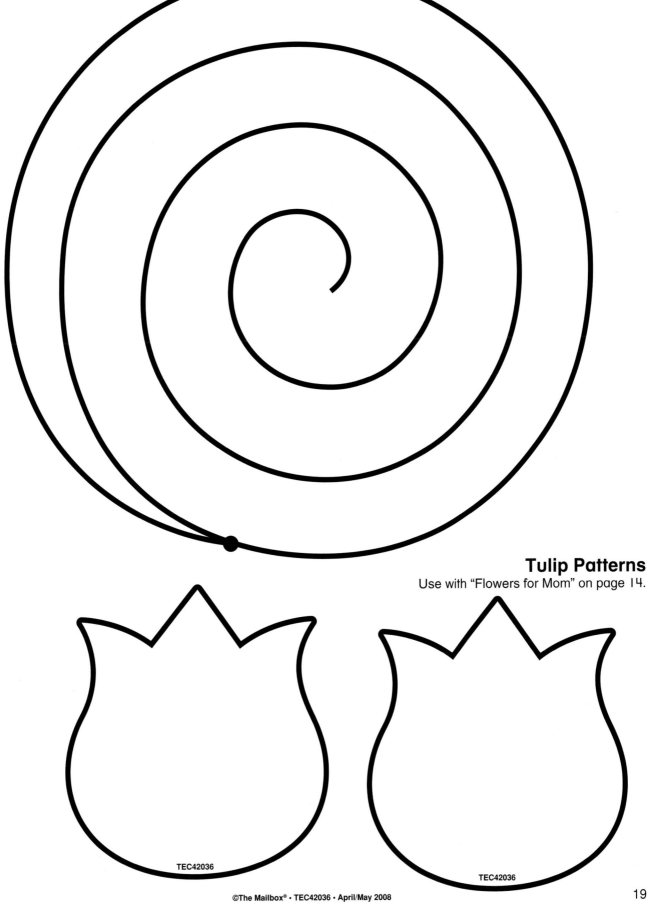

Tulip Patterns
Use with "Flowers for Mom" on page 14.

TEC42036

TEC42036

Butterfly Mat
Use with "Metallic Masterpiece" on page 15.

TEC42037

Turtle Head and Shell Patterns
Use with "Pond Pal" on page 16.

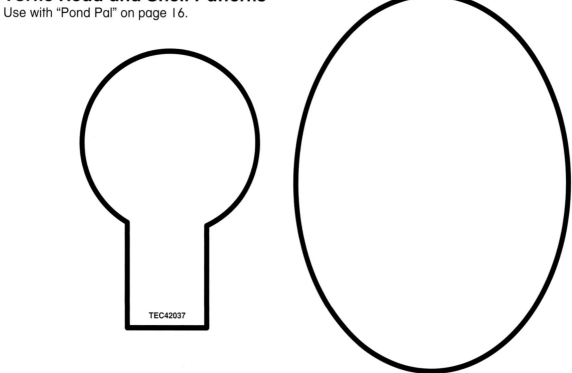

TEC42037

THE BOOK CORNER

The Book Corner

Roses Are Pink, Your Feet Really Stink
by Diane deGroat

Poor Gilbert learns a lesson about friendship the hard way! Put a fun twist on the lesson with this pocket chart activity. To prepare, write on a separate sentence strip each line of the poem shown, replacing each of several words with a blank space. Write each omitted word (and any punctuation that follows) on a separate heart cutout. Display the poem in a pocket chart and place the hearts in random order below it. To begin, have students read the words. Guide youngsters to use rhyming and other literacy skills to complete the poem with the hearts. Then prompt a class discussion about the poem's message. *Reading*

> Roses are red.
> Violets are blue.
> Be nice to your friends,
> And they will be nice to you!

Amazing Grace
Written by Mary Hoffman
Illustrated by Caroline Binch

There's something special about Grace! Students learn what it is with this introductory activity. In advance, address a large mailing envelope to your class. Decorate the envelope and label it with synonyms for the word *amazing*. Put the book in the envelope and seal it. Then arrange for a school staff member to deliver the package to your classroom.

After you accept the delivery, read the envelope and wonder aloud what is inside. Then open the envelope and remove the book with great fanfare. Read the title and point out that the words on the envelope have nearly the same meaning as the word *amazing*. Next, read the book aloud, encouraging students to think about why the author used that word to describe Grace. At the end of the story, students are sure to agree that Grace's determination and attitude are truly amazing! *Analyzing characters*

Julie Hays, Maryville, TN

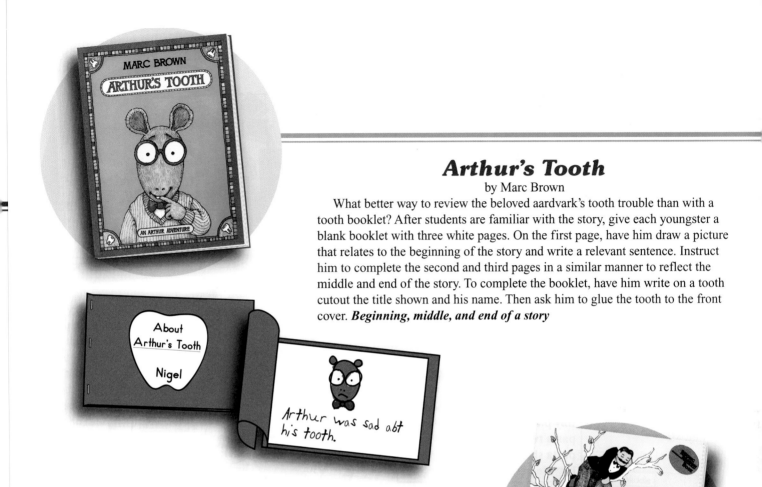

Arthur's Tooth
by Marc Brown

What better way to review the beloved aardvark's tooth trouble than with a tooth booklet? After students are familiar with the story, give each youngster a blank booklet with three white pages. On the first page, have him draw a picture that relates to the beginning of the story and write a relevant sentence. Instruct him to complete the second and third pages in a similar manner to reflect the middle and end of the story. To complete the booklet, have him write on a tooth cutout the title shown and his name. Then ask him to glue the tooth to the front cover. *Beginning, middle, and end of a story*

Caps for Sale: A Tale of a Peddler, Some Monkeys and Their Monkey Business
by Esphyr Slobodkina

With this follow-up activity, students don't trick monkeys to get the peddler's caps back. They count coins instead! Post a bare-branched tree on a bulletin board. Make several caps of various colors and write a grade-appropriate price on the back of each cap. Then display the caps on the tree so the prices are concealed. After you read the story to students, give each youngster some imitation coins. Next, invite a youngster to name a color. Remove a corresponding cap from the tree, reveal the price, and have the youngster read it aloud. Then ask each student to model the money amount. After you confirm the correct way(s) to model the amount, tack the cap at the bottom of the display to begin a stack of caps. Continue as described until all the caps are stacked for the peddler! *Modeling money amounts*

Butterfly Life Cycle Pattern and Word Cards
Use with *"The Very Hungry Caterpillar"* on page 24.

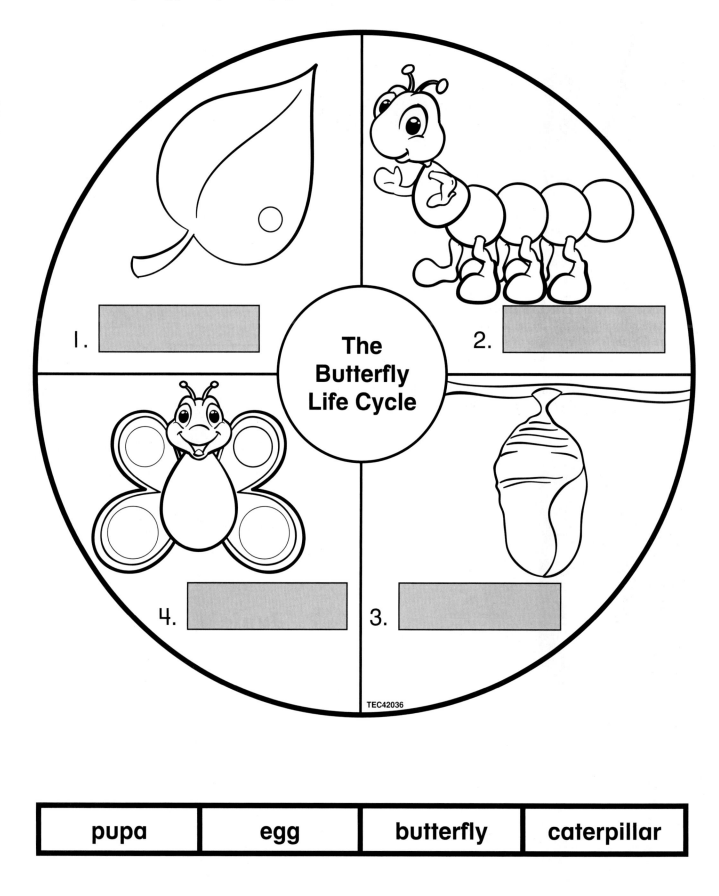

The Butterfly Life Cycle

1.

2.

3.

4.

TEC42036

| pupa | egg | butterfly | caterpillar |

BUILDING MATH SKILLS

Building Math Skills

Buggy Skills Check

Number sense

This easy-to-adapt activity allows you to assess a variety of math skills. Color and cut apart a copy of the ladybug cards on page 33. Working with one student at a time, assess one or more of the skills below as described. If desired, invite each youngster to use a magnifying glass to examine the cards or to look for designated ladybugs. It's a surefire way to spark her interest!

Counting: Have the child count the spots on chosen bugs.

Identifying sets: Arrange the cards faceup. Announce a number from 1 to 10. Then ask the youngster to find the ladybug with that many spots.

Comparing sets: Set out two cards and ask the child to tell which bug has more spots.

Matching sets and numbers: Instruct the child to match the ladybug cards with corresponding number cards.

Understanding addition: Show the child two ladybugs. Have her tell how many spots are on each bug and how many spots there are in all.

Jenny Baker
Beall Elementary
Frostburg, MD

What Comes Next?

Patterning

Nearly no advance preparation is needed for this idea! Place a variety of colorful plastic utensils in a basket, and set out a supply of white paper and crayons. To complete the activity, a child forms a pattern with the utensils. Then he uses the crayons to record the pattern on a sheet of paper. He makes and records different patterns in the same manner.

Katie Klipp, Bob Jones Elementary, Greenville, SC

Totals With Teamwork

Addition

For this hands-on activity, divide students into groups of three. Give each group six red cubes, six blue cubes, two dice, and a recording sheet similar to the one shown. The first child rolls a die, places the corresponding number of red cubes in front of the group, and writes the number on the recording sheet. The next youngster rolls a die, places that many blue cubes in front of the group, and writes the number. Then the third student determines the total number of cubes that have been set in front of the group and writes the sum. The youngsters switch roles and continue as described to complete the recording sheet.

Rozlyn M. Burrows
Delaware Academy Elementary
Delhi, NY

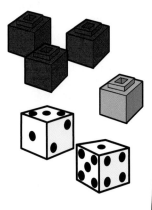

Names _Miller   Desmond   Katie_

Recording Sheet

1. $\underset{\text{red}}{2} + \underset{\text{blue}}{3} = \underset{\text{in all}}{5}$

2. $\underset{\text{red}}{4} + \underset{\text{blue}}{5} = \underset{\text{in all}}{9}$

3. $\underset{\text{red}}{3} + \underset{\text{blue}}{3} = \underset{\text{in all}}{6}$

4. $\underset{\text{red}}{1} + \underset{\text{blue}}{6} = \underset{\text{in all}}{7}$

5. $\underset{\text{red}}{3} + \underset{\text{blue}}{1} = \underset{\text{in all}}{4}$

Building Math Skills

Pages of Geometry

Identifying shapes in real-life objects

With this picture-perfect class book, students learn that math is everywhere! During a walk in and around the school, encourage youngsters to look for objects with geometric shapes. Take an individual photograph of each student pointing to a shape he found. Later, secure each photo to a separate sheet of paper. Ask each student to write a caption, similar to the one shown, for his picture. Then have him sign his name. Bind the completed pages into a class book titled "We See Shapes!"

Angie Kutzer
Garrett Elementary
Mebane, NC

Pasta Possibilities

Sorting

Stretch students' thinking with this hands-on activity! Place in an opaque container a class supply of uncooked pasta of various colors and shapes. Draw a large Venn diagram. Then label each circle with a chosen pasta attribute and the center of the diagram "Both." Place the diagram on the floor and gather students around it. Next, invite each student, in turn, to take a piece of pasta at random and place it on or outside the diagram to correctly categorize it. After all the pasta is correctly sorted, guide students to discuss the resulting groups. **For an easier version,** have youngsters sort the pasta in two or more ways without a Venn diagram.

Lidelle Corey
Chicod School
Greenville, NC

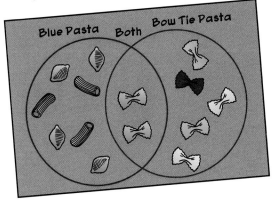

Hop to It!

Skip-counting

Use this variation of the traditional hopscotch game either indoors or outdoors. Label the boxes on a hopscotch grid with a chosen skip-counting sequence. (For indoor play, make a labeled grid on a shower curtain liner.) To play, invite a youngster to toss a beanbag on the grid. As the youngster hops to the box on which the beanbag landed, lead the class in saying the corresponding numbers. Then have the youngster pick up the beanbag, hop back to the beginning of the grid, and give the beanbag to the next student. **For more advanced students,** use a blank grid and ask youngsters to count by twos, fives, or tens by rote.

Karen Nelson
H.O.M.E. Center for Education
Kissee Mills, MO

Building Math Skills

Timely Tune

Telling time

Which hand is which? That's what students learn with this clock song! As you lead youngsters in each toe-tapping verse, point to the corresponding hand on a clock.

(sung to the tune of "Are You Sleeping?")

Here's the minute hand.
Here's the minute hand.
It is long. It is long.
There are 60 minutes.
There are 60 minutes
In one hour, in one hour.

Here's the hour hand.
Here's the hour hand.
It is short. It is short.
There are 24 hours.
There are 24 hours
In one day, in one day.

Kathryn Trimm
Glenn Harmon Elementary
Arlington, TX

Coin Caterpillars

Money

To prepare this small-group game, color and cut out a copy of the spinner pattern from page 35. Then use a brad to attach a paper clip to it. Give each student a copy of a game card on page 35. Set out a supply of imitation coins for game markers.

To take a turn, a youngster spins the spinner and names the coin. If he has a matching coin on his game card that is not covered, he puts a game marker on it. If he does not have a matching coin to cover, his turn is over. Students take turns as described until each player covers all his coins. **For more advanced students,** have each student name the value of the coins he spins and ask him to determine the total value of his caterpillar.

Diane L. Flohr
Orchard Trails Elementary
Kent City, MI

Clip to Answer!

Data analysis

This beginning graph is a snap to prepare. Program a horizontal 8½" x 11" sheet of paper as shown with a chosen question and two or three answer choices. Add illustrations if desired. Position a page protector horizontally, with the holes at the bottom, and slide the paper into it. Then tie a length of ribbon through each hole. Post the page protector within students' reach and secure the free ends of the ribbons. Place a class supply of personalized clothespins nearby.

Have each youngster respond to the question by clipping her clothespin to the ribbon that corresponds with her answer. Then guide students to analyze the results. To explore another topic, replace the programmed paper.

Erin Ropelato
Clinton, UT

Building Math Skills

It Takes Two!

Two-digit numbers

Use the number cube pattern on page 36 for both options below. To make a cube, cut out a copy of the pattern. Then fold it on the thin lines and secure the sides with clear tape.

Identifying numbers: Make two cubes as described above. Have two students roll the cubes, place them side by side, and then name the resulting two-digit number.

Place value: Make two different-colored cubes as described above. Designate one cube for tens and the other cube for ones. Give each student a four-by-four grid that you have programmed with two-digit numbers, using only the digits 1 through 6. Also give each student some game markers. Have students play as in the traditional game of lotto, except that to call a number, two students roll the cubes and arrange them to form a two-digit number. They tell the group how many tens and ones the number has and then announce the number.

adapted from an idea by J. J. Markle
Hanover, PA

There are two tens and four ones.

Valuable Lineup

Patterning, coins

This small-group activity is rich with skill-boosting possibilities! Have each youngster arrange several imitation coins in a chosen pattern. Then ask him to read his pattern by naming each coin or by identifying each coin's value. **For more advanced students,** follow up by asking each youngster to determine the combined value of his first three coins or the value of his entire coin lineup.

Karen Saner, Burns Elementary, Burns, KS

Handy Comparison

Nonstandard measurement

For this kid-pleasing activity, ask your school's principal to make a tracing of his hand. Cut out several copies of the tracing and write the principal's name on them. Help each youngster cut out and label tracings of her own hand. Invite each student to measure several classroom objects with the cutouts of the principal's hand and then with her own hand cutouts. No doubt youngsters will be eager to share the results with the principal!

Ellen Samuel
Ohlone Elementary
Watsonville, CA

Building Math Skills

"Sum" House!
Two-digit addition

This cute project has stellar reminders to add ones before tens. Make one copy of page 37 and then write a two-digit addition problem on each window. Give each student a copy of the programmed paper. Have him write his name on the roof and solve the problems. Then invite him to color the house, cut it out, and incorporate it into an illustration.

Nancy House
Gardens Elementary
Marysville, MI

Pond Favorites
Graphing

Here's a class activity that doubles as a display idea! Title a blue-backed bulletin board "What Would You Most Like to See at a Pond?" Draw and label a different pond animal on each of four colorful index cards. Post the cards in a column on the board, leaving a small amount of space between them. Next, have each youngster illustrate her answer on a separate white index card. Display students' cards to the right of your cards to create evenly spaced rows of like animals. Then number the resulting columns to complete the graph. After you discuss the graph with students, decorate the board with student-made cattails and grass.

Rita Skavinsky
Minersville Elementary Center
Minersville, PA

Homey Hives
Addition

What's the buzz? The mat and bees on page 38 can be used two different ways!

Adding sets: Have each child color a copy of page 38 and cut out the cards. Guide students to model several addition problems by placing a set of bees on each hive and determining the total number of bees. Then ask each youngster to glue some bees on each hive. Help her write the corresponding addition sentence below the hives.

Addition facts: For this partner game, give two students a copy of the mat and the bee cards. Also give them several cards with addition problems. Have each player claim a hive. To begin, each player takes a problem and states the answer. If the players' sums are different, the player with the greater sum puts a bee on her hive. If the players' sums are the same, each player puts a bee on her hive. Play continues as described with the remaining cards. The player with more bees wins.

adapted from an idea by Tara Viola
West New York Public School #2
West New York, NJ

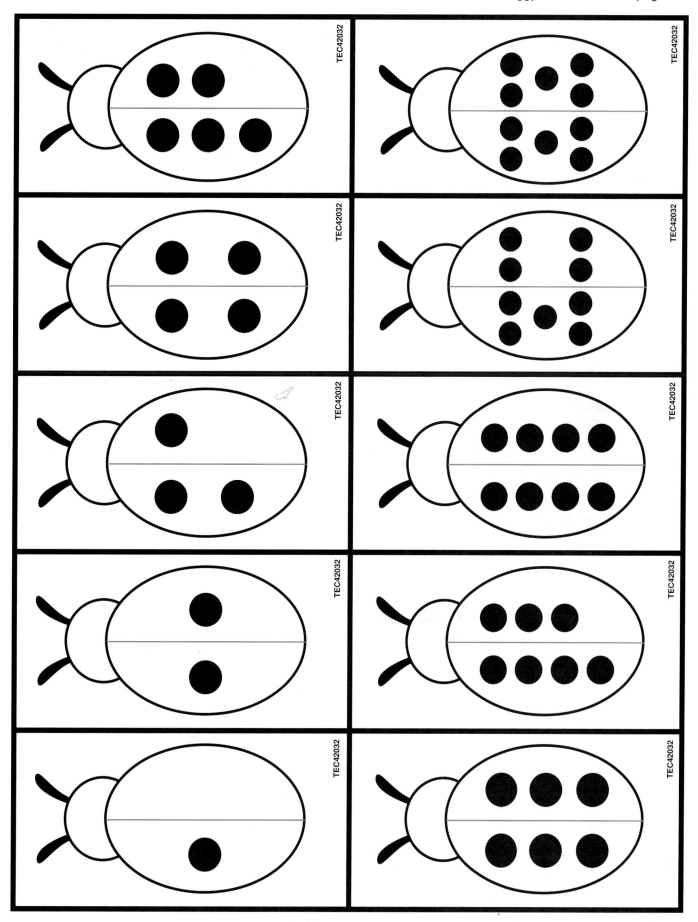

Yummy Cookies

Cut. Sort.

Glue. Explain your thinking.

Mel's Cookies

Max's Cookies

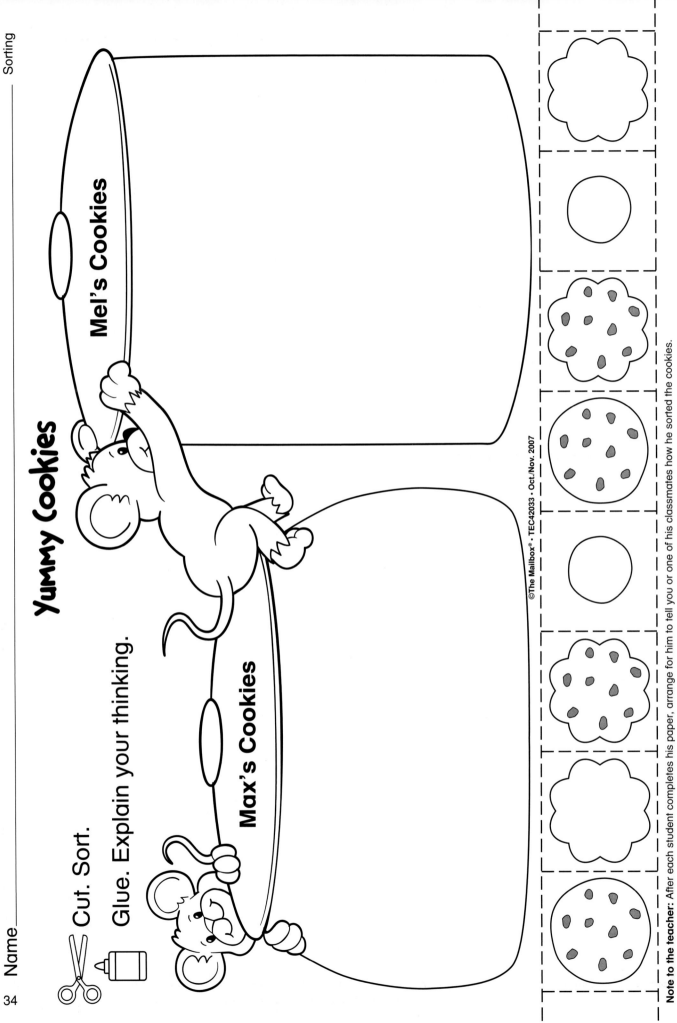

Note to the teacher: After each student completes his paper, arrange for him to tell you or one of his classmates how he sorted the cookies.

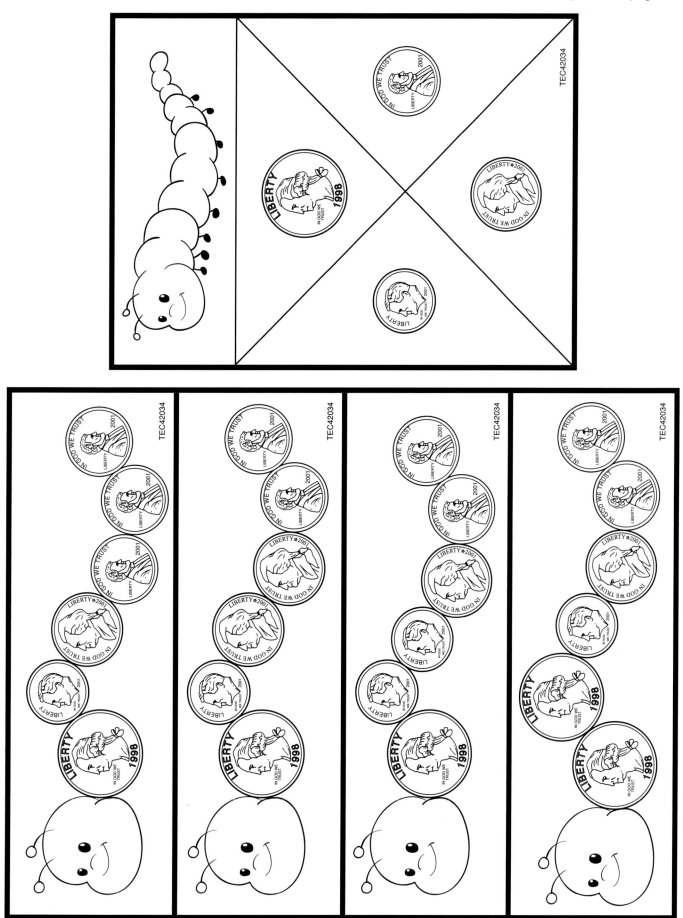

Number Cube Pattern

Use with "It Takes Two!" on page 31.

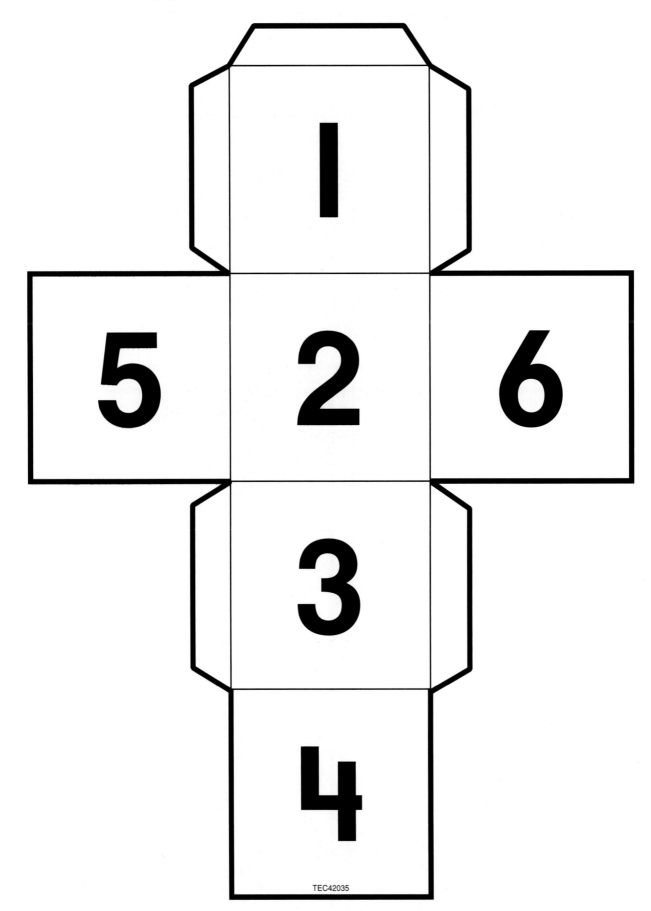

TEC42035

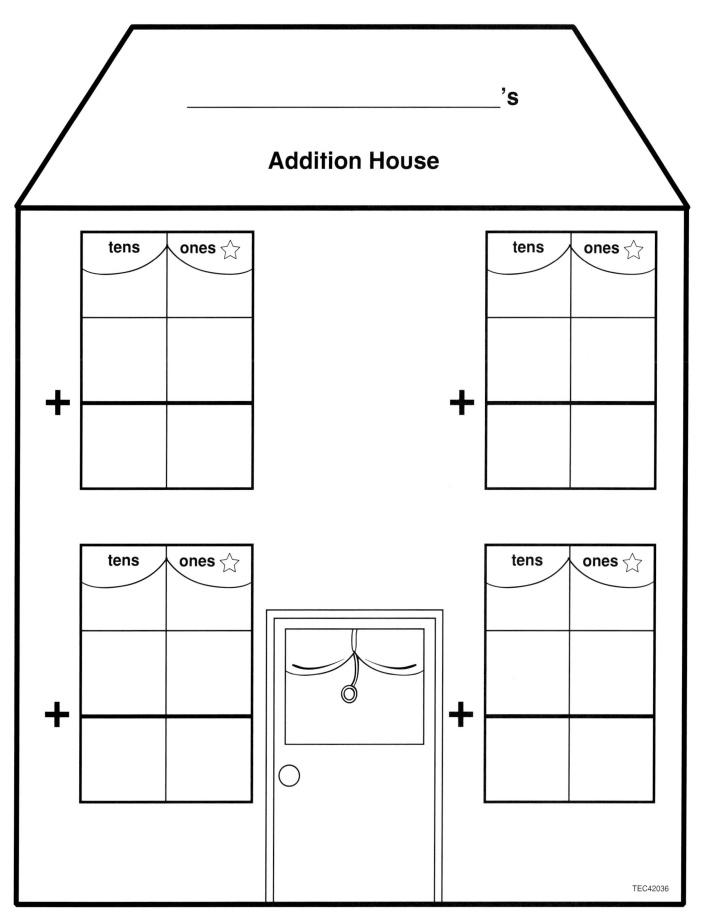

_____'s

Addition House

tens	ones ☆

+

tens	ones ☆

+

tens	ones ☆

+

tens	ones ☆

+

TEC42036

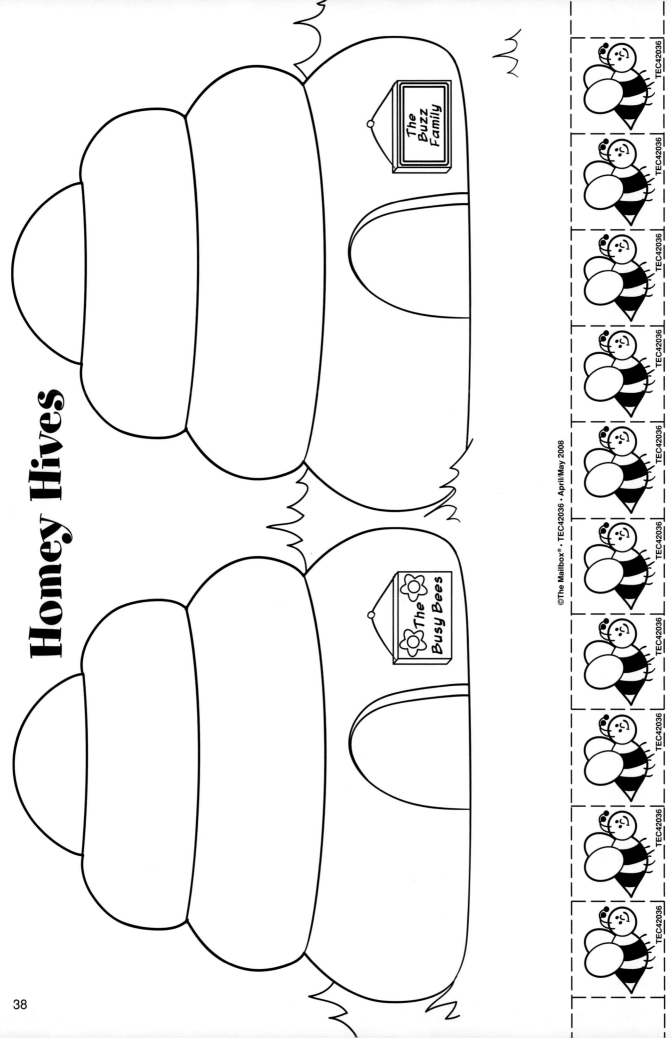

Homey Hives

The Buzz Family

The Busy Bees

Note to the teacher: Use with "Homey Hives" on page 32.

Classroom Displays

It's Going to Be a Colorful Year!

Making this hallway display is not only a great addition to a color unit, but it is also a simple art project for the beginning of the year. Have students use construction paper of different colors to make various school items. Showcase the artwork for open house or to set the tone for an exciting school year!

Nikki Buwalda, Randolph Elementary, Randolph, WI

Our Reading Tree

For this year-round display, post a bare-branched tree within students' reach. Add a leafy treetop and a title. Early in the fall, decorate the tree with apples labeled with letters or short *a* words. As the seasons change and students' skills progress, focus on different reading skills and update the tree with cutouts such as colorful fall leaves, snowflakes, and kites. (Remove the leafy treetop during winter.) It's an easy way to give students "tree-rific" skills practice!

Sandra Stalling, Stout Field Elementary
Indianapolis, IN

Students are sure to agree that making these dripping ice-cream cones is fun, hands down! Trace each child's hand on colorful paper with his fingers outstretched. Have him cut out the tracing, write his name on it, and then glue it to a cone. Title a jumbo ice-cream cone and arrange students' mouthwatering projects around it.

Roxeen Froio and Joanne Hubert, Florence V. Evans School, Marlton, NJ

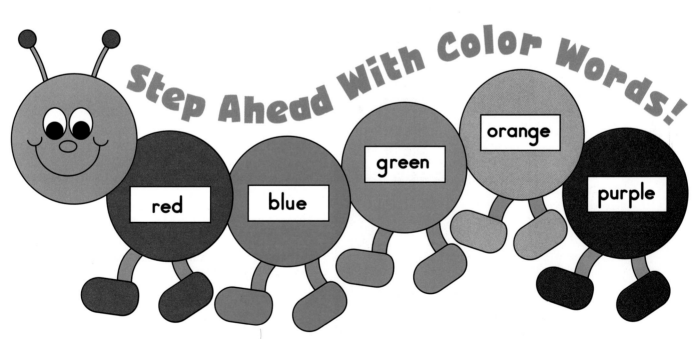

Count on students to use this reading and spelling reference again and again! Label circles of different colors with the corresponding color words. Glue two legs and feet to each circle. Then arrange the circles and a caterpillar head to make a caterpillar. If desired, post a title and embellish the display with grass and flowers.

Rebecca McGill, Tobey Elementary, Scotts, MI

Little Black Bats

Little black bats
Fly through the air.
They don't have feathers,
But they do have hair.

Little black bats
Hang by their toes.
Upside down is the way
They like to doze!

For this "spook-tacular" idea, give each youngster three adjacent sections of a sanitized foam egg carton. Instruct him to paint them with black acrylic paint. After the paint dries, have him fold a pipe cleaner in half, tape it to the project to make legs, and then paint two eyes. To showcase students' bats, display a moon cutout and the poem shown. Then post a leafless branch and hang the bats from it.

Kim Lavery, Sacandaga Elementary, Scotia, NY

juicy green grapes

crunchy orange carrots

cold pink ice cream

yummy yellow banana

shiny red apple

Serve up this idea as part of a nutrition unit, or use it to follow up *Lunch* by Denise Fleming. Have each youngster create a painting of a chosen food and then use an option below to write a caption. Display students' work as desired.

Color words: Write the corresponding color word and the name of the food.

Describing words: Write a phrase that includes a color word and another adjective.

Sentences: Write a complete sentence with correct capitalization and punctuation.

Katie Zuehlke
Bendix Elementary
Annandale, MN

CLASSROOM DISPLAYS

Have a Sweet Holiday!

Here's an adorable way to deliver heartfelt holiday and seasonal greetings. Have each child glue a photograph of himself to the center of a green heart. Instruct him to color stripes on two white candy canes and then glue the candy canes to the heart as shown. Arrange students' hearts with a greeting as desired.

Motrya Mayewsky
Arlington, VA

To make this "tree-rific" display, give each youngster a simple tree cutout with a trunk and a base. Have her glue precut construction paper and gift wrap circles all over the tree and write her name on the base. After she glues the tree to a sheet of paper, invite her to embellish it with glitter glue. Title a large tree and showcase students' projects around it.

Johanna Jansen, St. Agatha School, Portland, OR

For this New Year welcome, give each child two skate cutouts with precut lacing holes (patterns on page 48). After she laces the skates, instruct her to glue two vertical rectangles to the bottom of each skate. Then have her glue a foil-covered craft stick to each pair of rectangles to make blades. Ask her to personalize the blades and connect the skates with yarn. Showcase students' skates on a titled board with snowflakes.

Kelly Muldoon, Amsterdam Elementary, Hillsborough, NJ

Without telling students at first that they will make snowpals, ask each youngster to make three torn-paper circles of different sizes. Instruct him to tear a rectangle and a narrow strip from black paper and two long strips from brown paper. Have him glue the shapes together to make a snowpal and then draw a face and buttons. Display the snowpals as desired. **For a math connection,** ask each youngster to measure his snowpal's arms.

Sheila Criqui-Kelley
Lebo Elementary
Lebo, KS

CLASSROOM DISPLAYS

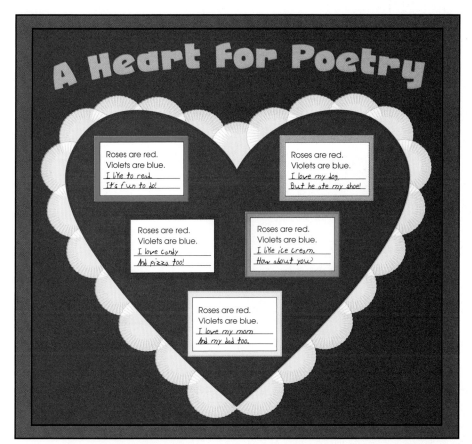

Coffee filters make it easy to create this Valentine's Day display! Post a large heart and then secure coffee filters under the edges of it to create a lacy effect. Help students complete holiday poems. Then post the poetry on the heart and title the frilly display.

Judy Newcomb
Acorn Elementary
Mena, AR

To spark interest in books, give each child a copy of the lion pattern on page 49. Have him write on the lion his name and the title of a book he enjoyed. Then ask him to draw a story-related illustration on provided paper and write a caption. Showcase each youngster's artwork with his lion. Complete the display with a title, a speech bubble, and an enlarged copy of the lion pattern (mask the words and writing lines).

Brooke Shaw, Irmo Elementary, Columbia, SC

There are no shenanigans here—just shining examples of students' work! Title a large pot of gold as shown and post it. Have each youngster personalize a shamrock. Then post her shamrock with a sample of her best work.

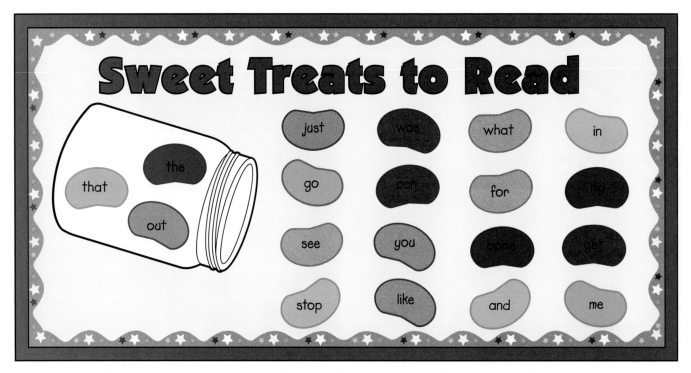

For this tempting word display, post a jar on a titled board. Write grade-appropriate words on jelly bean cutouts and then add the candies to the display. To review the words, ask students to find designated words or read the candies of a chosen color. For added fun, have a jelly bean challenge by asking students to see how quickly they can read all the words!

Deanne D'Imperio, Martin Luther King Elementary, Paterson, NJ

CLASSROOM DISPLAYS

All Aboard the Letter-Change Train!

bat · mat · sat · sad · mad · mud · mug

Loading cargo onto this train is skill-boosting fun! Help students write a series of words so each word is on a separate piece of paper and differs from the previous word by only one letter. Post the first word on a train engine cutout. Showcase the remaining words in order on separate boxcars. Add a title and then have students read the entire trainload of words!

Jill Mally, Standing Bear Elementary, Omaha, NE

To make a clock for this interactive display, cut out a colorful copy of each pattern on page 50. Hole-punch the carrots and secure them to the clock with a brad. Draw a bunny face on a four-inch circle and glue the circle to the clock as shown. Then glue two ears and two paws in place. Display several similar clocks within student reach. Then have students post the corresponding digital time below each clock.

adapted from an idea by Leslie Stephenson, Wetumpka Elementary, Wetumpka, AL

Skate Patterns

Use with "Skating Into 2008" on page 44.

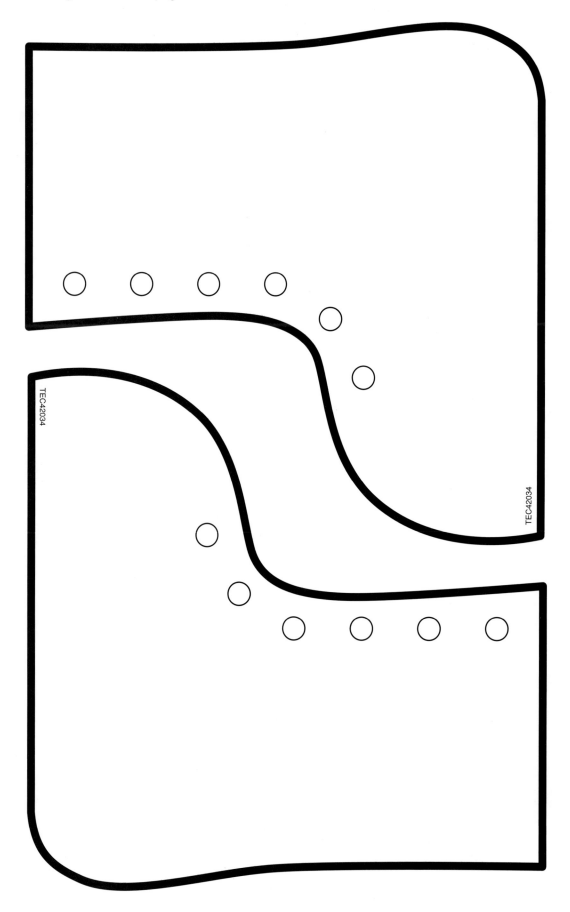

TEC42034

TEC42034

Name _____

Book: _____

_____

_____

Carrot Clock Patterns
Use with "Carrot Time!" on page 47.

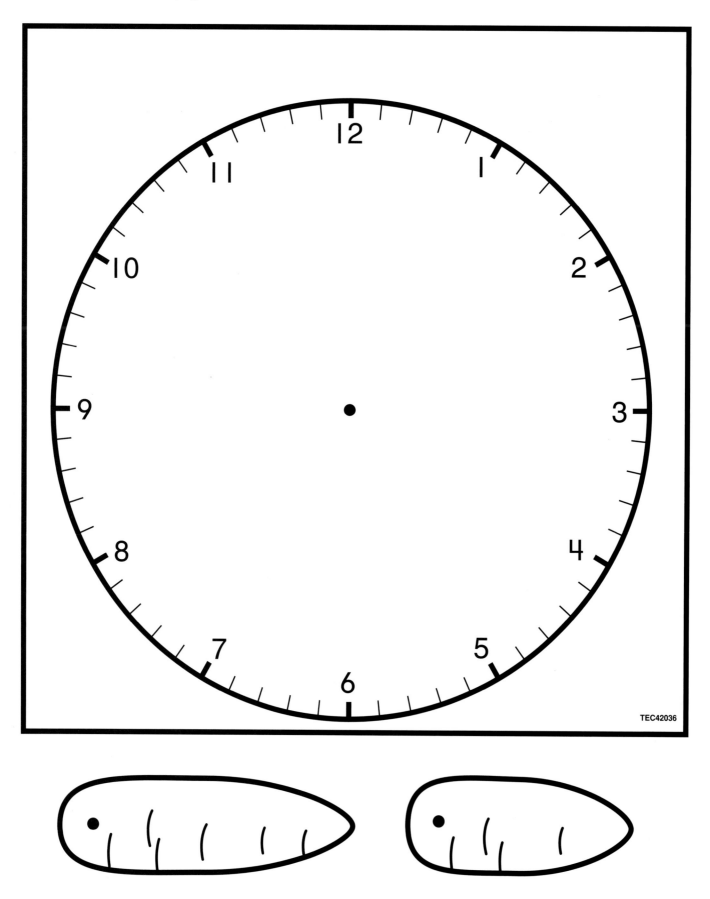

TEC42036

LEARNING CENTERS

Colorful Mix-Up
Literacy Center

Craft foam makes this color-word activity durable. Prepare a chosen version as described below. Then place all of the foam pieces in a container. Place at a center the container, a supply of paper, pencils, and a list of color words for a spelling reference. To complete the activity, a student chooses a color, arranges the foam pieces of that color to spell the corresponding color word, and then writes the word. She continues with additional colors as time allows. *Color words*

Easier version: For each color word, make a craft foam puzzle of that color with one puzzle piece per letter.

More advanced version: For each color word, use craft foam in the corresponding color to make die-cut letters that spell the word, or write the letters on separate craft foam rectangles.

Amber King, Berkeley Heights Elementary, Martinsburg, WV

Learning With Logos
Literacy Center

Youngsters will be thrilled to see how much they can read at this center! Collect a supply of logos with words from familiar products or fast-food restaurants so that you have two of each logo. Trim any excess packaging and mount each logo on a separate blank card. To complete the activity, a youngster pairs identical logos and reads them. **For a partner version,** two students spread out the cards facedown. Then they play as in the traditional game of Concentration. *Environmental print*

Paula Trueax, McNary Heights Elementary
Umatilla, OR

Attracted to Patterns
Math Center

Magnetic bingo chips are the manipulatives for this easy-to-prepare activity. Adhere a long strip of magnetic tape to the back of a ruler. Place the ruler and a supply of magnetic bingo chips at a center stocked with paper and crayons. To complete the activity, a student arranges the chips on the magnetic tape to form a pattern. Then he illustrates the pattern on a sheet of paper.

For a thematic variation, gather a supply of magnetic bingo chips that are the same color and an assortment of incentive stickers that relate to a chosen theme. Adhere a sticker to each bingo chip and have students make patterns based on the stickers. *Patterning*

Deborah Provencher, West Brookfield Elementary
West Brookfield, MA

Dragon's Treasure
Math Center

Here's a golden opportunity to reinforce counting. Color and cut out a copy of the game cards and label on page 62. Attach the label to a lidded container and put the cards inside. Arrange for two or three students to play at a time.

The players arrange the cards faceup in a circle. To take a turn, a student begins at any card. He counts to ten as he touches one card per number in a clockwise direction. If the last card he touches is a coin card, he takes it. If it is the dragon card, he leaves it and returns a coin card if he has one. Students take turns as described as time allows or until they take all the coin cards. **For more advanced students,** students skip-count to a designated number rather than count by ones to ten. *Counting*

Judy Frey, Lakeland Ridge Elementary
Sherwood Park, Alberta, Canada

Spotted!
Math Center

For this versatile idea, fold each of several sheets of colorful paper in half and cut a large butterfly wing along each fold. Unfold each paper. Then choose an option below.

Matching numbers and sets: For each set of wings, label a body cutout with a number. Decorate the wings with that many dots. A student matches the bodies and wings.

Addition combinations: For each set of wings, label a body cutout with a number. Set out paper, crayons, and pom-poms of two colors. A student assembles a butterfly. Then, to show one way to make the corresponding number, she places a combination of pom-poms on the wings. She records her work as desired.

adapted from an idea by Christine M. Vohs, Blue Valley Montessori School
Overland Park, KS

In Harmony
Literacy Center

To prepare this rhyming activity, color a copy of the center mat on page 63 and a copy of the activity cards on page 64. Code the backs of the rhyming pairs to make the activity self-checking. Put each set of cards in a separate resealable plastic bag. To complete the activity, a student spreads out a designated set of cards faceup. He puts two cards with pictures whose names rhyme in the boxes on the mat and names the pictures. Then he turns the two cards over. If the backs of the cards match, he stacks the cards facedown near the mat. If the backs of the cards do not match, he tries again. He continues as described to correctly pair all the cards. *Rhyming*

Catherine Broome-Kehm, Melbourne Beach, FL

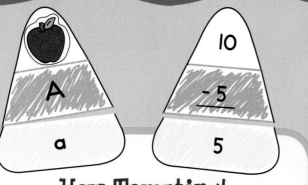

How Tempting!
Literacy or Math Center

For this easy-to-adapt idea, choose an option below. Program several identical candy corn cutouts as described. Then cut off the bottom section of each candy. To complete the activity, a youngster spreads out the candy pieces faceup. He matches each bottom section with the correct upper portion. Then he flips the upper portion of each candy to check his work.

Letter knowledge: Write an uppercase letter on the middle section of each candy. Write the matching lowercase letter on the bottom section and the back of the middle section. If desired, glue on the top section a picture whose name begins with the corresponding letter.

Addition or subtraction: Write a math problem on the upper portion of each candy. Write the answer on the bottom section and the back of the middle section.

Katie Klipp, Bob Jones Elementary
Greenville, SC

Syllable Feast
Literacy Center

There's no need to shop around; this phonological awareness idea is sure to please! Divide and label a sheet of paper as shown and then copy it to make a class supply. Place the papers, several grocery store sale circulars, scissors, and glue at a center. When a student visits the center, she cuts out a picture of a food. Then she says the name of the food, clapping once for each syllable. After she determines how many syllables the word has, she glues the picture in the corresponding section of a paper. She sorts several different pictures in the same manner. *Oral segmenting*

Angie Kutzer, Garrett Elementary
Mebane, NC

Before and After
Math Center

Use this versatile activity to reinforce nearly any range of numbers. To prepare, write a different number greater than 1 on each of several blank cards. Make a supply of recording sheets similar to the one shown. To complete the activity, a student scrambles the cards and then stacks them facedown. He takes the top card and writes the number in the first box on a recording sheet. Then he writes the numbers that come directly before and after that number in the corresponding blanks. He continues as described to complete the paper. *Number order*

adapted from an idea by Sara Heitschmidt
St. John the Apostle Catholic School
North Richland Hills, TX

Name Darius

Recording Sheet

3 [4] 5
1 [2] 3
5 [6] 7
2 [3] 4

3

Wild Sorting
Literacy Center

This approach to phonics uses disposable animal plates. Choose two or more initial consonants, initial consonant blends, or short vowels to reinforce. Gather plates featuring animals whose names have the corresponding phonics elements and label the plates accordingly. Use clip art or old phonics workbooks to make picture cards for students to sort. Code the back of each card for self-checking. After a youngster names each picture and puts it on the corresponding plate, she flips the cards to check her work. *Phonics*

Julie Lewis, J. O. Davis Elementary, Irving, TX

Framed!
Math Center

Picture this: a fresh way to give students measurement practice! Gather a few picture frames of different sizes. Remove the glass and backings. Place the frames at a center stocked with paper and either rulers or nonstandard units of measure. When a student visits the center, she traces the outer edges of a frame on a sheet of paper. Then she measures each side of the tracing and writes the measurements near the corresponding lengths. She's sure to notice that the opposite sides of a rectangle are equal! *Linear measurement*

adapted from an idea by Suzanne Moore
Irving, TX

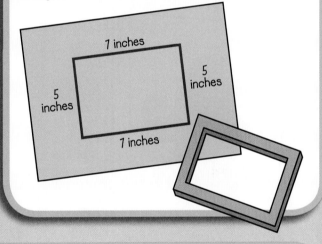

Roll, Read, and Write
Literacy Center

Nearly no preparation is needed for this word wall idea! Place near your word wall a die and a supply of recording sheets like the one shown. Have two or more students sit near the word wall. To take a turn, a youngster rolls the die and announces the number rolled. The students look on the wall for a word with that many letters. (They try to find a word that they have not written yet.) If a youngster rolls a number and there is no matching word, he rolls again. Once the youngsters find a word, they read it aloud and write it on their papers in the appropriate column. Students take turns as described for the allotted time. *Word recognition*

Sheila Criqui-Kelley, Lebo Elementary, Lebo, KS

Name _Parker_

Recording Sheet

1	2	3	4	5	6
		she	have		friend
		was	very		
			come		

Learning Centers

Mitten Measurement
Math Center

For this capacity activity, place at a center crayons, paper, a few different mittens, and a supply of math cubes. First, a youngster illustrates a chosen mitten. Next, she estimates how many cubes will fit in the real mitten and writes her estimate. Then she determines the actual number, writes the number, and circles it. **For an easier version,** have students use recording sheets similar to the one shown. *Capacity with nonstandard units*

Katie Zuehlke, Bendix Elementary, Annandale, MN

Name Kara

How many cubes can the mitten hold?
Guess: 20 cubes
Check: 16 cubes

Just "Write" Shopping
Literacy Center

This differentiated activity is a bargain! Make one copy of page 67. Write a chosen letter in each circle on list C. Then make copies of each list on different-colored paper for easy management. Make picture cards of appropriate foods, including the foods on list A. Place the lists, picture cards, and paper lunch bags at a center. A student takes an assigned list and completes the activity as described below. *Reading, writing*

List A: He checks off the items on the list as he puts the corresponding cards in a bag.
List B: He chooses several picture cards, lists the items, and then puts the cards in a bag.
List C: He finds pictures of foods whose names begin with the designated letters. He writes the words and puts the cards in the bag.

Juanita Stokes, Payne Elementary, Washington, DC

Grayson's
Shopping List A
☑ apples
☑ bread
☐ eggs
☐ hot dogs
☑ milk
☑ pizza

Snow Cones for Sale!
Math Center

To prepare this coin-counting activity, color a copy of the center mat on page 65 and a copy of the activity cards on page 66. On the back of each coin card, write the corresponding value. Put the cards in a resealable plastic bag. To complete the activity, a student spreads out the cards faceup. She puts a coin card on the mat and then puts the matching value card below it. She flips the coin card to check her work. If the values are the same, she returns the two cards to the bag. If the values are not the same, she tries again. She continues as described with the remaining cards. *Counting coins*

Catherine Broome-Kehm, Melbourne Beach, FL

Snow Cones for Sale!
Put a coin card.
Put the matching card.
Check.

40¢

7¢

Learning Centers

My Love List

I love my mom.
I love bskbal.
I love my dog.

Love Lists
Literacy Center

This writing activity gets to the heart of Valentine's Day! Place at a center crayons, story paper, and a heart template. When a child visits the center, he makes three or more tracings of the heart on a sheet of paper. Inside each tracing, he illustrates a different person, place, or thing that he loves. Then he titles his paper and writes a sentence about each illustration. ***Writing***

Valuable Cards
Math Center

Coin stampers make it easy to prepare these partner activities! Glue together two pink circles and two pink rectangles as shown. Then add marker details to make a piggy bank. Choose an option below and program blank cards as described. To complete the activity, a student shuffles the cards and stacks them facedown. Then each youngster takes a card. If the cards have the same value, the students put them on the bank. If the cards have different values, the student whose card has the greater value takes both cards. The students continue as described with the remaining cards. Then each youngster compares the number of cards she has with the number of cards on the bank.

Sets of pennies: Use a penny stamper to program 20 cards so there are two cards with one cent, two cards with two cents, and so on.
Combinations of coins: Use stampers to program an even number of cards with individual coins and sets of coins, making some cards of equal value.

Stacy Schriever
Prairie Lincoln Elementary
Columbus, OH

Serve and Sort!
Math Center

Use any three varieties of pasta for this graphing idea. Make a blank graph with simple illustrations of the chosen pasta. Then copy the graph to make a class supply. Place up to ten pieces of each type of pasta in each of several resealable plastic bags, making each assortment unique. Label each bag with a different letter. A student takes a bag and writes the letter on his paper. Then he sorts the pasta and completes the graph. **For more advanced students,** have each youngster write about his graph using words such as *more, less,* and *equal*. ***Graphing***

Mary Richards
Monroe Elementary
Janesville, WI

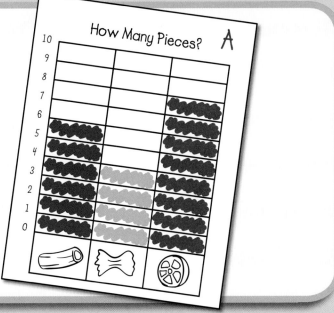

How Many Pieces? A

Learning Centers

Shape-o!
Math Center

Here's a winning approach to solid figures. To prepare this small-group game, color and cut out a copy of the spinner pattern on page 68. Attach a paper clip to the spinner with a brad. Place at a center the spinner, game markers, and one copy of a gameboard (page 68) for each group member.

To take a turn, a player spins the spinner. If the spinner lands on "Super Shape!" she marks a chosen shape on her gameboard. If the spinner lands on a shape, the player names it and marks an object of the same shape. (If no matching objects are unmarked, her turn is over.) Players take turns as described until one player marks four objects in a row. *Solid figures*

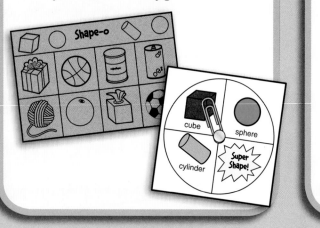

Super Sandwiches
Literacy Center

For made-to-order word fun, make several bread slice cutouts and purple rectangles (jelly). Write a chosen consonant on each slice of bread and a vowel on each serving of jelly. Place the sandwich supplies at a center along with paper and paper plates. To complete the activity, a student forms words by making jelly sandwiches. He puts each sandwich on a separate plate and writes each word. For differentiated practice, see the suggestions below. *Forming words*

Initial consonants: A student makes just one sandwich and then changes the first letter to make different words.

Vowel digraphs: Write a vowel on each of several tan rectangles (peanut butter) and have students make peanut butter and jelly sandwiches.

Melanie Snodgrass
Council Grove Elementary
Oklahoma City, OK

Pup on the Go
Literacy Center

To help students bone up on word families, color a copy of the center mat on page 69 and a copy of the activity cards on page 70. To complete the activity, a student places a picture-word card on each large box on the mat. She stacks the word cards faceup nearby and then sorts them by rime. Then she reads each group of words. **For more advanced students,** have youngsters write each group of words after they correctly sort the cards. *Word families*

Catherine Broome-Kehm
Melbourne Beach, FL

Learning Centers

Writing to Go
Literacy Center

Since this activity is self-contained, students can take it to their seats! Prepare the cards as described below. Laminate the resulting strips for reuse. Then place in a container the strips, wipe-off markers, and paper towels or other materials that students can use for cleaning the strips.

Spelling: Make one copy of page 71. Color and cut out chosen cards. Then glue the cards on separate sentence strips. Write on the back of each strip the corresponding word. To complete the activity, a child selects a strip, names the corresponding picture, and then writes the word. He flips the strip to check his work.

Handwriting: Write a chosen letter or word on each strip and have students practice writing it.

Amy Crawford-King, Oceanair Elementary, Norfolk, VA

Swat!
Literacy Center

You can use this partner activity to reinforce any reading words! Write several words on separate blank cards. Place the cards and two flyswatters at a center. When students visit the center, they spread the cards out faceup. Then they take turns gently swatting cards and reading aloud the corresponding words. For a variation, after a youngster swats and reads a word, he uses it in a sentence. ***Word recognition***

Sheila Criqui-Kelley
Lebo Elementary, Lebo, KS

Colossal Cones
Math or Literacy Center

To prepare this mouthwatering activity, make one ice cream cone cutout and four ice cream scoop cutouts per student. For math, write on each cone the three numbers in a chosen addition and subtraction fact family. For literacy, write a rime on each cone. Then place the cutouts at a center stocked with crayons, paper, and glue. Have each student complete the activity as described below and then glue her cutouts on a sheet of paper to make a jumbo ice cream treat.

Fact families: A student takes a cone. She writes each number sentence in the corresponding fact family on a separate ice cream scoop.

Word families: A student takes a cone and reads the rime. She writes on each of four ice cream scoops a different word that contains the rime.

Summer Andrus, Draper Elementary
Draper, UT

$14 - 8 = 6$

$14 - 6 = 8$

$8 + 6 = 14$

$6 + 8 = 14$

6
8
14

Learning Centers

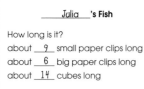

__Julia__'s Fish

How long is it?
about __9__ small paper clips long
about __6__ big paper clips long
about __14__ cubes long

A Measurable Catch
Math Center

To get students in the swim of comparing measurements, gather a supply of three different manipulatives for students to use as units of measure. Place at a center the manipulatives, recording sheets similar to the one shown, and a class supply of fish cutouts. Also set out construction paper, glue, crayons, and glitter glue. To begin, a youngster writes her name on a recording sheet. Next, she measures the length of a chosen fish with each type of manipulative, in turn, and records the measurements. Then she glues the fish and recording sheet to a sheet of paper and decorates the fish as desired. ***Nonstandard measurement***

Sue Fleischmann, Catholic East Elementary
Milwaukee, WI

Super Cheesecake
Literacy Center

For tempting practice with end punctuation, color a copy of the center mat on page 72 and a copy of the activity cards on page 73. Write the correct punctuation on the back of each card and then scramble the cards. To complete the activity, a student stacks the cards faceup. Then she reads each sentence and places it on the mat beside the appropriate end mark. After she sorts all the sentences in this manner, she flips the cards to check her work. ***End punctuation***

For more advanced students, after a youngster checks her work, have her choose several sentences and write them with the correct punctuation on provided paper.

Catherine Broome-Kehm, Melbourne Beach, FL

Flower Patch
Math Center

How does this garden grow? With addition! Gather a supply of adhesive dots of two different colors. Place the dots, a number cube, white paper, and crayons at a center. To complete the activity, a student rolls the number cube. Then he puts the corresponding number of like-colored dots on his paper, leaving space between them. He rolls the cube again to find out how many dots of the other color to add to his paper. Once his paper has two sets of dots, he incorporates each dot into a flower illustration. Then he labels his work to show how many flowers there are in each set and how many flowers there are in all. ***Beginning addition***

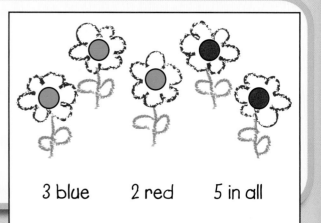

3 blue   2 red   5 in all

Learning Centers

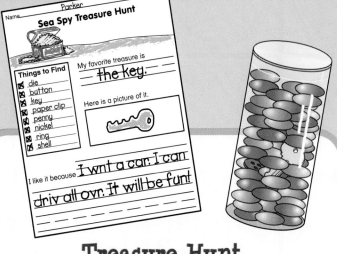

Treasure Hunt
Literacy Center

If your students like the I Spy book series, they're sure to enjoy this activity! List eight small items (treasures) on a copy of page 74. Then make student copies of the paper. Gather the items and a clear plastic container with a lid. Nearly fill the container with the items and beads or decorative glass stones. Secure the lid with clear packing tape. To complete the activity, a student moves the container around to shift its contents. When he sees a listed item, he draws an X in the corresponding box on his paper. After he finds all the treasures, he completes the rest of the paper. *Writing*

Katie Klipp, Bob Jones Elementary, Greenville, SC

Totally Tubular
Literacy Center

For this compound word activity, cut several cardboard tubes into short lengths. Choose several compound words. Write on separate tubes the two words that form each compound word. Place the tubes at a center along with craft sticks and paper. When a student visits the center, he arranges tubes on craft sticks as shown to form compound words. Then he lists the compound words on a sheet of paper. *Compound words*

Heather E. Graley
Grace Christian School, Blacklick, OH

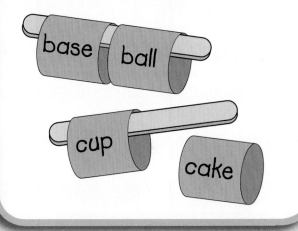

Fishy Sums
Math Center

Reel in just-right skill practice! Tie one end of a string to a magnet and the other end to a dowel to make a fishing pole. Program several fish cutouts for an option below and then attach a paper clip to each fish. Spread out the fish facedown on a pond cutout. Have students complete the activity as described.

Beginning addition: Write an addition problem on each fish and set out a supply of plastic worms. A student catches a fish, uses the worms to solve the problem, and then writes the corresponding addition sentence on provided paper.
Adding three numbers: Write an addend on each fish. A student catches three fish. She arranges them in a column so the numbers are in the order in which she wants to add them. Then she writes and solves the problem on provided paper.

Andrea M. Singleton, Waynesville Elementary
Waynesville, OH

Game Cards and Label

Use with "Dragon's Treasure" on page 53.

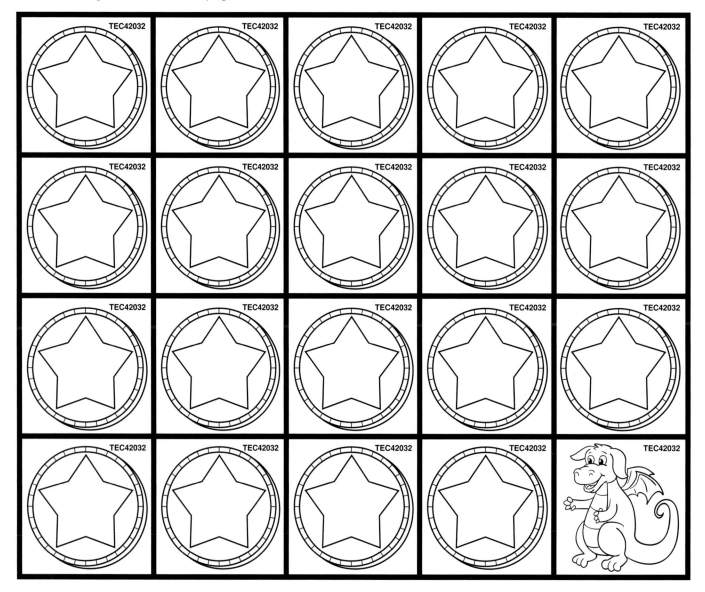

In Harmony

Match rhyming cards.
Name the pictures.
Check.

Activity Cards

Use with "In Harmony" on page 53.

box

fox

cat

bat

mop

top

pen

hen

dog

log

fan

can

Snow Cones for Sale!

Put a coin card.
Put the matching card.
Check.

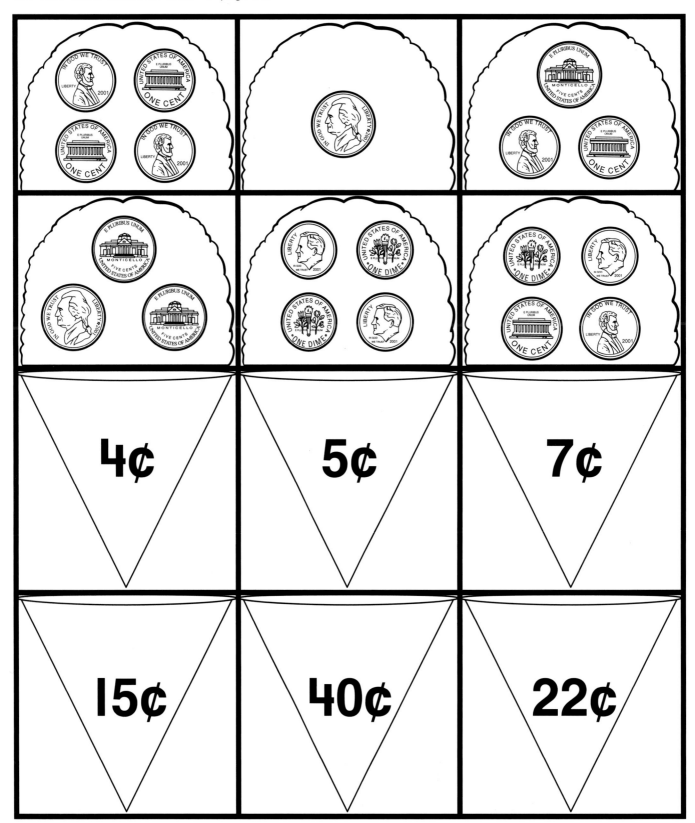

Shopping List A

_____'s

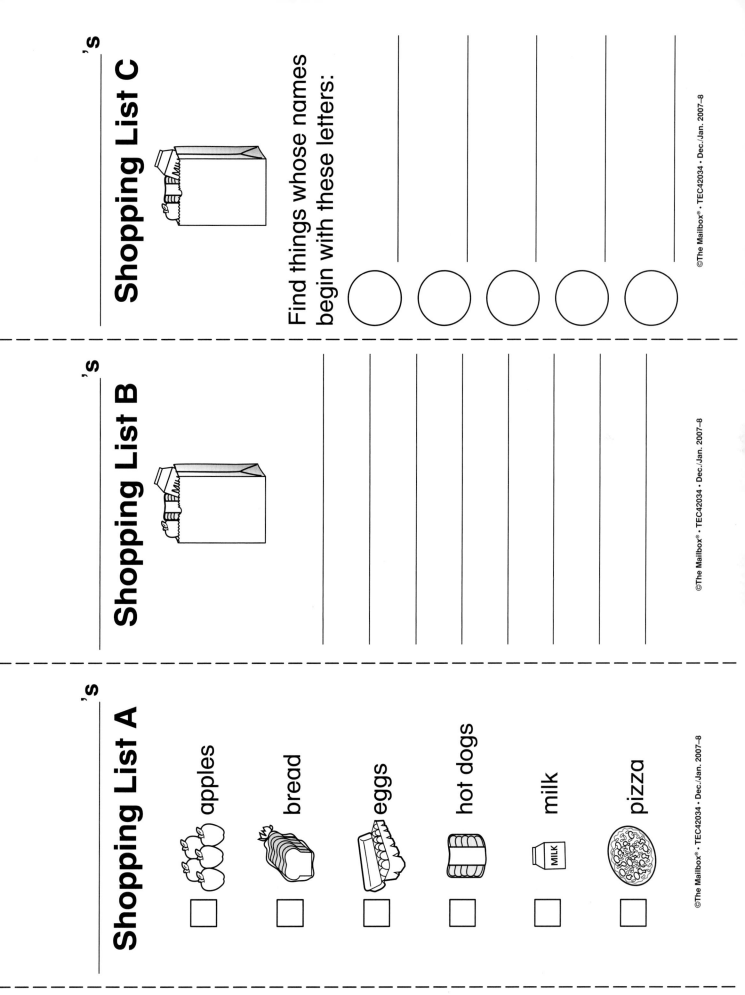

apples ☐

bread ☐

eggs ☐

hot dogs ☐

milk ☐

pizza ☐

Shopping List B

_____'s

Shopping List C

_____'s

Find things whose names begin with these letters:

Note to the teacher: Use with "Just 'Write' Shopping" on page 56.

Gameboards and Spinner Pattern

Use with "Shape-o!" on page 58.

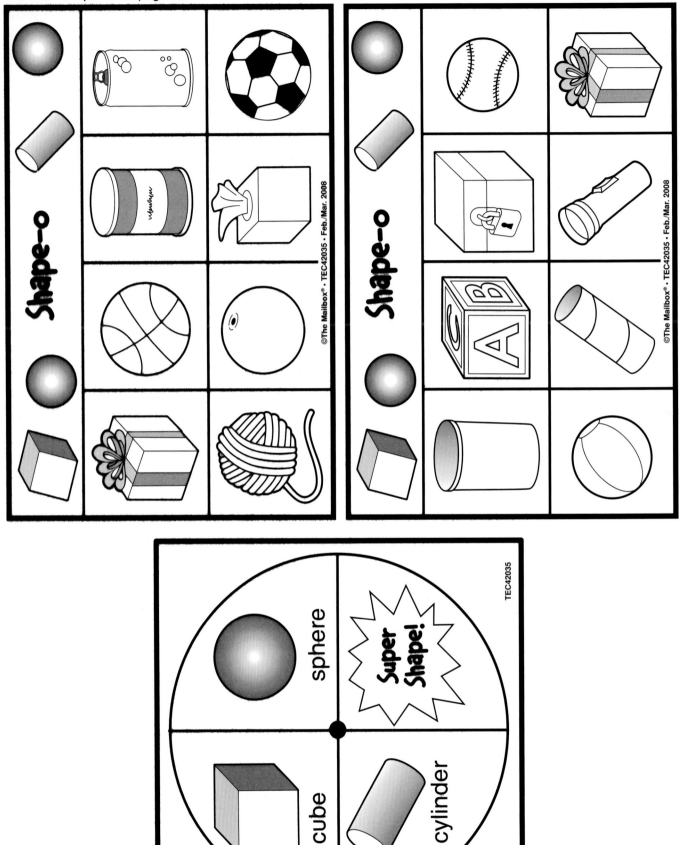

©The Mailbox® • TEC42035 • Feb./Mar. 2008

©The Mailbox® • TEC42035 • Feb./Mar. 2008

TEC42035

Pup on the Go

Sort.
Read.

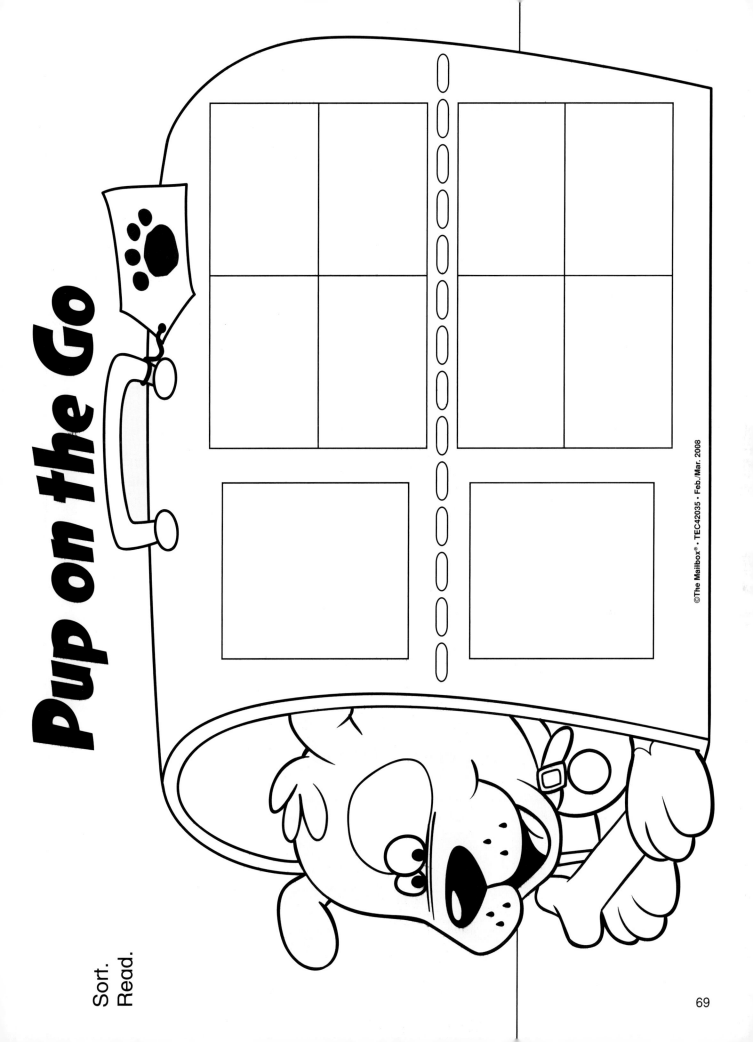

get	hen	bake	day
met	men	rake	way
set	pen	take	play
wet	then	snake	stay

Short-Vowel Words

Long-Vowel Words

TEC42036

TEC42036

TEC42036

TEC42036

TEC42036

TEC42036

TEC42036

TEC42036

TEC42036

TEC42036

TEC42036

TEC42036

TEC42036

TEC42036

TEC42036

TEC42036

Super Cheesecake

Read.
Sort.
Check.

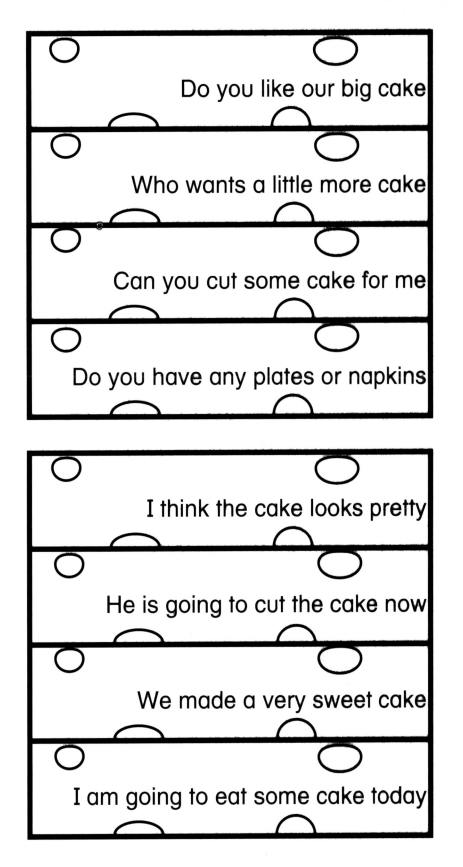

Do you like our big cake

Who wants a little more cake

Can you cut some cake for me

Do you have any plates or napkins

I think the cake looks pretty

He is going to cut the cake now

We made a very sweet cake

I am going to eat some cake today

Sea Spy Treasure Hunt

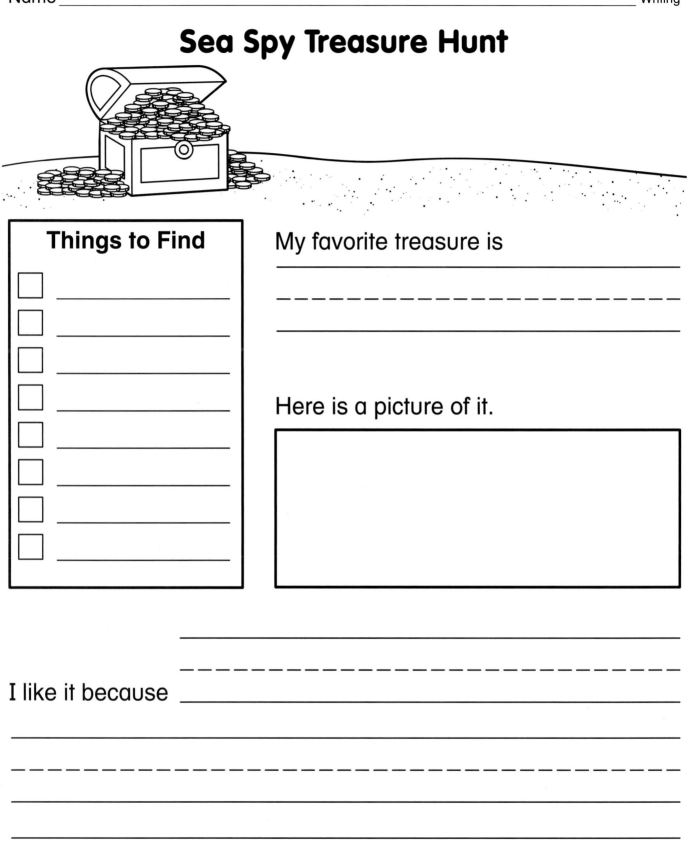

Things to Find

☐ _____

☐ _____

☐ _____

☐ _____

☐ _____

☐ _____

☐ _____

☐ _____

My favorite treasure is

_____

_ _ _ _ _ _ _ _ _ _ _ _ _ _ _ _ _ _ _

_____

Here is a picture of it.

_____

I like it because _____

_____

_ _ _ _ _ _ _ _ _ _ _ _ _ _ _ _ _ _ _

_____

_ _ _ _ _ _ _ _ _ _ _ _ _ _ _ _ _ _ _

_____

Management Tips & Timesavers

Management Tips & Timesaver's

Minute Movements

To make it easier for students to focus during instructional time, help them get their wiggles out with these ideas. After youngsters have been seated awhile, use the rhyme shown to give them an opportunity to stretch. During a transition from one location to another, encourage students to "fly," tiptoe, walk like Frankenstein's monster, or move in another silly way. It takes just a few minutes and helps youngsters expend some energy! *Terri Ross, Merrill Elementary, Beloit, WI*

> Stretch to the ceiling.
> Stretch to the floor.
> Stretch to the window.
> Stretch to the door.
> Stretch way up high
>   and way down low.
> Now stretch as far as
>   you can go!

End of the Line

Since students often vie for the last place in line, designate a student as the End Friend. It prevents disagreements about who should be last, and it avoids any misunderstandings that a less familiar word, such as *caboose*, may cause. Plus, children love the catchy rhyme! *Bobbie Redd-Hallman, Don Stowell School, Merced, CA*

Folders at Hand

Every paper has a place with this organizational tip. Label sticky notes with the categories of forms, notices, and other papers you need to keep track of. Secure each sticky note on the tab of a separate file folder and then file the papers in the appropriate folders. When the contents of a folder are no longer current or you empty the folder for another reason, remove the sticky note and relabel the folder for a different set of papers. No more wasted folders! *Michelle Littleton, Pioneer Park Elementary, Lawton, OK*

Everyone Writes!

Use this skill-boosting idea to keep students actively engaged during shared-writing activities. While one student writes a letter or word on chart paper or the classroom board, have his classmates write the same letter or word on individual whiteboards. It not only reduces off-task behavior, but it also reinforces important skills! *Beth Wineberger, Southold Elementary, Southold, NY*

Math Tubs

If you're looking for an easy way to give students skill-based morning work, try this! Label each of several plastic tubs with a chosen math topic. Then stock the tubs with relevant familiar activities. Set out the tubs before students arrive in the morning, and they can get to work without interrupting your morning duties. The tubs are also convenient for volunteers to use with individual students at other times of the day. *Wendy Russell, Bingham Elementary, Springfield, MO*

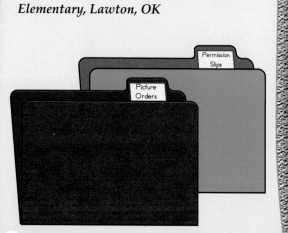

Management Tips & Timesavers

Crayon Keeper

If your students often lose crayons in their desks, try this! For each child, adhere a strip of magnetic tape to the back of an eight-count crayon box. Then ask the youngster to attach the box to the side of her desk. When it's time for her to color, have her remove the box from the desk. She'll find the colors she needs right away! *Michelle McElhinny, Forest Heights Elementary, Gastonia, NC*

Do Not Disturb

When you call a student away from an activity for small-group or individualized instruction, he may worry that a classmate will take his place. To ensure that doesn't happen, have him mark his place with a card you have labeled "Save." It lets students know that he plans to return to the activity, and it puts the youngster at ease! *Lynn Edmiston, Plumb Elementary, Clearwater, FL*

Piece by Piece

This motivational idea is a perfect fit for either academic or behavioral class goals. Assemble a children's puzzle on a piece of poster board and then trace the outer edges of it. Secure the first puzzle piece with rubber cement. Number the back of the remaining puzzle pieces sequentially as you take the puzzle apart. Divide the pieces among a few containers labeled with ranges of numbers. Whenever you want to recognize students' progress toward a designated goal, have a youngster add the next piece to the puzzle. After the puzzle is complete, reward the class as desired. *Hilda Fields, Georgetown Elementary, Savannah, GA*

Individualized Attention

Here's an organized way to have classroom volunteers give students extra help and enrichment. Place in a container an activity for a chosen skill, corresponding instructions, and a list of students who need individualized attention for the skill. When a volunteer visits your classroom, have her take the container and work with the youngsters as described. When she thinks a student has mastered the designated skill, have her circle his name on the list. After you check his progress, update the list if needed. *Kim Criswell, Wilson, KS*

Picture File

Save time preparing phonics activities with this clip art tip. Make copies of picture cards from back issues of *The Mailbox®* magazine. Store the cards in an expanding file with alphabetized sections. If desired, label sections for phonics elements such as digraphs and blends. Finding the pictures you need will be as easy as A, B, C! *Casey Cooksey, Bruce Elementary, Bruce, MS*

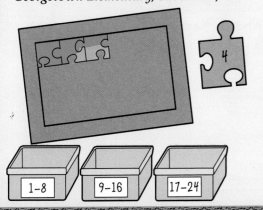

Management Tips & Timesavers

Attractive and Neat!

Make piles of jumbled paper clips a thing of the past! Attach a strip of magnetic tape around a pencil cup. Then place separate paper clips on the tape. Whenever you need a paper clip, it will be right at your fingertips! *Lisa Hixson, Stewart Elementary, Washington, IA*

Literature Reminder

If you sometimes forget for which storybooks you have activities, try this! Print "activity on file" or a similar phrase on adhesive labels. Whenever you file an idea for a book that you have in your classroom library, attach a label to the book on the inside of the front cover. Later, when you select the book for storytime, the label will alert you to check your files. *Sheila Criqui-Kelley, Lebo Elementary, Lebo, KS*

Towers of Ten

To streamline preparation for Unifix cube activities, keep like-colored cubes snapped together in towers of ten. The towers make it a snap to hand out the cubes in chosen quantities and colors. Plus, at the end of an activity, it's easy for you and your students to check that all the cubes have been returned! *Nancy Carpenter, Silver Lake Elementary, Federal Way, WA*

Out of This World!

Promote positive behavior with this stellar approach! Display a set of labeled planet cutouts in a row on a classroom wall, beginning with the planet closest to the sun and continuing in order. Post a star cutout at the first planet. Each time students exhibit exceptionally positive behavior, advance the star one planet. After you place the star on the last planet, reward students as desired for their achievement! *adapted from an idea by Debbie Heinzen, Brookdale School, Bloomfield, NJ*

On Their Own

Color-coded folders make it easy to manage different reading groups. Assign each student in the same group a pocket folder of the same color. Place in each set of folders appropriate independent assignments. Also place in each folder a list of chosen learning centers. While you're working with one group, have the other students work on the assignments in their folders. If a youngster finishes his assignments with time to spare, he returns them to the folder and visits a designated center. Since the expectations are clear for students, they can work on their own without interrupting you! *Susan Flippen, Douglass Elementary, Memphis, TN*

Michael

What Is Next?

1. A B C — word center
2. book baskets
3. computer

Management Tips & Timesavers

In Full Bloom

Watch students' positive behavior blossom with this incentive idea! Write a different class reward on each petal of a poster-size flower. Divide the stem into several sections. Display the flower and then post a bug cutout at the bottom of the stem. Each time your students exhibit especially good behavior, move the bug up one section. After you move the bug to the last section, invite students to choose a reward. *Angie Kutzer, Garrett Elementary, Mebane, NC*

longer recess

no homework

guest reader

movie

special snack

A Friendly Reminder

If your students sometimes forget to write their names on their papers, try this! Before each student turns in an assignment, have a neighboring classmate check that his name is on the paper. If his name is missing, no doubt a friendly reminder from the classmate will prompt the youngster to write it! *Katy Hoh, W. C. K. Walls Elementary, Pitman, NJ*

Reusable Class List

To keep track of which students have turned in something or completed a certain task, put a copy of your class list in a plastic page protector. Use a wipe-off marker to title the page protector and mark students' names as appropriate. After you no longer need the information, wipe the page protector clean to use the class list again. It's a simple way to cut down on wasted paper! *Elizabeth Arway, St. Benedict School, Holmdel, NJ*

Field Trip Money

✓ Amy
Bailey
Carmen
✓ Erica
George
✓ Henry
Juanita

Mikayla
✓ Pedro
Rachel
Riley
Stephen
✓ Tanner
Violet

Decorating Timesaver

This picture-perfect strategy makes it easy to reuse your best display ideas. Before you take down a display, take a photo of it. Attach the photo to a large envelope. Then place the display title and a sample of any projects in the envelope. Prepare envelopes for different displays in the same manner and file the envelopes by month. The resulting collection of tried-and-true ideas is sure to be a convenient resource! *Michelle Mesamore, First Baptist Church Kindergarten, Pelham, AL*

Sticker Storage

Save time spent looking for just the right stickers with this organizational idea. Cut sheets of stickers to fit in storage pages with pockets for trading cards or business cards. Put groups of stickers in the pockets and then secure the pages in a three-ring binder. The storage system makes it easy to see a variety of stickers at once. Plus, it keeps the stickers in good condition! *Andrea Hetzke, Oakdale Christian Academy, Chicago, IL*

Management Tips & Timesavers

Coded Nametags

This kid-pleasing idea helps field trip chaperones keep track of their charges. Divide students into groups and assign a chaperone to each group. Give each chaperone a card with her name, the names of her group members, and a different sticker. Put a matching sticker on each group member's nametag. Then chaperones can identify their group members at a glance! *Cindy Marshall, Prospect Elementary, Meridian, ID*

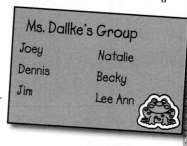

Ms. Dallke's Group
Joey   Natalie
Dennis   Becky
Jim   Lee Ann

Joey

Photo Finish

Use this tip at the end of the school year to make it easier to set up your classroom for back-to-school. Before you pack up classroom decorations and materials, take digital pictures of various classroom areas. When it's time to set up the room again, refer to the photos. It will be a snap to put everything in its place! *Amy James, Olive Branch Elementary, Portsmouth, VA*

Cupcake Containers

If you're running low on paint cups, save clean and empty plastic cupcake containers from class parties or other occasions. After you remove the lids, the containers are perfect for holding paint. If you have any extra containers, use them for sorting activities or manipulative storage. It's a sweet way to recycle! *Jenny Barnett, Sumter County Primary, Americus, GA*

Book Buddies

Looking for a way to get silent reading time off to a quick start? Enlist the help of book buddies! Number baskets of independent reading books. Each week designate students as book buddies and assign them numbers that match the numbered baskets. When it's time for silent reading, have each buddy take the appropriate basket to his group's reading area. At the end of the reading period, ask the buddies to collect the books and return the baskets. *Lori Hathaway, Murlin Heights Elementary, Dayton, OH*

Feed the Fish!

For this positive reinforcement idea, attach blue paper to the back of a fishbowl. Decorate the inside of the bowl with fish stickers and sand or aquarium gravel. Also place paper strips in a small lidded canister labeled "Fish Food." Whenever a student achieves a goal or demonstrates especially good behavior, invite her to write her name on a strip and drop the strip in the fishbowl. At the end of each week, draw a few strips from the fishbowl and reward the corresponding youngsters as desired. *Maria A. Cano, Hubert R. Hudson Elementary, Brownsville, TX*

OUR READERS WRITE

Our Readers Write

Welcome Gifts

Before the school year begins, I have an open house for my students and their parents. I mail each youngster a nametag to wear for the occasion. During the event, I give each child a decorative package containing a few items, such as a notepad, a small package of crayons, and a novelty pencil. The treats make students feel welcome. Plus, they keep youngsters occupied while I share information with their parents.

Sandra Miller, Mount Calvary School, Erie, PA

Whose Birthday Is Next?

Rather than take up precious wall space with a birthday display, I showcase the information in a class book. I purchase a photo album with self-adhesive pages. I title 12 pages with the months of the year in chronological order, writing each month on a separate page. I write each child's name and birthdate on a cupcake cutout. I mount his photo on the cupcake and then add the cupcake to the corresponding page. My students read the book time and again, so they quickly learn the order of the months!

Amy Finn, John Allen Elementary, Soddy-Daisy, TN

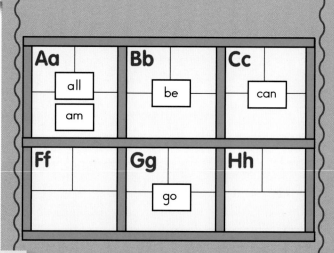

No Measuring Needed!

If you have tape and a cinder block or brick wall in your classroom, then you have the makings for a nifty word wall. Mark off 26 sections with colorful masking tape, using the blocks or bricks as guides for making straight lines and equal-size sections. Then label the sections alphabetically. Since you don't have to put up paper or measure the sections, you'll have a ready-to-use word wall in minutes!

Patty Henderson
Early Childhood Learning Center
Titusville, PA

Year at a Glance

My students enjoy this timeline display because it's about a topic near and dear to their hearts: their school year! Throughout the year I take photos of class activities, special events, and classroom visitors. Once I enlarge the photos and mount them on tagboard, I display them along with captions chronologically on a hallway wall. At the year's end, I give the photos to students as souvenirs.

Roxanne Ward, Meadowvale Elementary, Toledo, OH

August 28
First day of school

September 24
Apple orchard field trip

October 12
Firefighters' visit

Our Readers Write

Point It Out!

Use this idea to turn any ruler into a colorful pointer. Make two identical construction paper shapes and then use markers to add any desired details. Glue the shapes together along the edges, leaving an opening at the bottom for the end of a ruler. Laminate the shapes. Then slit the opening and slide the ruler inside. With one ruler and several interchangeable shapes, you can create a variety of pointers!

Rosemary Cliburn, Christian Home and Bible School, Mount Dora, FL

Decorative Cover-Up

Keep cluttered shelves out of sight with this decorating tip. Drape a plastic tablecloth over the front of the shelving and secure the top of it with clear packing tape. Whenever you want to retrieve items from the shelves, gently lift the tablecloth or move it aside. Students love tablecloths with colorful designs and characters, and the coverings really brighten a room!

Cindy Schumacher
Prairie Elementary
Cottonwood, ID

Sorting Reminder

At math time, my students and I sing this catchy song to the tune of "London Bridge." It helps them learn and remember several ways to sort things.

Lauri Moreno
Lujan-Chavez Elementary
El Paso, TX

> There are many ways to sort,
> Ways to sort, ways to sort.
> There are many ways to sort.
> Here are four.
>
> You can sort by color or shape,
> Color or shape, color or shape.
> You can sort by color or shape,
> Size, or texture!

Letter-Perfect Harmony

When it comes to promoting letter recognition, this idea couldn't be easier! I write the alphabet on sentence strips so that the strips correspond with the phrasing in the traditional alphabet song. I post the strips within students' reach, and I encourage youngsters to point to each letter or touch it as they sing the familiar tune. My students' letter recognition skills have improved greatly since I displayed the alphabet this way.

Nancy Verkley
Welch Elementary
Cincinnati, OH

A B C D

E F G

H I J K

L M N O P

Spotlight on Science

I have a year-round bulletin board titled "Animal of the Week." Each week I display pictures of a different animal along with some relevant facts. We read fiction and nonfiction books about the animal and do a related art project. Youngsters are always eager to find out what animal will be featured next.

Cynthia Jamnik
Our Lady Queen of Peace School
Milwaukee, WI

Our Readers Write

Invisible Names

I hear lots of oohs and ahs from my students when I use this idea to assign special helpers in October. I make a class supply of white construction paper pumpkins with colorful stems. Then I write each student's name on a different pumpkin with a white crayon using thick, heavy lines. Each day I have youngsters paint two or more pumpkins with watered-down paint to reveal who the special helpers are. The honored youngsters love to take the spooky pumpkins home at the end of the day!

Sue Fleischmann
Child and Family Centers of Excellence
Waukesha, WI

Conference Organizer

To make sure I remember everything I want to cover during parent-teacher meetings, I use a simple folder system. I have each student personalize a file folder. On a copy of a form I created, I note the student's strengths, areas to work on, and any additional information I want to discuss with her parents. I attach the form to the inside of the folder and add samples of the youngster's work to the folder. The folders put everything I need at my fingertips. Plus, they're convenient for parents to take home after we meet.

Heather Harris
Middleton Elementary
Middleton, TN

Skills for the Season

Construction paper and craft foam cutouts make it easy for me to prepare a variety of practice activities in a jiffy. I program seasonal cutouts to make sequencing activities, two-piece puzzles, and Concentration games. For example, in the fall, I use pumpkin, leaf, and acorn cutouts to make an alphabet sequencing activity, several uppercase and lowercase letter puzzles, and a reading Concentration game. When it's time for small-group skill practice, I give each group a different activity to complete.

Kim Criswell
Wilson, KS

Where Are They?

I use a small photo album of my pets to reinforce positional words. I show students each photo and ask them to tell where the pets are in relation to other objects. For example, a youngster might say, "The dog is on the rug" or "The cat is beside the chair." The photos are also great writing prompts!

Mary Flynn
Ocotillo Elementary
Tucson, AZ

Shake a Snack!

Each of your students can have a hand in making this no-cook recipe. Have students measure the dry ingredients into a plastic gallon container with a lid. After you secure the lid, sit with youngsters in a circle. Have them sing, count by ones, or skip-count as they shake the container and pass it around the circle. Then add the oil and shake the container again. For a richer flavor, set the snack mix aside for a few hours before serving it.

Shirley Burdick
Waseca, MN

Snack Mix Ingredients

3 c. bite-size pretzels
4 c. small cheese crackers
4 c. dry cereal, such as Chex
1 tsp. dried dill weed or oregano
1 small envelope of dry ranch
   dressing mix
½ c. vegetable or corn oil

Hidden Turkey

This Thanksgiving game gives students practice following directions. To begin, I instruct a volunteer to wait out of sight while another child hides a stuffed toy turkey in the classroom. Then I have students give the volunteer clues with positional words to lead him to the turkey. As an alternative, I label the room with cardinal directions and have children use those words. After the volunteer finds the turkey, I invite him to hide it for the next player.

Sheila Criqui-Kelley
Lebo Elementary
Lebo, KS

Bags and Boxes

To spark students' interest in learning centers, I store activities in a variety of visually appealing containers. For example, I use gift bags for seasonal activities and empty cookie tins for cookie-shaped activity cards. I also use empty tissue boxes to house game cards, and I decorate some of the boxes to look like gifts. The possibilities are endless!

Paula Trueax
McNary Heights Elementary
Umatilla, OR

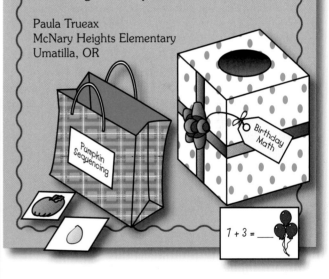

Quite a Quilt

At the end of our study of Native Americans, I write each letter of the alphabet at the top of a separate paper square. Then I have students illustrate on each square something that relates to Native Americans and has a name that begins with the corresponding letter. After we label the artwork, I arrange the squares on a board to create an alphabetical quilt. It's a fun review of the topic!

Taryn Lynn Way
Los Molinos Elementary
Los Molinos, CA

Count on It!

When I teach addition and subtraction, I use number lines and game pawns. I have each student move a pawn on a number line to solve math problems. Since children are familiar with playing board games, the pawns help them remember not to count their starting points!

Sheila Gonzales
Rockbrook Elementary
Lewisville, TX

December Display

This variation of "The 12 Days of Christmas" reinforces sets, number words, and describing words. To prepare, I title a bulletin board and then divide it into 12 sections. I label the sections sequentially with the corresponding numbers and number words. I have my students color sets of 1 to 12 holiday and seasonal pictures. Then I post each set and a descriptive phrase in the appropriate section of the board. The display is a wonderful visual aid when students sing the song!

Deanne D'Imperio
Martin Luther King School #30
Paterson, NJ

The 12 Days of a Merry Christmas

| **1** one red stocking | **2** two ringing bells | **3** three yummy cookies | **4** four wrapped presents |

Where in the World?

I make map skills relevant for my students with holiday mail. I ask students to bring in the envelopes in which holiday cards are mailed to their families. Whenever a youngster brings an envelope to school, we read the return address and find the corresponding state or country on a map. I also invite the youngster to tell who sent the card since that makes the geography lesson even more meaningful!

Laura Boeve
Beverly Elementary
Beverly Hills, MI

Colorful Kente

To honor African culture before Kwanzaa or at any time of year, share *Kente Colors* by Debbi Chocolate with your students. Then tie the book to your curriculum with the ideas below.

Susan Miller Geisler
Oakmont Elementary
Fort Worth, TX

Follow-Up Ideas

Social Studies: Help students find Africa on a map.

Patterning: Have youngsters make a class book of colorful geometric patterns.

Vocabulary: List selected color words, such as *emerald*, and have students name color words with nearly the same meanings.

Science: Discuss the colors of nature in the book. Then ask students to write about colors they observe in nature.

Yummy Wreath

Here's a supersimple snack for holiday celebrations. To make one, a child spreads green-tinted cream cheese on one half of a bagel. Then he decorates the bagel with pieces of red maraschino cherries. It's a great alternative to sugary treats!

Randi Austin
Stoutland R-2 School District
Stoutland, MO

Tray Graph

Save time preparing graphing activities with the help of ice cube trays! To create a simplified graph with two rows, I display two ice cube trays end to end. I label the rows and post a question. To complete the graph, students simply put manipulatives, such as Unifix cubes or pom-poms, in the appropriate sections of the trays.

Jill Davis, Kendall-Whittier Elementary, Tulsa, OK

Is Winter Your Favorite Season?

Yes

No

Party Planning

Watch for sales on party goods after New Year's Day. They're a perfect opportunity to stock up on supplies for 100th Day celebrations! I buy festive hats, noisemakers, and decorations that have been marked down. I have students make labels that say "100 Days" and use them to cover any holiday slogans on the hats and decorations. The store-bought supplies add a special touch to our school-year milestone.

Jeanne Taylor
Cincinnati Christian School
Fairfield, OH

Welcome to the Class!

When a youngster joins my class midyear, I have students make a class book for her. Each student writes and illustrates a letter to the new classmate with information about our class or school. Then I bind the letters into a book and present it to the new class member. The project encourages the entire class to make the newcomer feel welcome!

Stacey Helders-Pevan
Somerset Elementary
Somerset, WI

Dear Hailey,
We do journals every day. We have two recesses.
From Brett

Paint Stick Pointers

My students love these pointers since they're easy for them to handle and the decorations are unique. I paint several paint sticks. Then I decorate them with arts-and-crafts supplies, such as glitter, ribbon, and small painted wooden figures (available in craft stores). The wooden figures are inexpensive and relate to all sorts of themes and topics!

Janet Hatfield
Eagle Elementary
Eagle, NE

Action-Packed Math

Here's how I promote fitness during our busy day. I make a poster with photographs of students demonstrating six different exercises. I number the photographs from 1 to 6. To determine what exercise students will do, I instruct a youngster to roll a die, name the number rolled, and then describe the corresponding exercise. To determine how many times students will do the exercise, I ask a different student to roll two dice and announce the sum of the numbers rolled. Students get exercise as well as addition practice!

Diane Billman
McKitrick Elementary
Lutz, FL

Our Readers Write

Imagine!

Invite students to wonder "What If?" with this National Black History Month idea. Tell students about the achievements of several black inventors, such as the ones listed to the right. Then have each child imagine what life would be like without a chosen invention. Ask him to write and illustrate his thoughts on story paper. It's a great way to help students recognize the importance of several historic achievements!

Chandra Wright
West Handley Elementary
Fort Worth, TX

Inventors and Their Inventions
George Washington Carver: more than 300 products from peanuts
Frederick Jones: refrigeration system for trucks and railroad cars
Jan Matzeliger: machine used in making shoes
Garrett Morgan: traffic light
Joseph Winters: folding ladder mounted on a fire wagon

Calling All Vowels!

My students sit in groups at tables, and I label each table with a vowel. When it's time for youngsters to line up or come to an activity, I call the groups by the vowel sounds. After students are familiar with the sounds, I call out words with chosen vowels instead of announcing just the vowel sounds. Since students are eager to hear their groups called, they listen carefully and sharpen their phonics skills in the process!

Andrea Vinson
Joseph J. Pleviak Elementary
Lake Villa, IL

held the door for Mom

helped Dad with the baby

Terrific For Teeth

For National Children's Dental Health Month, I make a toothbrush booklet for each student. To make one, I fold a long strip of paper in half lengthwise. I staple two white covers and several pages between the paper as shown. I ask each youngster to write her name on her booklet handle and carefully cut the front cover so it looks like bristles. Then I have her complete the pages with sentences and illustrations that promote good dental hygiene.

Sara Wendahl
St. Mary's Elementary
Waukesha, WI

Camisha

100 Acts of Kindness

The 100th day of school is near Valentine's Day, so we create one display for both celebrations. To begin, we divide 100 heart cutouts among our students. Each youngster takes his hearts home, along with a note of explanation. When a youngster shows kindness to someone, an adult family member notes the good deed on a heart and the child adds an illustration. After all the hearts are returned to school, we arrange them in a large heart shape on a hallway wall.

Michele Holmes, Heather Menduke,
Kimberly Schwarz
Dogwood Hill Elementary
Oakland, NJ

Our Readers Write

Sweet Treat

At the end of our butterfly unit, I give each student a Lepidoptera lollipop! To make one, I use a permanent marker to draw a face and two antennae on the wrapper of a lollipop. Next, I cut a rectangle from a colorful napkin. I pinch the rectangle in the middle, wrap clear tape around it, and then tape it to the lollipop to make wings. My students love to show off their butterfly vocabulary by saying, "Thank you for the Lepidoptera lollipops!"

Diane L. Tondreau-Flohr
Kent City Elementary
Kent City, MI

Display Updates

One of the best decorating ideas I've tried is an ongoing thematic display. I use bulletin board trim to make a large rectangle on a wall. I title the resulting display area with the name of the theme. Then I showcase samples of relevant student work with a sign that says, "Look What We Are Learning!" When we begin a new theme, I simply change the title and work samples. Since I don't need to replace any bulletin board paper, it's easy to update the display!

Maria Farnham
J. P. Ryon Elementary
Waldorf, MD

The pictures in this book are really funny. They made us laugh.

Three Rs Mascot

During our recycling unit, my students and I collect clean, recyclable trash items. Once we have an assortment of items, we brainstorm how we can create a figure with them. I glue the items together as agreed upon by the group. Then I display the figure in the hallway with a sign that reads, "Mr. Recycle says, 'Reduce, reuse, recycle!'" At the end of the school year, we give the figure to a recycling center for display.

Debbie Shaner, Woodward Elementary
St. Louis, MO

Goodbye Gift

Looking for a perfect thank-you present for a student teacher? Try this! Purchase a few books that your students enjoyed reading with her. Then mount inside each book a group photograph of the youngsters along with student comments about the book. The intern not only gets books for her future classroom, but she also gets picture-perfect mementos!

Angela Phillips
Richard Bryan Elementary
Las Vegas, NV

Geometry Hero

To help my students remember the attributes of a cylinder, I draw a face on a large cylinder. Then I attach a colorful cape to the cylinder and label the cylinder with a large C. When I introduce the prop to students, I say, "It stacks! It rolls! It slides! It's Super Cylinder!" My students love it, and now they can easily identify cylinders!

Lori Billings
Washington Elementary
Gallipolis, OH

Graphing Ease

Painters' tape is a great tool for math time! I use it to make a graph grid on a wall. Then I add a title and labels. To complete the graph, I give each student a person cutout with his name on it. The youngsters illustrate their cutouts and then post them on the graph with reusable adhesive. Since the grid and cutouts can be reused, they save me lots of time.

Crystal Howard
Queens Creek Elementary
Swansboro, NC

More Can Play!

I make Concentration games for a variety of themes and skills. Instead of having just a few students play a game on a table or the carpet, I arrange the cards in a pocket chart. That way more children can easily see the cards and play at one time!

Susanne Ward
Caledonia Centennial Public School
Caledonia, Ontario, Canada

$8 + 8 =$

16

No Laminating or Hole-Punching

When I make class books, I save time and materials by using plastic page protectors. I slip each child's page in a top-loading page protector. Then I secure the page protectors with metal rings or place them in a three-ring binder. At the year's end, I remove each child's page from its page protector and invite him to take it home. Students are pleased to show their families their work. Plus, I can reuse the page protectors the following year!

Jill Haertner
Hondo First Baptist Church School
Hondo, TX

Globe Matchup

This approach to geography is a hit among my students! I put tracing paper on a globe and loosely trace the outer edges of each continent. I use the tracings as patterns and make corresponding felt cutouts. Then I have students match the cutouts to the correct places on the globe and help them name the continents. For reinforcement, I put the globe and cutouts at a learning center.

Ruthanne Fridley
J. Andrew Morrow Primary School
Towanda, PA

Nifty Notecards

Since I often send personal notes to parents, I came up with this quick and easy idea for making attractive notecards. First, I use watercolor paints to paint stripes all over an 8½" x 11" sheet of white paper. After the paint dries, I cut the paper into quarters (to 4¼" x 5½"). Then I cut two small sheets of construction paper in half lengthwise. I fold each resulting strip in half and then glue the paintings to the front of the folded paper. In nearly no time at all, I have four beautiful cards!

Carol Cochuyt
Fleming Island Elementary
Orange Park, FL

Top Banana

Here's how I put a fresh spin on the traditional student-of-the-day idea. Each morning before my students arrive, I place a plastic banana on a child's desk to designate him as the top banana. The honored youngster has several special jobs, such as helping at calendar time and being the line leader. My students are always eager to see who will be the next top banana!

Mary McGowan
Will L. Lee Elementary
Richmond, MI

Beach Parfait

Making this delicious snack is a great way to end an ocean unit. To make the snack, a child crushes a whole graham cracker in a plastic bag. She pours the crushed cracker (sand) into a clear disposable cup. Then she puts one-half cup of blue-tinted vanilla pudding on the sand. Finally, she tops the snack with whipped cream!

Anne Hoffman
The Young School
Columbia, MD

Unequaled Math Mats

Special workmats make it fun for my students to practice using greater than, less than, and equal to signs. To make a mat, I use brads to attach two tagboard strips to the middle of a tagboard rectangle. To use the mat, I have a student place a set of objects or a number card on each half of the mat. Then I ask him to compare the sets or numbers by making the appropriate math sign with the strips.

Jessica Wells
Baker Elementary
Moorestown, NJ

91

Beautiful Borders

I use gift wrap to add a festive touch to my bulletin boards. I accordion-fold strips of gift wrap. Then I make scalloped, zigzag, or other decorative cuts along the top of each folded strip. After I unfold the strips, they're ready to add to a display!

Linda Rasmussen
Donner Springs Elementary
Reno, NV

Ride and Look

Before I take my class on a bus for a field trip, I make a list of different points of interest we will see on the way. Once we are on the bus, I give each student a copy of the list and a crayon. Whenever a student sees a designated sight, I have him mark it on his paper. The scavenger hunt keeps my youngsters busy during the entire bus ride!

Kris McLouth
Court Street Elementary
Lancaster, NY

Key Volunteers

Here's a picture-perfect way to thank adults who help in your classroom. Place a reduced picture of your class in a key ring photo frame. Attach a card with a desired message. Then have students present the keepsake to the deserving adult.

Diane Bonica
Deer Creek Elementary
Tigard, OR

Ms. Jones, you were a key part of our year!

Deer Creek Elementary

Gift For Dad

This Father's Day magnet is a hit with my students! To make one, instruct a student to write the message shown on a baseball cutout. Then have him glue a photograph of himself below the message and sign his name. Laminate the baseball for durability and then put a magnet on the back of it.

Stacy Maneri
Moriah Central School
Moriah, NY

You're an all-star dad!

Love, Mark

Letter, Letter, Word

When I need a fun spelling game, I have students play this variation of Duck, Duck, Goose. I ask students to sit in a circle. I choose one student to be It and I whisper a word to her. Next, the youngster walks around the outside of the circle, touching a different classmate's head as she names each letter in the word. After she says the last letter, she announces the word as she touches the next student. This classmate stands up and chases her around the circle. The first student who reaches the recently vacated spot quickly sits down in it. To continue, I whisper a different word to the student who is still standing.

Jennifer Braden
Bangor Township Schools
Bay City, MI

SIMPLE SCIENCE

Melt and Mix!
Making predictions

For this cool approach to mixing colors, make a supply of red, yellow, and blue ice cubes. Divide students into small groups and give each group three clear plastic cups. Instruct the students in each group to put two ice cubes in each cup so that each cup has a different color combination. Have the students label each cup with two adhesive dots in the corresponding colors. Next, ask volunteers to predict what will happen to the ice cubes of each color combination. Instruct each youngster to illustrate or write her prediction on provided paper. After the ice partially melts, ask students to discuss and record their observations.

For an easier version, have students experiment with a different color combination on each of two days. Encourage students to use the results from the first day to help them make reasonable predictions on the second day.

Susan Braun
Roanoke Elementary
Roanoke, IN

I wonder whether all of the shells have ridges.

Under Investigation
Making and recording observations

Students will feel like scientists at this open-ended center! Place a supply of paper in a three-ring binder and title the binder "Our Science Log." Place the binder, a magnifying glass, a ruler, and a supply of pencils and crayons at a center. If desired, also provide a date stamp for dating entries in the log. Every week or so, set out different science-related items for students to explore. For example, you might set out seashells, rocks, leaves, plants, or pieces of bark.

When a student visits the center, he explores the items and records his observations in the log. Encourage students to make specific observations about details such as color, shape, size, and texture. Periodically set aside time for the young scientists to report their observations to the group. To prompt further exploration, comment on the observations and wonder aloud about other details that students may investigate. **For more advanced students,** post questions at the center to guide students' investigations.

Ty Powell
21st Century Academy
Chattanooga, TN

SIMPLE SCIENCE

Nighttime Song
Identifying nocturnal animals

After students are familiar with this catchy tune, lead them in additional verses about different nocturnal animals if desired. To follow up, post the song with student illustrations of the featured animals.

(sung to the tune of "Are You Sleeping?")

Nocturnal animals, nocturnal animals
Stay awake at night, stay awake at night.
Raccoons are nocturnal.
Opossums are nocturnal.
Awake at night. Awake at night.

Nocturnal animals, nocturnal animals
Stay awake at night, stay awake at night.
Owls are nocturnal.
Foxes are nocturnal.
Awake at night. Awake at night.

Nocturnal animals, nocturnal animals
Stay awake at night, stay awake at night.
I go to sleep, I go to sleep.
Good night, good night!

adapted from an idea by Myra Ingram
Yorktown Elementary Math, Science, and Technology Magnet
*   School*
Yorktown, VA

Weather Watchers
Describing the weather

With this daily activity, the forecast is for increased home-school communication! To make a microphone, secure a foam ball to one end of a cardboard tube. Cover the ball with foil and the tube with paper. Then attach a length of yarn to the open end of the tube. To prepare a take-home envelope, sign the letter on a copy of page 99. Cut apart the letter and report form. Then glue the letter to the front of a large envelope. Next, laminate the envelope for durability and the form for daily use. Slit the opening in the envelope. Then place the form and a wipe-off marker in the envelope.

Send the envelope home with each student on a rotating basis, asking each child to complete the report for the next school day with an older family member. When it is time for a youngster to present the day's weather report, hold the microphone and introduce the child with an announcer voice. Then pass the microphone to the child and have her read her report. Students will not only increase their science and math skills, but they will also boost their speaking skills!

Sally Williams
Mirror Lake Elementary
Villa Rica, GA

SIMPLE SCIENCE

Watchful Groundhog
Understanding how shadows form

Getting ready:
- Set up an overhead projector.
- Collect several small familiar objects that form distinctive shadows.

Activity: Turn on the overhead projector and point out to students how the light shines when it is unobstructed. Next, place an object on the projector and encourage students to tell what they notice. *(A shadow is cast.)* Guide youngsters to realize that when an object blocks light from shining on a surface, a shadow is formed. To follow up, place several items on the projector while concealing them from students' view. Designate a volunteer as a groundhog. Then lead the class in the first line of the chant shown. After the volunteer responds by completing the second line, invite him to point out the item he identified. To continue, rearrange or replace the items and then invite a different student to be the groundhog.

Cherie Rissman
Urbandale, IA

> Groundhog, Groundhog, what do you see?
>
> I see a [fork's] shadow in front of me!

Penny-Wise
Making and testing predictions

Getting ready:
- Get a penny, a paper towel, an eyedropper, a small container of water, and a marker.
- Post a sheet of chart paper.
- Gather a small group of students.

Activity: Put the penny on the paper towel and have students predict how many drops of water will fit on it. Record the predictions. Then use the eyedropper to put a drop of water on the penny. After you draw a tally mark on the paper, invite students to examine the penny at eye level and describe what they observe. *(The water bulges.)* Next, have youngsters add water to the penny one drop at a time and help you keep a tally of the number of drops. Once the water rolls off the penny, compare the actual number of drops with students' predictions. Since surface tension holds the water on the coin, a surprising number of water droplets can fit on it! No doubt your young scientists will be eager to test the results, so arrange for them to repeat the investigation with different coins.

Christina Kutz
North Olmsted, OH

Simple Science

Tadpole Transformation
Frog life cycle

Getting ready (for each student):
- Copy the frog patterns from page 100 onto green construction paper to make one head and body, two front legs, and two back legs.
- Cut one 2½" x 6" green construction paper rectangle.
- Gather five brads.

Activity: Have each child cut out the patterns and then use brads to attach two front legs and two back legs to the body. Instruct him to trim the rectangle to make a tadpole tail and then attach the tail to the body with a brad. Ask him to cut two eyes from white paper scraps. Then have him draw black pupils on the eyes, glue the eyes to the frog, and draw two nostrils. After each child has completed his project, instruct him to tuck the legs behind the body and keep the tail extended so it looks like a tadpole. Then, as you share the information below, have each youngster use his project to model how a tadpole changes as it grows.

Mary Alsager, Irving Primary School, Highland Park, NJ

A tadpole grows hind legs.
It develops lungs and grows front legs.
It becomes a tiny frog and absorbs its tail.

Amazing Changes
Butterfly life cycle

To reinforce a lesson about a caterpillar's metamorphosis into a butterfly, teach students the first verse below. Then lead them in singing additional verses, replacing the first, second, and fourth lines with the next line in the sequence shown. Conclude the song by repeating the first verse. It's a sure-fire way to help students remember that the life cycle continues!

(sung to the tune of "The Farmer in the Dell")

[A butterfly lays some eggs.]
[A butterfly lays some eggs.]
Hi-ho, metamorphosis!
[A butterfly lays some eggs.]

The eggs begin to hatch.
The caterpillar eats and eats.
It becomes a chrysalis.
We all watch and wait.
The chrysalis cracks and splits.
Out comes a butterfly.

Diane L. Tondreau-Flohr, Kent City Elementary, Kent City, MI

SIMPLE SCIENCE

Build a Bug!
Identifying the parts of an insect
Getting ready:
- Make a supply of construction paper ovals in various sizes and colors.
- For each student, make a label for each of the following insect parts: head, thorax, abdomen, legs, eyes, antennae, wings.

Activity: Each student selects three ovals to make the body of a chosen type of insect. He cuts from construction paper six legs and other appropriate features, such as eyes, antennae, and wings. Next, he arranges the ovals and cutouts on a sheet of paper to form the insect and adds any desired marker details. After he glues the pieces to the paper, he glues the appropriate labels in place. (He discards any extra labels.) He draws lines from the labels to the corresponding parts of the insect as needed for clarity. Then he titles the resulting diagram and signs his name.

Ana Catasús-Perez, Mother of Christ Catholic School, Miami, FL

Cool Colors
Making and testing predictions
Getting ready:
- Divide a horizontal sheet of paper into three sections and label them as shown. Copy the paper to make a class supply.
- Make red and blue ice cubes with tinted water so there is one ice cube per student.
- Brighten a pitcher of lemonade with yellow food coloring.

Activity: Give each student a serving of lemonade in a clear plastic cup. Instruct her to illustrate the lemonade in the first section of her paper. Also have her draw and color in that section a separate illustration of either a red or blue ice cube. Ask her to silently predict what will happen if she adds an ice cube of that color to her lemonade. Instruct her to record her prediction in the second section of the paper. Then have her put an ice cube of the chosen color in her cup. After she stirs the lemonade with a plastic spoon, ask her to record her observations in the third section of the paper.

Andrea Singleton, Waynesville Elementary, Waynesville, OH

Weather Report

Good morning! Here is the weather forecast for

_____.

date

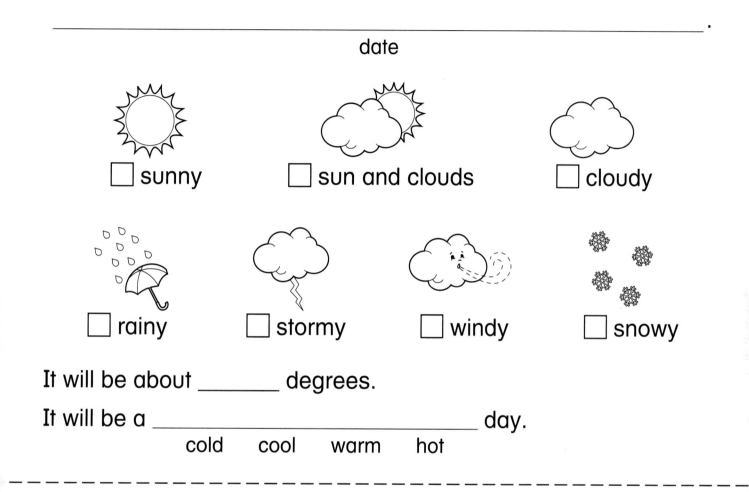

☐ sunny   ☐ sun and clouds   ☐ cloudy

☐ rainy   ☐ stormy   ☐ windy   ☐ snowy

It will be about _____ degrees.

It will be a _____ day.

cold   cool   warm   hot

Dear Family,

    Your child will be our student meteorologist tomorrow and announce the weather in class. Please check the local weather forecast with your youngster. Then help him or her fill out the enclosed report. Have your child practice reading the report and return it to school tomorrow. Thank you!

Sincerely,

Note to the teacher: Use with "Weather Watchers" on page 95.

Frog Patterns
Use with "Tadpole Transformation" on page 97.

head and body

front leg

back leg

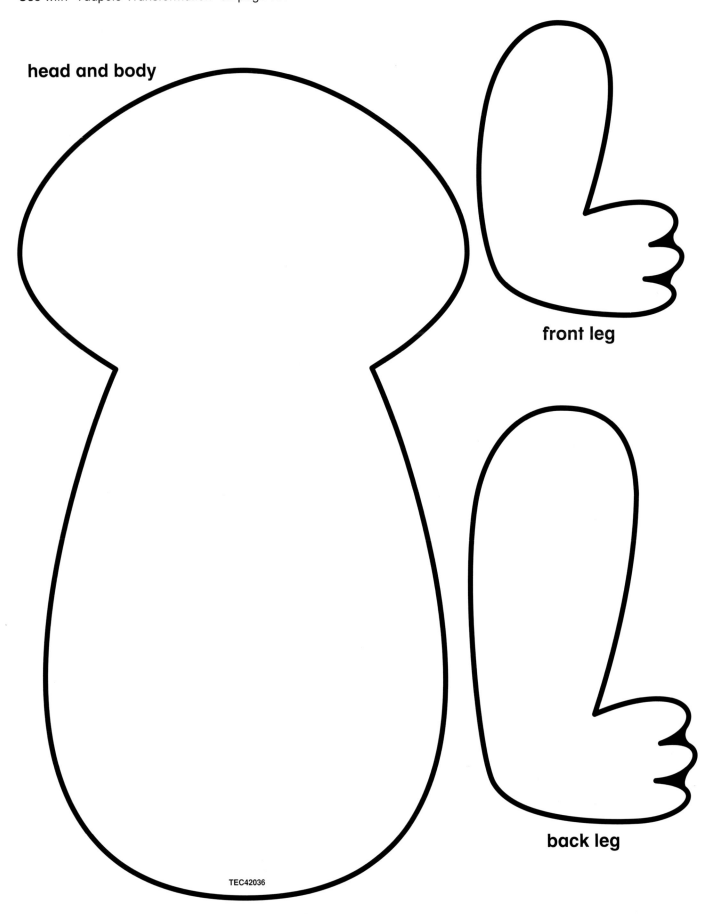

TEC42036

SKILLS FOR YOUNG READERS

Skills for Young Readers

Mr. Pointer
Concepts About Print

This adorable pointer is sure to make group reading activities much-anticipated experiences! Place a dowel in the pointer finger of a garden glove and then stuff the glove with cotton. Embellish the pointer finger with facial features and a bow. Use craft glue and string to secure the cuff to the dowel. Position the thumb and fingers as shown and glue them in place.

When it's time for a group reading activity, lead students in singing the first song below as you take out the pointer. Use the pointer to help students track print and focus on particular words. For added fun, pretend that the pointer whispers comments to you. To conclude the activity, sing the second song with students as you put the pointer away.

(sung to the tune of "Yankee Doodle")

Mr. Pointer, please come out.
We need you here today.
We like reading lots of words
And you can point the way!

(sung to the tune of "Good Night, Ladies")

Goodbye, Pointer. Goodbye, Pointer.
Goodbye, Pointer, until we read again!

Lisa Jarosh
St. Elizabeth Elementary
Pittsburgh, PA

Picture Pairs
Rhyming

For this group activity, gather two small tissue boxes. Color and cut out enlarged copies of the picture cards on page 114. Glue a picture to each side of both boxes so that the pictures in each rhyming pair are on different boxes. Sit with students in a circle. To begin, pass each box to a different student. Next, have the youngsters roll the boxes and then name the pictures that are on top. If the words rhyme, each student in the group gives a thumbs-up. If the words do not rhyme, each student gives a thumbs-down and a volunteer names words that do rhyme with the two pictures. The activity continues as described until each student has had a turn rolling a box.

Kathryn Davenport
Partin Elementary
Oviedo, FL

Mouse, house!

Looking for Letters
Environmental Print

To make this appetizing class book, cut the front from a package of food whose name begins with a chosen letter. Have students identify the name of the food and its initial letter. Write the letter near the top of a sheet of paper. Then mount the packaging on the paper. Repeat the activity to make a page for each alphabet letter, reviewing each previously prepared page with students before making a new page. (For less common letters, consider using foods that have the letters anywhere in their names.) Bind the pages in alphabetical order between two covers. Then title the book "Our Food Alphabet."

Karen Knecht
Dalton Elementary
Baton Rouge, LA

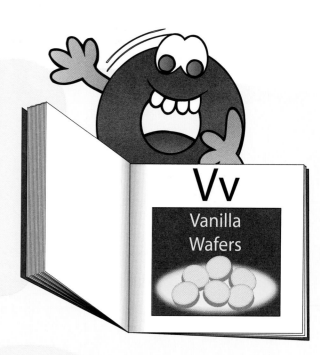

Mystery Alphabet
Letter Knowledge

Stretch students' thinking with this intriguing display idea! Secretly place in a paper lunch bag several small, like items whose names begin with a chosen letter. Draw the letter block-style very lightly on a sheet of tagboard.

To begin, hold the tagboard so the letter will be facing students when it is cut out, but avoid letting them see the drawing. Cut out the letter, pausing periodically for students to guess what it is. After it is cut out, tell students that the bag holds items whose names begin with the letter. Shake the bag to give them a clue. Once students correctly guess what is in the bag, have them glue the contents to the letter. Then post the letter on the wall. Repeat the activity over a few weeks to create a unique display from *A* to *Z!*

Sarah Currier
Glendale Elementary
Savage, MN

Empty the Box!
Letter Knowledge or High-Frequency Words

Here's a versatile idea that's perfect for when you have just a few minutes. Draw a large cube on the board. Then write several letters or high-frequency words on the cube. Next, tell students that the goal is to empty the box quickly. To do this, a youngster goes to the board, names a letter or word, and then erases it. He quickly returns to his seat and passes the eraser to the next student. That student takes a turn in the same manner. The activity continues as described until the box is empty.

Marie Mahon
Fountain Inn Elementary
Fountain Inn, SC

Skills for Young Readers

Alphabet Hunt
Letter Knowledge

It's a snap to prepare this activity with a word-processing program. Choose several letters to reinforce. Then type several rows of the uppercase and lowercase forms of the letters, varying the order of the letters and leaving space between them. Give each child a copy of the list and several counters.

Next, write on the board the uppercase and lowercase forms of a chosen letter. Have students name the letter. Then ask each youngster to place a counter on each occurrence of the letter on his paper. Instruct him to give a thumbs-up when he thinks he has marked all the matching letters. After each child signals in this manner, tell students how many counters they should have on their papers and encourage them to check their work. Then instruct students to clear their papers. Write a different letter on the board to continue. **For a word recognition version,** use high-frequency words or word families instead of letters.

Kelsey Strohm
Milton, WI

Stop and Start!
Comprehension

Retelling stories gets a green light with this idea. To make a story traffic sign, cut out two equal-size paper circles, one red and one green. Tape a craft stick to one circle to make a handle. Then glue the other circle on top so that the edges are aligned. After a read-aloud, sit with students in a circle and hold the sign with the green side facing them. Have a volunteer begin retelling the story. At a chosen point in the retelling, signal the volunteer to stop by turning the sign to the red side. Then name a different student, turn the sign to the green side, and have that youngster continue the retelling. Continue as described until students retell the entire story. Since you control who tells the story and for how long, it's easy to accommodate various skill levels. Plus, students are sure to pay close attention so they are ready for their turns!

Gretchen Braun, Letort Elementary
Washington Boro, PA

Colorful Questions
Word Recognition

Looking for a fun way to give students practice reading words in context? Try this! Gather a few die-cut shapes of different colors. Display the shapes in a pocket chart with questions that have the incorrect color words, like the ones shown. Write the response shown for each question, leaving space for the color word. Add the responses to the chart and place a supply of color word cards nearby. Then have students read the sentences and complete the responses with the correct word cards.

Andrea Goodman, Goodrich Elementary
Milwaukee, WI

Is it yellow?
No, it is red.
Is it green?
No, it is orange.

(sung to the tune of "If You're Happy and You Know It")

If you're reading and get stuck,
[check the picture.]
If you're reading and get stuck,
[check the picture.]
If you're reading and get stuck,
That's one thing that you can try.
If you're reading and get stuck,
[check the picture.]

Suggestions for additional verses:
look for chunks.
start the word.
ask, "What makes sense?"

Simple Solutions
Reading Strategies

Use this versatile song to help youngsters remember what good readers do when they come to words they don't know. As students become familiar with different strategies, teach them corresponding verses.

Christi Lee, B. F. Adam Elementary
Houston, TX

A "Lotto" Pizza
Number Words

To prepare this small-group game, make a few copies of the pizza gameboard on page 115. Program the gameboards with chosen numbers from 1 to 10, writing one number on each circle and making each board unique. Copy the boards to make a class supply. Make one copy of the spinner for each group. Cut out each spinner and attach a paper clip to it with a brad. Each group also needs one gameboard per player and a supply of round red counters (pepperoni slices).

To play one round, one player spins the spinner and reads the corresponding word. Each player who has the matching number on her pizza places a counter on it if it is not already marked. Then the next player spins the spinner and announces a number for players to mark. Play continues as described until one or more players marks all her numbers and calls out, "Delicious!"

Cris Edwards, Gardendale, AL

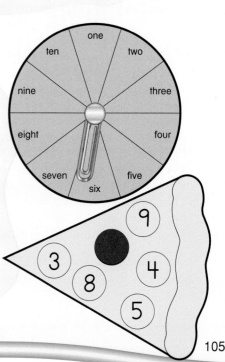

105

Skills for Young Readers

The three bears went for a walk.

Five-Finger Reminder
Comprehension

No materials are needed for this handy retelling strategy! To introduce the strategy to students, read aloud a story with a clear beginning, middle, and end. Then ask each student to hold up a closed hand. Next, invite a volunteer to retell a significant event that happened at the beginning of the story. Once he finishes telling about it, have each youngster raise his thumb. Have volunteers continue the retelling with three events or details from the middle of the story, and instruct each student to raise his next finger after each addition to the story. Then ask a youngster to recap the end of the story and have each student raise his last finger. To celebrate the students' successful teamwork, invite each student to give a classmate a high five.

Andrea Taylor, Southwest Elementary, Jacksonville, NC

Stop the Music!
Letter identification

For this letter-perfect group activity, place a name card for each student in a container. Have youngsters arrange their chairs in a circle with the chairs facing outward. Then place a different alphabet letter card on each chair. To begin, play some lively music and instruct students to walk in the same direction around the chairs. After a few moments, stop the music. At this signal, each child takes the card on the nearest chair and sits down. Next, take a name card at random. Ask the corresponding child to identify the letter on her card. Then have the group name a word that begins with that letter. Resume the music to continue play.

For a version with words, instead of using cards with letters, use cards with reading words or words from antonym word pairs. After a youngster identifies a word, ask her to use it in a sentence or have her name an antonym.

adapted from an idea by Rhonda Urfey
Allan A. Greenleaf Elementary, Waterdown, Ontario, Canada

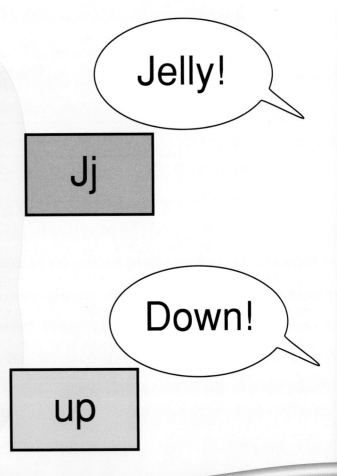

Winning Words
Word recognition

This skill-boosting version of tic-tac-toe is easy to manage for different reading levels. Make a desired number of gameboards like the one shown, each with a tic-tac-toe grid and decorative stickers. Write one word per grid space, using different-colored markers to program boards for different reading levels. Laminate the boards for reuse and set out wipe-off markers.

To play, students take turns as in the traditional game, except that before a player can claim a grid space, he needs to read the corresponding word correctly. The game ends when one player claims three spaces in a row and is declared the winner, or when every space has been claimed and the game is declared a draw.

Margo Parker, Lee F. Jackson Elementary, White Plains, NY

All Aboard!
Phonemic awareness

With this idea, it's full speed ahead with segmenting and blending! Have three students stand side by side. Hand a train engine cutout to the first student and a paper train car to each of the other two students. Explain that the train engine represents the beginning sound of a word, the second car represents the middle sound, and the last car represents the final sound. Next, say, "All aboard!" and name a word with three sounds. Then, beginning with the first child, have each youngster raise her part of the train as she says the corresponding sound in the word. Then ask the youngsters to blend the sounds.

For a word-making variation, use a sticky note to program each part of the train with the appropriate letter. Have students add or substitute different train cars to make new words.

Pick a Pair!
Initial consonant blends

Either a small group or a pair of students can play this phonics game. To prepare, write each *l* blend (*bl, cl, fl, gl, pl, sl*) on two separate index cards. Color and cut out a copy of the blend picture cards on page 116. Then glue each picture card on a separate index card. Have students play as in the traditional game of Concentration, pairing each picture card with the corresponding initial consonant blend.

Laura Wanke, Pecatonica Elementary, Pecatonica, IL

Skills for Young Readers

Rainbow Reading
Word recognition

To track students' reading vocabularies, draw a large rainbow on an 8½" x 11" sheet of paper. Write chosen words on alternating sections of the rainbow so that the more difficult words are on the outer sections. For easy coloring later, label each section with the first letter of the appropriate color word if desired. Make a copy of the rainbow for each student.

After a youngster can easily read the innermost group of words, ask her to color the corresponding section of the rainbow. Encourage her to practice reading each successive group of words and color the rainbow as described to record her progress. Once she masters all the words and finishes coloring the rainbow, instruct her to cut it out. Then have her glue the rainbow on blue paper and add cotton for clouds. It's sure to be a bright reminder of her achievement!

Debbie Hill, Stone Elementary, Crossville, TN

In a Flash!
Letter-sound associations

A set of alphabet flash cards is all you need for this small-group activity! Show a card to the first student. Have him identify the letter and say a word that begins with that letter. Then ask the next student to use the word in a sentence. After she says an appropriate sentence, show her a different card. Ask her to identify the letter and name a word that begins with that letter. Continue around the group as described. Since the activity is fast-paced, there's no doubt students will be eager to have more than one turn!

Carla Purdy
Fairmount Elementary
Fairmount, GA

For Poems and More!
Skill review

This versatile idea reinforces a variety of skills. Give each child a copy of a poem, song, or reading passage. After students are familiar with the reading material, make one copy of the form at the bottom of page 117. Program it to correspond with the reading material. Then have each child complete a copy of the programmed form. What a simple way to check his progress!

Sheila Criqui-Kelley, Lebo Elementary, Lebo, KS

I need to find -at words.

Drive or Park?
Long and short o

For this fun twist on sorting words, make a supply of car cutouts (pattern on page 117). Write a long *o* word on each of several cars. Then write a short *o* word on each remaining car. Label a paper road and a sheet of paper as shown and place them on the floor. Have students sit nearby. Next, invite a volunteer to take a car and read its word. If the word has the long *o* sound, each youngster pantomimes turning a steering wheel and the volunteer puts the car on the road. If the word has the short *o* sound, each youngster puts her hands in her lap and the volunteer "parks" the car in the lot. After students sort the rest of the cars in the same manner, they read each group of words.

adapted from an idea by Lyndsey Daiga
Keystone Schools, Fort Wayne, IN

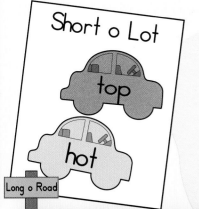

Point It Out!
Letter or word recognition

Nearly no advance preparation is needed for this activity. List several letters or words on the board. Then divide students into two groups. Have the students in each group line up behind one another facing the board. Give the first student in each line a pointer. Next, name a featured letter or word and have the two students quickly point to it. For a letter activity, ask them to name a word that begins with the letter. For a word activity, ask them to spell the word aloud. Then instruct each youngster to pass his pointer to the next student in his group and go to the end of the line. Continue as described until each youngster has had a turn.

Tammy Lutz, George E. Greene Elementary, Bad Axe, MI

can
man
pan
fan
ran
tan

Skills for Young Readers

Bear. Big!

Round and Round
Letter-sound associations

Have students sit in a circle for these variations of the traditional game of hot potato.

To review one letter, get a small object whose name begins with a chosen letter. Have students pass the object around the circle while you play some music. After a few moments, stop the music. Then ask the child holding the object to name it and say another word that begins with the featured letter. Resume the music to continue.

To review several letters, play some music as students pass around a small paper bag containing pictures whose names begin with different letters. Stop the music after a few moments. Then instruct the child holding the bag to remove a picture, name it, and state the corresponding beginning letter. After he sets the picture aside, resume the music. Continue as described until the bag is empty.

Angela Ward, Pearcy Elementary, Arlington, TX

Card Mix-Up
Initial consonant digraphs

For this group activity, put digraph cards like the ones shown in a pocket chart to create column headings. Color and cut out a copy of the picture cards on page 118. Then display the cards in the chart, putting some of them below the wrong digraphs and leaving one row empty so students can easily move the cards among the columns.

To begin, notice with mock surprise that the cards are scrambled. To correct the mix-up, direct students' attention to the first card. Then have each student give a thumbs-up if the card is in the correct column and a thumbs-down if it is not. Verify the correct response. If the card is below the wrong digraph, ask a youngster to move it to the correct column. Continue as described with the remaining cards.

Beverly Wells, Hopkins Road Elementary, Richmond, VA

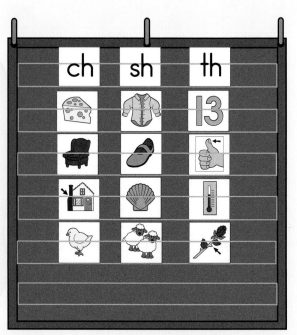

Shopping Spree
High-frequency words

A trip to Word Mart gives students valuable reading practice! To prepare, make a class supply of high-frequency word cards. Make three more sets of cards with the same words, making each set a different color. Write each different word on a separate paper lunch bag. Place the word cards around your room. To begin, give each child a bag. Then have her "shop" for her word by finding all the corresponding word cards and putting them in the bag. To "check out" from Word Mart, ask her to read the cards to you.

For more advanced students, give each youngster a list of different words (ingredients for word soup) and a plain paper lunch bag. Arrange for her to find one card for each listed word and complete her shopping trip as described above.

Sapna Datta, Endeavor Elementary, Orlando, FL

Prereading Predictions
Prior knowledge

Encourage students to think ahead with this nonfiction idea! Display a student photograph or a person cutout. Above it post a laminated thought bubble and small connecting bubbles. To begin, read the title of a chosen nonfiction book to students and briefly show them several illustrations. Next, have students brainstorm words they think are in the book; then list the words on the thought bubble. After you read the book aloud, ask students to draw a checkmark beside each listed word they heard during the reading. Then prompt a group discussion about any unmarked words.

Peggy Campbell-Rush, Union Township School, Hampton, NJ

Perfect Pairs
Rhyming

Sticky notes make this small-group activity a favorite! Make a 3" x 4" grid and write a consonant-vowel-consonant word in each grid space. For each word, write a rhyming word on a separate blank card. Post the grid and place a supply of sticky notes nearby. Next, take a card and read aloud the corresponding word. Encourage students to find a rhyming word on the grid. Then have a youngster read the word and cover it with a sticky note. Continue as described until all the words on the grid are covered. **To modify the skill,** feature different pairs of words such as antonym-word pairs or words that form compound words.

Cheryl Latil, Magnolia Park Elementary, Ocean Springs, MS

Skills for Young Readers

Breezy Review
Letter-sound associations

To make a windsock, a youngster writes an assigned letter on a horizontal 9" x 12" sheet of construction paper. She illustrates the paper with pictures whose names begin with the letter and then labels the pictures. Next, she turns the paper over and tapes several paper strips along the bottom edge of the paper. Then she turns the paper back over and writes the featured letter on the strips several times.

To complete the project, roll the paper into a cylinder with the strips to the inside. Staple the overlapping edges together. Then tape the ends of a length of string to the inside of the cylinder on opposite sides to make a hanger.

Kathryn Davenport, Partin Elementary, Oviedo, FL

Stepping Ahead
Antonyms or words with oo

Since students get to move around for this activity, it's sure to be a hit! Write each student's name on a separate craft stick and then stand the sticks in a container. Decide whether to focus on antonyms or words with *oo*. Then program a class supply of footprint cards (pattern on page 119) with corresponding words, writing one word per card. Arrange the cards in a large circle on the floor.

To begin, play some lively music and have students walk around the circle. After a few moments, stop the music and have students stand still. Next, take a stick at random and read the name aloud. Have the named student read the word on the nearest footprint. Then, for antonyms, ask him to say a word with nearly the opposite meaning. For words with *oo*, have him use the word in a sentence. Resume the music to continue.

Angela Jackson, Flemingsburg Elementary, Flemingsburg, KY

Glad!

Crash!
Letter-sound associations or word recognition

For this small-group game, use an option below to program two copies of the game cards on page 120. Color the cards and cut them out. Have a group member stack the cards facedown. To take a turn, a player takes the top card. If it shows a car, he responds as indicated below and keeps the card. If it shows *Crash!* he sets the card aside and puts any other cards he has at the bottom of the stack. The players take turns as described until no cards are left in play.

Letter-sound associations: Write a letter on each car. A child names the letter and a word that begins with the letter.
Word recognition: Write a reading word on each car. A child reads the word and uses it in a sentence.

Amanda Duffell, Landis Elementary, Landis, NC

The Story Tree
Comprehension

Branch out with story elements! Post a large bare-branched tree and label the trunk with the title of a familiar storybook. Write each story element on a bird cutout (pattern on page 119) and then post the birds on different parts of the tree. Next, give each child a leaf cutout. Have her describe and illustrate on the leaf an assigned story element. (More than one child may have the same story element.) Post the completed leaves near the appropriate birds. The result will be a "tree-rific" tool for discussing the story!

Kathryn Davenport, Partin Elementary, Oviedo, FL

Pick a Word!
High-frequency words, comprehension

Here's a kid-pleasing way to give students practice with reading sentences. Write several sentences on a magnetic whiteboard, replacing a high-frequency word in each sentence with a blank. Write the missing words on separate index cards and then spread out the cards facedown on a desk. Next, have a volunteer take a card and read its word aloud. Then ask the class to read the incomplete sentences. After the volunteer determines in which sentence the word belongs, have him post the card in place with a magnet. Then ask a different student to take a card. Continue as described until only one card remains on the desk. Then have a volunteer put it in place and read all the sentences!

Deborah Carlberg, Stewartsville Elementary, Goodview, VA

Picture Cards
Use with "Picture Pairs" on page 102.

TEC42032

TEC42032

TEC42032

TEC42032

TEC42032

TEC42032

TEC42032

TEC42032

TEC42032

TEC42032

TEC42032

TEC42032

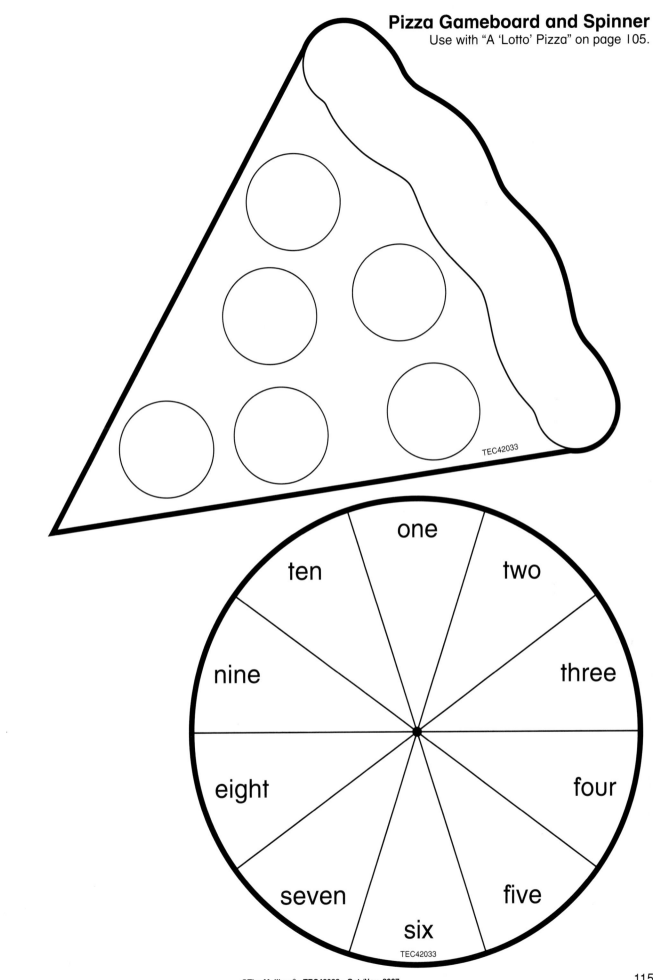

TEC42033

one

ten

two

nine

three

eight

four

seven

five

six

TEC42033

Blend Picture Cards

Use with "Pick a Pair!" on page 107.

TEC42034

TEC42034

TEC42034

TEC42034

TEC42034

TEC42034

TEC42034

TEC42034

TEC42034

TEC42034

TEC42034

TEC42034

TEC42035

Name_____ Reading

Search for Words!

1. Find these words: [   ]. Circle them with a red crayon.

2. Find three word wall words. Circle them with a yellow crayon.

3. Find _____ words. Circle them with a blue crayon.

4. Find a word that rhymes with _____. Underline it.

Picture Cards

Use with "Card Mix-Up" on page 110.

TEC42036

TEC42036

TEC42036

TEC42036

TEC42036

TEC42036

TEC42036

TEC42036

TEC42036

TEC42036

TEC42036

TEC42036

TEC42037

Bird Pattern
Use with "The Story Tree" on page 113.

TEC42037

Game Cards

Use with "Crash!" on page 113.

'Tis the Season

'Tis the Season

Tasty Treat

Refrigerated biscuits make preparing this apple snack as easy as pie! Purchase enough Pillsbury Golden Layers biscuits or similar biscuits so that there is one per child. Also purchase apple pie filling. (A 20-ounce can of filling is enough for more than 40 children.) To make a mini pie, a child splits a biscuit in half horizontally and places the halves on a piece of personalized aluminum foil. He puts a spoonful of pie filling on one biscuit half and then places the other biscuit half on top. After he seals the edges of the biscuit with a fork, he sprinkles a mixture of cinnamon and sugar on top. To bake students' pies, follow the biscuit baking instructions.

Cindy Schumacher
Prairie Elementary
Cottonwood, ID

Nuts About Fall

Use this lotto game for either letter or word recognition. Program a few copies of the gameboard on page 128, writing one letter or word per box and making each gameboard unique. Make one copy of each programmed gameboard and then cut apart the boxes to make caller's cards. Have each child color and cut out a copy of a programmed gameboard and a copy of the acorn cards on page 128. To play, take a caller's card at random and read it aloud. Instruct each student with a corresponding gameboard space to cover it with an acorn card. Continue the game as described until one or more students cover all of their gameboard spaces and call out, "Hooray for fall!"

Hooray for Fall!

at

it

and

I

Agreed!

Pay tribute to Constitution Day with this look at rules. To begin, invite students to tell why they think playground rules are important. Point out that the rules help youngsters get along and stay safe. Next, tell students that a long time ago an important group of men wrote rules for the United States for similar reasons. Then show students a picture of the U.S. Constitution.

To follow up, write student-generated playground rules on a large piece of paper. Have each child sign his name with a novelty pen. Afterward, take photos of students following the rules on the playground. Then display the playground constitution and photos near your classroom door. Each time students head to recess, they'll be reminded of the expectations!

Our Playground Constitution

We, the kids in room 12, promise to
take turns
share
play safely

Kaylee

Eric

Shante

Cameron

Hunter

Mia Arizona

Kieye

Ben

'Tis the Season

What's Inside?

Imagine hiding something in a pumpkin shell. That's what students do with this fall project! Give each child a copy of the sentence frame shown sized to fit a nine-inch circle. Have him complete the sentence, illustrate it, and then glue it on a nine-inch orange circle. To make a pumpkin, ask him to sponge-paint the back of a nine-inch white paper plate orange. After the paint is dry, have him glue to the plate a stem and the pumpkin sentence shown. Then staple the plate to the circle on the left-hand side.

Melissa Barker
Montgomery Elementary
San Antonio, TX

Turkey Sightings

This booklet project is a gobblin' fun approach to math! To prepare, make three copies of the first booklet page on page 130. Write the following words, each in the first blank on a separate page: *Two, Three,* and *Four.* For each student, copy the programmed pages as well as the illustrated booklet page and turkey cards on page 130. Arrange the pages in numerical order and place the illustrated page behind them. Then staple the pages between two construction paper covers.

To complete his booklet, a youngster writes a title and his name on the front cover. Next, he colors and cuts out the turkey cards. He glues the indicated number of turkeys on the first three pages and completes the sentences. Then he circles pairs of tracks on the last page. He determines how many turkeys there would be if each pair of tracks were made by a different turkey and then writes that number in the blank.

Angie Kutzer
Garrett Elementary
Mebane, NC

In Gratitude

For this poetic Thanksgiving idea, have each youngster complete a copy of the poem shown and then mount it on a larger piece of construction paper. Punch two holes side by side in the top of the paper. Then thread a length of ribbon through the holes and tie a bow. Whether you display the poems or encourage youngsters to present them to loved ones, they're sure to convey the heart of the holiday!

Giving Thanks
I am thankful for ___Mom___,
___My sister___,
And ___My house___.
They are special to me
And make me as happy as I could be!

123

'Tis the Season

Sensory Celebration

This holiday idea pairs writing and art. Have each youngster write about a chosen holiday on a copy of the writing form on page 132. Then ask her to mount the form on a larger piece of construction paper. To make a festive background, place a sheet of white paper in a shallow box and then squeeze a small amount of holiday-colored paint on it. Instruct the youngster to roll a Ping-Pong ball back and forth through the paint until a desired effect is achieved. Then remove the paper from the box. After the paint dries, staple the child's work to the painting.

Name Laura   Writing
Holiday Clues
I see   candles.
I hear   singing.
I smell   latkes.
It must be   Hanukkah!

Mittens for Kittens

Students look up, down, left, and right with this math game! Have each child color a copy of page 133 and then cut along the dashed lines. Next, instruct him to draw a colorful dot at each of three grid intersections. To play one round, name a grid location and ask each child to find it. If a child drew a dot at that location, he puts a pair of mittens on it. Continue the game as described until one or more students wins by placing all his mittens on his grid and calling out, "The kittens have found their mittens!"

Kim Criswell, Wilson, KS

Remember Dr. King's dream today
Where we live, learn, and play.

I will shr. I will not fite.

Peace and Equality

Pay tribute to Martin Luther King Jr. with this poster project. For each student, cut two wedges (wings) from the outer part of a small white paper plate. To begin, ask each student to illustrate how she will model Dr. King's dream of all people living in harmony. Have her write a caption or dictate a caption for you to write. Next, give each youngster a colorful copy of the poster label and a white copy of the dove pattern on page 132. Invite her to color the dove's beak and the poster label. After she cuts out the label and dove, have her fringe-cut the dove's tail. Then instruct her to glue one wing to the front of the dove and one wing to the back of it. Finally, ask her to glue the dove on a sheet of construction paper along with the label and illustration.

'Tis the Season

Mail Call!

To deliver Valentine's Day fun, choose an option below and prepare the activity as described. Decorate the bags. Then have students put each card in the correct bag.

Letter-sound associations: Cut out a copy of the illustrated heart cards on page 134. Write each of the following letters on a separate white paper lunch bag: *c, d,* and *f.*
Addition: Write a sum on each of a few white paper lunch bags. Program blank heart cards (patterns on page 134) with corresponding problems.

Marline Schindewolf, Moran Elementary, Osceola, IN

Find the Gold!

When students are not present, turn over a few chairs. Nearby, sprinkle glitter and leave a note with the following message: "To find the pot of gold, you must look in the [office], or so I'm told." Place a similar note in the designated location and other places to create a trail of clues. Place a class supply of foil-wrapped candy coins at the last location.

When students return and notice the disorder, suggest that a leprechaun dropped the note during his search for gold. Encourage students to find the gold before the leprechaun does, and use the notes to lead them on the search. After students find the gold, write about the experience as a class or have each youngster draw a map that shows where the gold was hidden.

Johnna Young, Rocky Gap Elementary, Rocky Gap, VA

Colorful Combinations

For this sweet activity, give each youngster several jelly beans of two different colors (patterns on page 135). Choose an option below. After each child completes an activity form as described, ask her to glue it to a sheet of paper along with the jelly beans and some cellophane grass.

Number and color words: Have a child complete a copy of the first form on page 135.
Addition stories: Give a child a copy of the second form on page 135. Instruct her to write the appropriate numbers, color words, and addition sentence.

Andrea Goodman, Goodrich Elementary, Milwaukee, WI

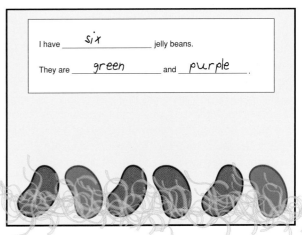

I have _____six_____ jelly beans.
They are _____green_____ and _____purple_____.

125

'Tis the Season

Spring Happenings

For this class book activity, title a sheet of chart paper "What Happens in the Spring?" List each child's response and write her name beside it. Later, give each child a strip of paper with her sentence and name. Instruct her to cut between the words. Have her glue her name and the sentence on a large sheet of paper, leaving space between the words. Then ask her to illustrate her work. Bind students' completed papers into a class book. Then ask each child, in turn, to lead students in reading her page as she points to the words.

Jacqueline Vandermeulen, Immanuel Christian School
Winnipeg, Manitoba, Canada

Flowers grow in the spring.
Abby

Sing and Read

Here's a toe-tapping approach to literacy! Give each child a copy of the song on page 137. After you teach youngsters the song, use the ideas below.

Word recognition: Ask students to determine how many times the word *spring* appears.
High-frequency words: Have youngsters highlight the words *and, are, is, now,* or *the.*
Compound words: Challenge students to find the two compound words.
Contractions: Ask students to identify the contractions.

adapted from an idea by Deborah Garmon
Groton, CT

Busy Bees

Once students are familiar with this addition game, they can take it home and play it with their families! Have each child color a copy of page 136 so the like flowers are the same colors. Then ask him to cut apart the cards. Pair students and give each youngster a game marker and a sheet of paper.

To play, each twosome uses one gameboard and one set of cards. The players put the cards in a disposable cup, and each player puts his marker on a different space with an arrow. Next, Player 1 takes a card at random. If the card shows a flower, he moves in a clockwise direction to the first matching flower. Then he names the corresponding addition fact and writes it on his paper. If the card shows a bee, he moves to a flower of his choice and then names and writes the appropriate fact. Player 2 takes a turn in the same manner. Alternate play continues as time allows, with the players reusing the cards as needed.

Just Beachy!

Program a few copies of the gameboard on page 139 for an option below, making each gameboard unique. Cut apart one copy of each programmed gameboard to make caller's cards. Give each child a copy of a programmed gameboard and the game markers from page 139. Instruct students to play as in the traditional game of lotto.

Letter-sound associations: Write a letter on each gameboard space. To call a letter, say a word that begins with the letter.
Place value: Write a two-digit number on each gameboard space. To call a number, say how many tens and ones it has.

On the Shore

Display this summery song as desired. After students are familiar with it, have them find the color words, the rhyming words, or chosen high-frequency words.

Margaret Southard
Cleveland, NY

> (sung to the tune of
> "Twinkle, Twinkle, Little Star")
>
> Seashells, seashells on the shore—
> Pick some up and look for more.
> Pink shells, white shells, big and small,
> In our pails we let them fall.
> Seashells, seashells on the shore
> Once lay on the ocean floor.

Berry Picking

For this small-group addition game, make one copy of each game mat and several copies of the game cards from page 140. Write a sum on each basket on the large mat and a corresponding addition problem on each strawberry. Cut out the cards, the bear mat, and one copy of a programmed mat for each player. Stack the cards facedown.

To take a turn, a player takes a card. If it shows a problem, he puts it on his basket with the correct sum. If it shows a bear, he takes a berry card from his mat, puts it on the bear's basket, and sets the bear card aside. (If he does not have a berry card, he simply sets the bear card aside.) Players take turns until no cards are left in play. Then they compare the contents of the baskets. **For a word family version,** program the large mat with rimes and each strawberry with a corresponding word.

adapted from an idea by Beth Marquardt
St. Paul's School of Early Learning, Muskego, WI

Gameboard and Acorn Cards

Use with "Nuts About Fall" on page 122.

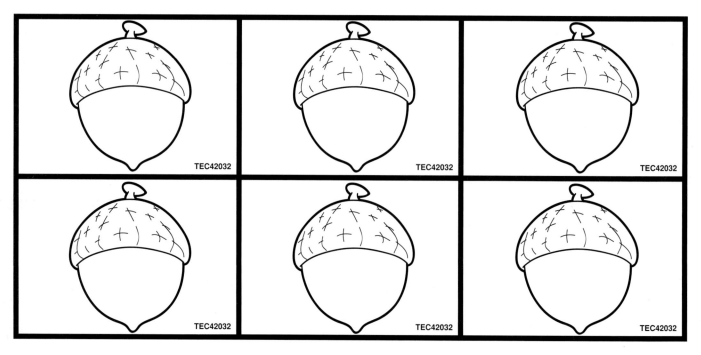

Name _____

Delicious!

Color to show what comes next.

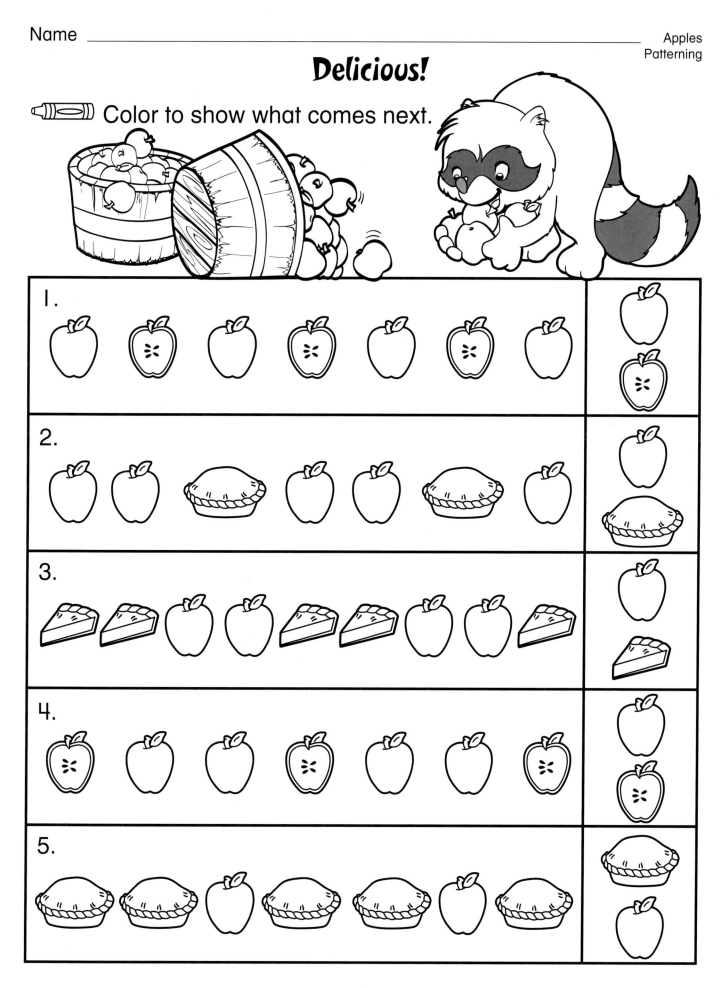

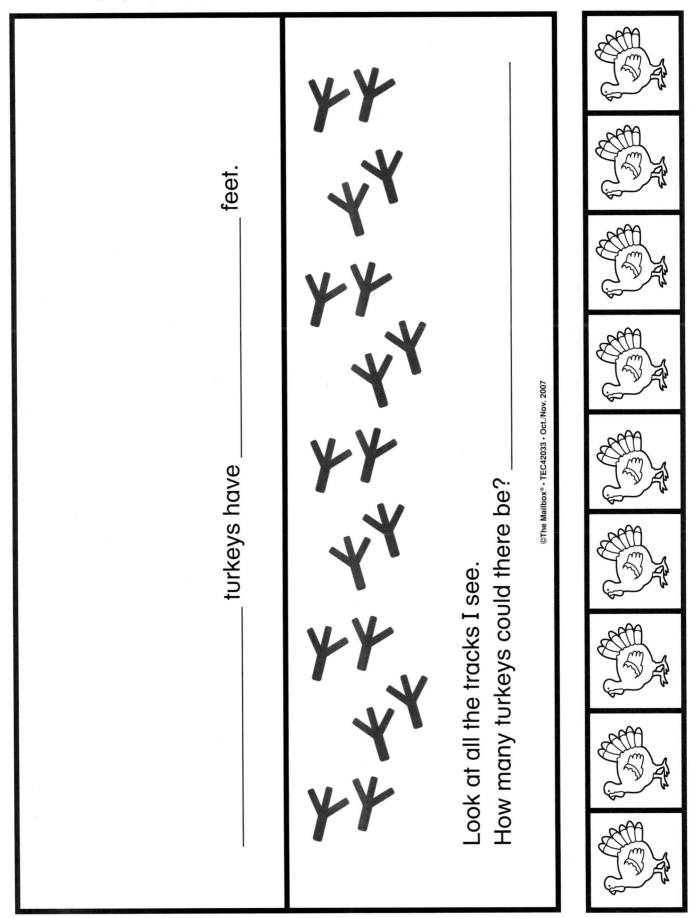

_____ turkeys have _____ feet.

Look at all the tracks I see.
How many turkeys could there be?

©The Mailbox® • TEC42033 • Oct./Nov. 2007

130

Mr. Patches

Read.
Color.
Write.

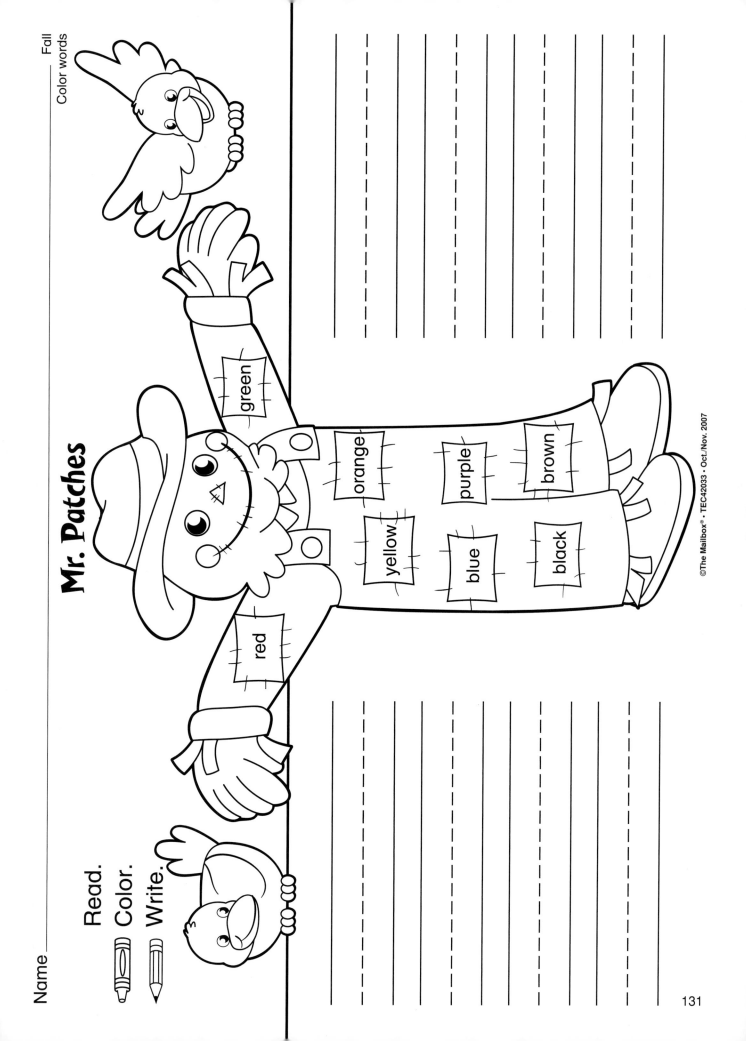

green

orange

purple

brown

yellow

blue

black

red

Writing Form

Use with "Sensory Celebration" on page 124.

Name _____ Writing

Holiday Clues

I see _____

I hear _____

I smell _____

It must be _____

TEC42034

Poster Label and Dove Pattern

Use with "Peace and Equality" on page 124.

Remember Dr. King's dream today
Where we live, learn, and play.

TEC42034

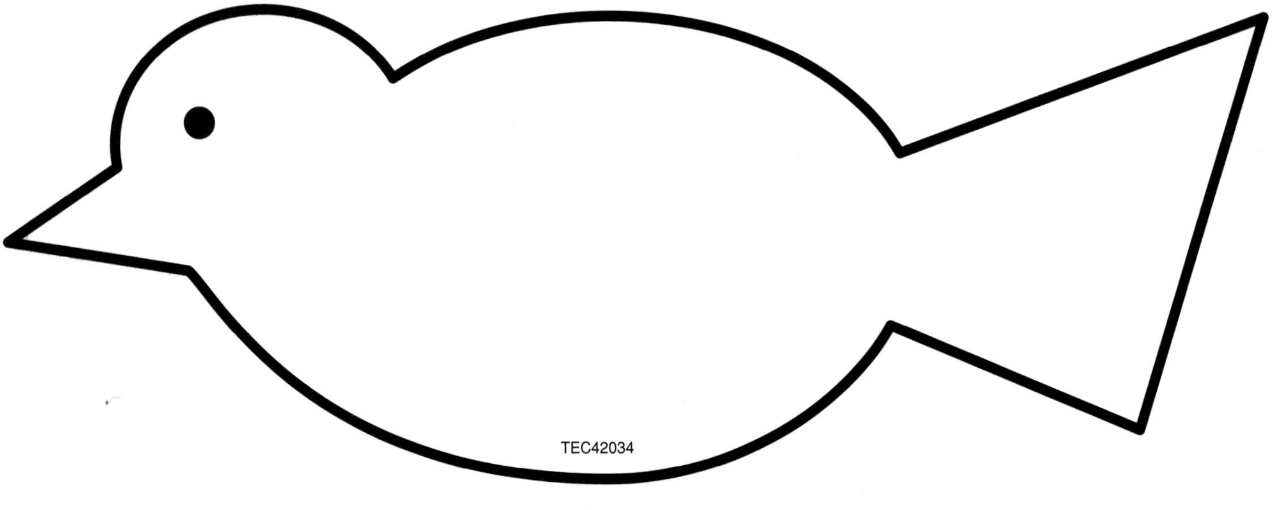

TEC42034

Mittens for Kittens

Listen for directions.

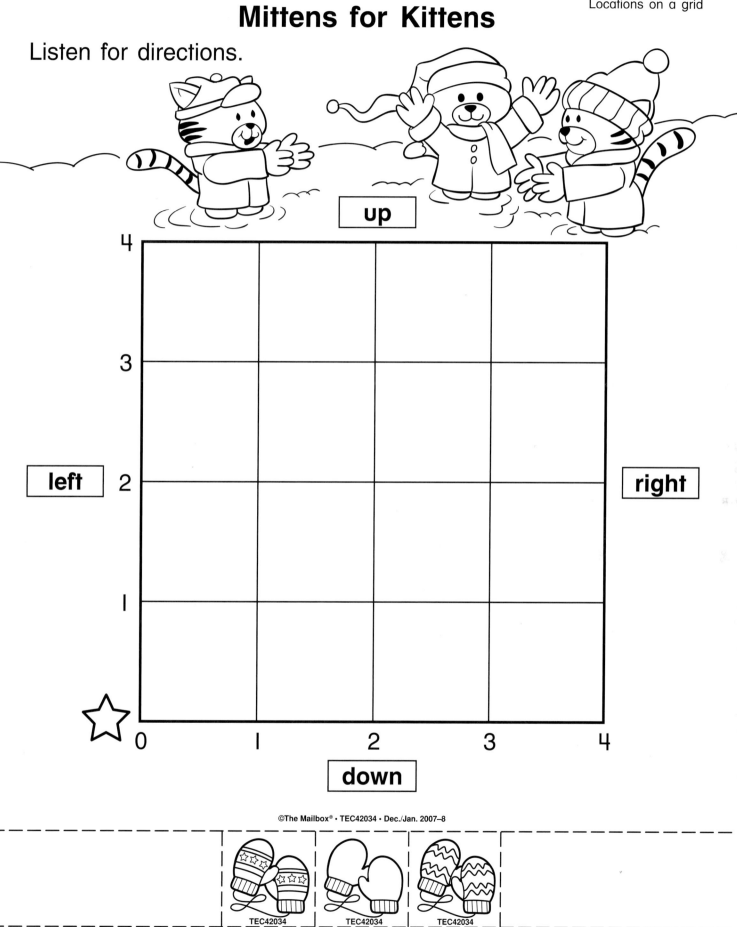

©The Mailbox® • TEC42034 • Dec./Jan. 2007–8

Note to the teacher: Use with "Mittens for Kittens" on page 124.

133

Heart Cards

Use with "Mail Call!" on page 125.

TEC42035   TEC42035   TEC42035

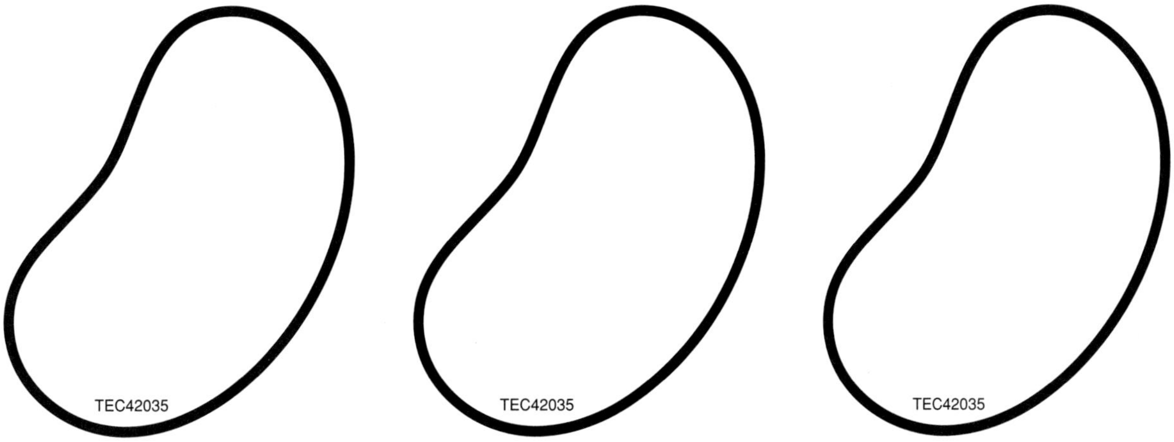

I have _____ jelly beans.

They are _____ and _____.

I have _____ _____ jelly beans.

I have _____ _____ jelly beans.

I have _____ jelly beans in all.

_____ + _____ = _____

Busy Bees

8 + 9 9 + 6 9 + 9

6 + 8 7 + 7

9 + 7 7 + 9

6 + 9 9 + 8

8 + 8 8 + 6

5 + 9 7 + 8

9 + 9 9 + 5 8 + 7

©The Mailbox® • TEC42036 • April/May 2008

Note to the teacher: Use with "Busy Bees" on page 126.

Hello, Spring!

(sung to the tune of "Up on the Housetop")

Winter is gone and now it's spring.

Flowers bloom and robins sing.

The sunshine is warm; it's nice and bright.

The butterflies are a pretty sight!

Spring, spring, spring! Now it's here.

Spring, spring, spring! Give a cheer!

Winter is gone and now it's spring.

Let's shout, "Hooray! We're glad it's spring!"

Note to the teacher: Use with "Sing and Read" on page 126.

Rainy Day Fun

✂ Cut. 🖊 Glue in order.

✏ Write.

1. _____

_____

_____

2. _____

_____

_____

3. _____

_____

_____

4. _____

_____

_____

Super Sand Castle

©The Mailbox® • TEC42037 • June/July 2008

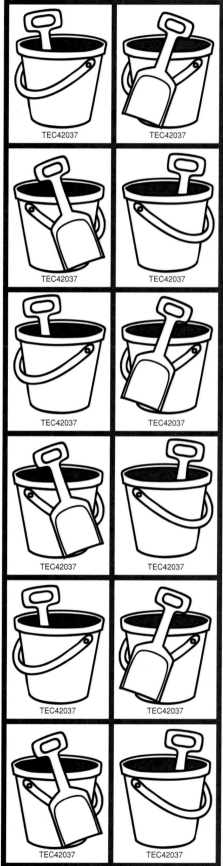

TEC42037

TEC42037

TEC42037

TEC42037

TEC42037

TEC42037

TEC42037

TEC42037

TEC42037

TEC42037

TEC42037

TEC42037

Game Mats and Game Cards

Use with "Berry Picking" on page 127.

My Berry Baskets

Berries for Bear

TEC42037

TEC42037

TEC42037

TEC42037

TEC42037

TEC42037

Hungry Bear

TEC42037

©The Mailbox® • TEC42037 • June/July 2008

WRITE ON!

Write On!

Month by Month

Track students' writing and drawing progress with this monthly activity. At the beginning of each month, make one copy of page 148 and write the current month in the blank below the name line. Then give each student a light-colored copy of the page. (The color will make it easy to distinguish the activity from other writing tasks.) Have each youngster write her name where indicated. Then encourage her to draw a self-portrait in the box and write below it as appropriate for her skill level. Provide additional writing paper if necessary. Keep each student's completed work on file or instruct her to add it to her journal. Since the task is the same each month, it will be easy to see her progress throughout the year!

Suzanne Ward, Seneca Unity Public School, Caledonia, Ontario, Canada

Focused on Feelings

To prepare this two-sided **class book**, program one side of a sheet of paper with the sentence starter "I smile when…" and the other side with the sentence starter "I frown when…" To begin, give each child a two-sided copy of the paper. Have each child complete the sentences himself or dictate sentence endings for you to write. Then instruct him to illustrate each sentence with a drawing or photo of himself. Stack students' completed papers with the smile sentences on top. Sandwich the papers between two covers and bind the entire stack at the top. Title and decorate the covers as desired.

Josephine Flammer, Brook Avenue School, Bay Shore, NY

Colorful Contributions

This multicolored approach to **shared writing** increases student ownership as well as home-school communication. Gather a small group of students near a sheet of chart paper. Choose a writing topic with student input and then have youngsters take turns dictating sentences. Write each child's sentence(s) with a marker of a different color. After the writing is complete, arrange for each student, in turn, to take the paper home overnight in a special folder. With the different colors of writing, youngsters can easily point out their contributions to their families! **For more advanced students,** invite youngsters to help write their sentences.

Stephanie Affinito, Glens Falls, NY

Write On!

Writing Resource

Here's a simple way to keep **frequently used words** at students' fingertips. Type a list of words your young writers often use (other than the ones on page 149), such as word wall words and students' names. Then copy the list and page 149 back-to-back to make a two-sided word reference for each student. Have each youngster write his name on his paper and then use crayons to color-code the color words. After he adds any other desired crayon details, ask him to keep the word reference in his journal or another easily accessible location. It's sure to help him become a more independent writer!

Carolyn Carr, Mountainview Elementary, Morgantown, WV

In Disguise

Spark a bumper crop of **imaginative writing** with this seasonal idea. Draw a face on a pumpkin. Disguise the pumpkin with a simple prop or two, such as a paper crown, a clown wig and nose, a cowboy hat and bandana, or a pair of plastic eyeglasses with a mustache. Then place the pumpkin at the front of the classroom or at your writing center. Nearby place a supply of writing paper or copies of a form similar to the one shown. After each child writes about the pumpkin, change the disguise for more writing fun!

Katie Klipp, Bob Jones Elementary, Greenville, SC

Seasonal Sentences

This approach to **descriptive details** can be used any time of the year. For each student, stack three sheets of paper and position them vertically. Slide the top two sheets upward about one inch and then slide the top sheet up about one more inch. Fold the papers forward to create six graduated pages. Staple the fold to make a booklet. To begin, each student titles her booklet "In the [Season]" and signs her name. Next, she labels the pages with verbs as shown. She uses each verb in a descriptive sentence on the corresponding page. Then she illustrates her work.

143

Write On!

Things That ★☆ Four-Star Writers Remember

★ name
☆ date
☆ picture
★ spaces between words

Star Quality

To help students become more independent writers, try this stellar **self-assessment idea**. Choose four details that you would like students to double-check before they turn in writing assignments. Then list the details on a poster like the one shown. Encourage students to refer to the poster whenever they write. After students' skills progress, add a different detail to the poster and change the title to match. No doubt youngsters will be thrilled to graduate from being four-star writers to five-star writers!

Helaine Rooney, Lakewood Elementary, Rockville, MD

cold snow

Winter Is...

By Tasha

Excellent Evergreen

You can use this "tree-rific" **booklet** in a variety of ways! To make a booklet, stack two 9" x 12" sheets of white paper and position them vertically. Slide the top paper up about 1½ inches. Then fold the papers forward to create four graduated pages. Lightly draw two diagonal lines to make the sides of a tree. Staple the tree at the top and then cut along the lines.

Give each youngster a booklet and ask her to color the front of it green. Then instruct her to write on the pages as desired. For example, you might have her write about winter, Christmas, or a seasonal read-aloud. Have her complete her booklet with a title, her name, and cover decorations such as tufts of cotton (snow) or colorful circles (ornaments).

Cindy Barber, Fredonia, WI

Super Soup

If desired, introduce this **seasonal activity** by reading aloud *Chicken Soup With Rice: A Book of Months* by Maurice Sendak. To begin, give each child a copy of page 150. Have him complete the sentence with the name of a chosen kind of soup. Then instruct him to write about the soup or respond to a soup-related prompt. After he finishes writing, instruct him to color the illustration and then mount his work on colorful paper. Display students' completed papers on a board titled "Warm Up With Writing!"

Amy DuBois, Orchard Farm Elementary, St. Charles, MO

Name Eddie   **Super Soup**   Writing

In a bowl or in a cup,
Tomato soup   warms me up!

I like tomato soup. I put milk in it. Then I stir it. It looks funny.

Write On!

Bedtime!

What better topic for writing **steps in sequence** than something students do every day? If desired, introduce the activity by reading aloud *Froggy Goes to Bed* by Jonathan London. Give each youngster a copy of page 151. (Provide additional copies if necessary.) Ask each child to illustrate his bedtime routine in the small boxes. Then have him refer to the word bank as he writes the steps.

Aris Velez, Southwest Elementary, Bayshore, NY

Creativity With Cutouts

Here's a simple way to **spark enthusiasm for writing**. Every once in a while, designate a writing time as Cool Cutout Hour. Set out a selection of cutouts and novelty pens and pencils. Ask each youngster to glue a cutout on a sheet of paper. Invite him to decorate the cutout or incorporate it into an illustration. Then have him use a chosen writing utensil to write something related to the cutout. For example, he might write a caption or share a relevant personal experience. Students are sure to have a variety of creative ideas!

Jo Fryer, Kildeer Countryside School, Long Grove, IL

Weekend Letters

Promote home-school communication with this approach to **letter writing!** Format a page with writing lines for a friendly letter and then make two copies. Title one copy "Student Letter" and the other copy "Parent Letter." Then, for each student, make a booklet with alternating copies of the papers, beginning with a student letter.

At the end of each week, have each youngster write in her booklet a letter to her parents telling them what happened at school that week. Ask her to take the booklet home and have her parents write a response to her letter on the page that follows it. Instruct her to return the booklet to school on Monday for more letter-writing fun!

Sheila Criqui-Kelley, Lebo Elementary, Lebo, KS

Write On!

Flowerpot Planner

Here's a **prewriting** strategy that's perfect for budding writers. Give each student a copy of the graphic organizer on page 152. Have him write a topic on the flowerpot, and ask him to illustrate or write a relevant detail on each flower. Encourage him to refer to the completed graphic organizer as he writes about the topic. It's sure to keep his writing focused!

Karen Luba, Racine, WI

Winged Wonder

Watch students' **writing motivation** soar with this clever project! For each child, fold in the sides of a 9" x 12" sheet of paper so they meet in the middle of the paper. Have each child make two butterfly wings and one butterfly body (patterns on page 153). After she decorates the wings, ask her to glue a wing on each folded half of the paper so the wings' straight edges are aligned. Next, have her glue the body to the paper, as shown, and draw two antennae. Then instruct her to unfold the paper and complete the project as described below.

Greeting card: Write on the project a message for Mother's Day or another occasion.
Poem: Write a spring poem on provided paper. Then glue it to the middle section of the project and illustrate the two blank sections.
List: Write a list of spring things on provided paper and then glue it to the project.

Diane L. Tondreau-Flohr, Kent City Elementary, Kent City, MI

Show-and-Write!

Looking for a way to help students choose **writing topics** that are important to them? Start with show-and-tell! After a brief show-and-tell time, have each student illustrate an object that he or a classmate shared with the group. Then ask him to write about it, including details such as his feelings and thoughts about the object or his reaction to it. If desired, give each child a show-and-tell journal and make this special writing time a weekly activity!

Mary Davis, Keokuk Christian Academy, Keokuk, IA

I shod a pikshur of Austin. He is my babe brudr. I am happy becuz he is comin home frm the hspl today. I cant wate!

Write On!

The ants go marching nine by nine.
The little one stops to read a sign.

Ant Parade

To introduce this **rhyming class book**, teach students the traditional song "The Ants Go Marching." Then, for each number 1 through 10, enlist students' help to write two sentences, similar to the ones shown, so the first sentence is like the song and the second sentence is a revised song line. Type each pair of sentences and the last two lines of the song. Mount the pairs of sentences on separate sheets of paper. After students illustrate the sentences, bind the papers in order between two covers.

Sheila Crawford, Kids Kampus, Huntington, IN

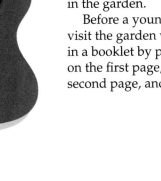

Name *Jason*

Describe It!

mnt chklt chip
ice crem

see

green like my
shrt
small chips

taste

mint
good

feel

crnche
cold

Deliciously Descriptive

The **graphic organizers** on page 154 make writing with details a treat! Have each youngster complete a copy of a graphic organizer as described below. Ask him to refer to it as he writes a description or story on provided paper. If desired, bind his completed writing into a booklet and then invite him to decorate the cover with an ice cream illustration and a plastic spoon.

"Describe It!" A child writes the name of his favorite frozen treat in the box. Then he writes how it looks, tastes, and feels.

"Cool Story Planner": A child writes details about a time he ate ice cream or another frozen treat.

adapted from an idea by Ada Goren, Winston-Salem, NC

Writers' Garden

What's the buzz? This simple display is a great **prewriting** tool! Make five large construction paper flowers with pencil cutouts for stems. Post the flowers in a row to make a writers' garden. Draw black lines and eyes on a yellow pom-pom to make a bee and then glue it to one end of a craft stick. Place the resulting pointer and a supply of blank five-page booklets in the garden.

Before a youngster writes about a personal experience, invite her to visit the garden with a classmate. Have her rehearse what she will write in a booklet by pointing to the first flower as she tells what she will write on the first page, the second flower as she tells what she will write on the second page, and so on. It's sure to help her organize her thoughts!

Name _____

Look at me and my writing in _____!

Name _____

Number Words

1 one
2 two
3 three
4 four
5 five
6 six

7 seven
8 eight
9 nine
10 ten
11 eleven
12 twelve

Color Words

red
orange
yellow
green
blue

purple
brown
black
white
pink
gray

COLORFUL CRAYONS
8 LARGE CRAYONS

Days of the Week

Sunday   Monday   Tuesday   Wednesday   Thursday   Friday   Saturday

©The Mailbox® • TEC42033 • Oct./Nov. 2007

Note to the teacher: Use with "Writing Resource" on page 143.

Super Soup

In a bowl or in a cup,

_____

warms me up!

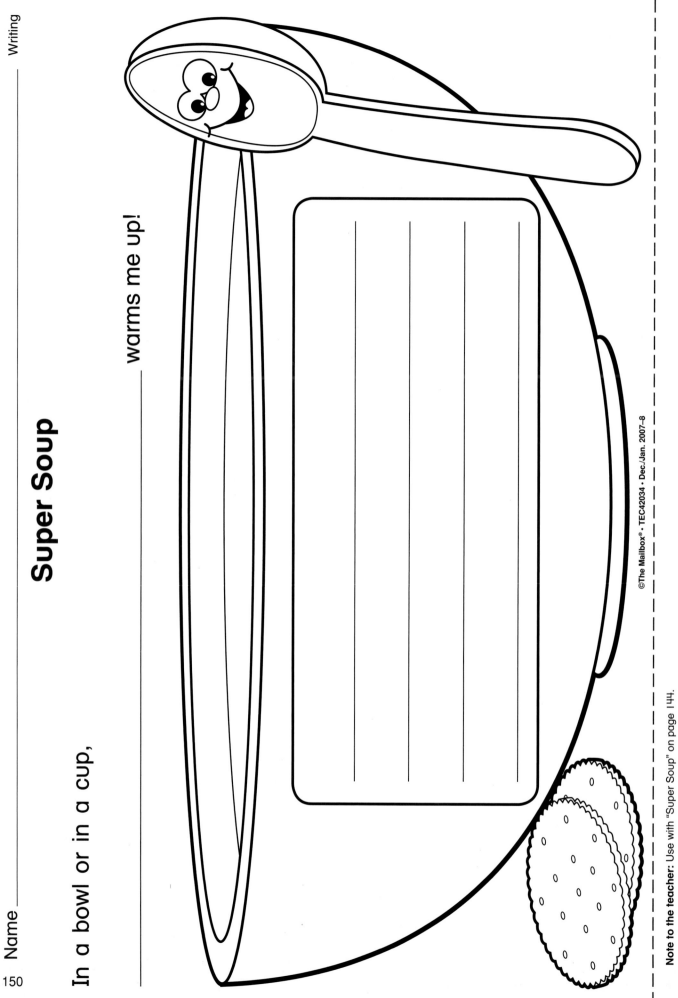

Note to the teacher: Use with "Super Soup" on page 144.

How I Get Ready for Bed

Word Bank

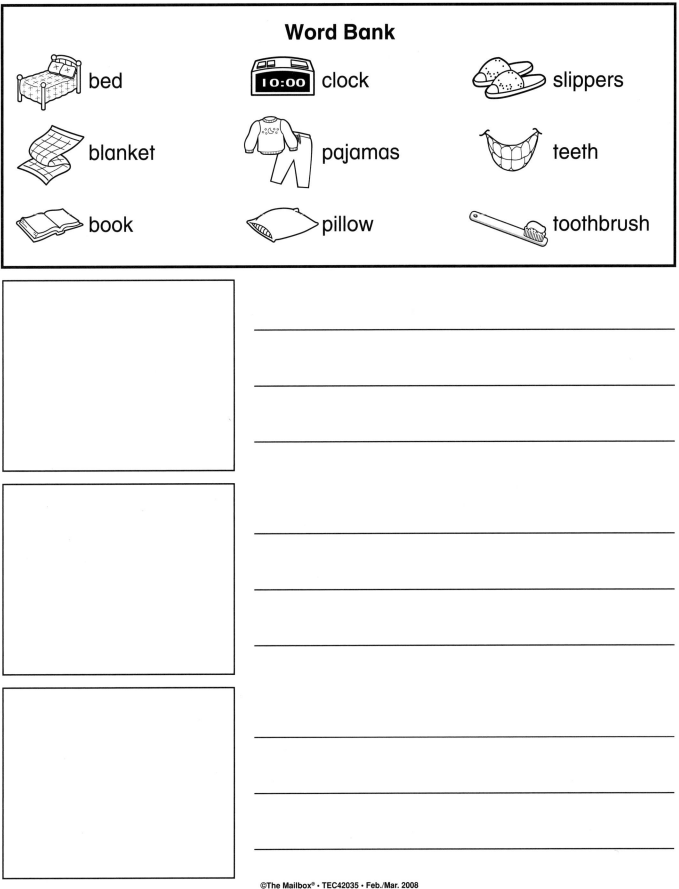

bed

clock

slippers

blanket

pajamas

teeth

book

pillow

toothbrush

Note to the teacher: Use with "Bedtime!" on page 145.

Flowerpot Planner

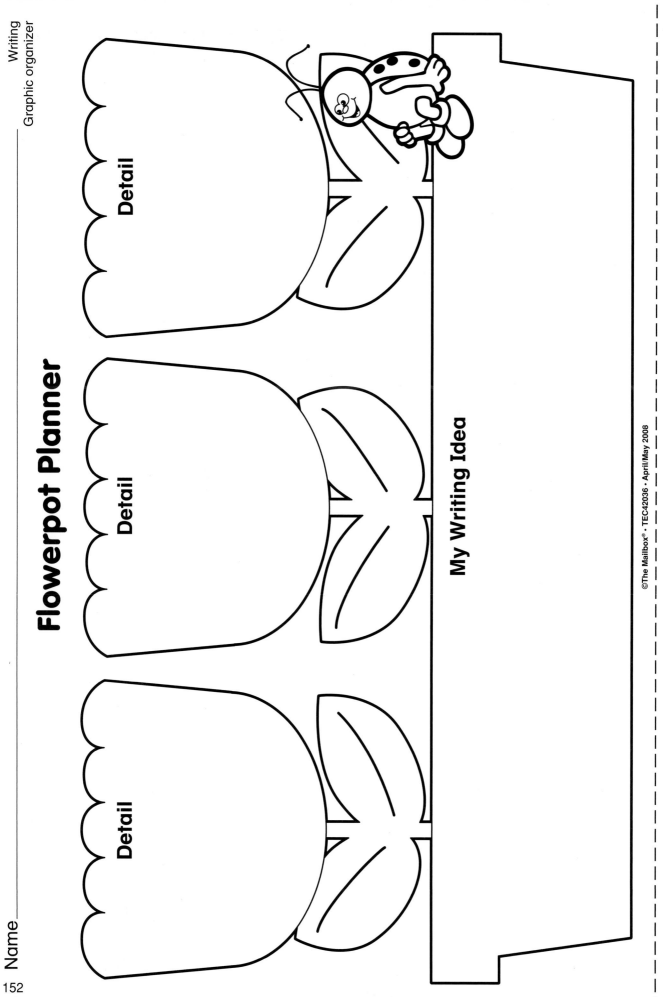

Detail

Detail

Detail

My Writing Idea

Note to the teacher: Use with "Flowerpot Planner" on page 146.

Butterfly Wing and Body Patterns

Use with "Splendid Spring Mobile" on page 14 and "Winged Wonder" on page 146.

TEC42036

Name _____

Describe It!

[ ]

see

taste

feel

Name _____

Cool Story Planner

who

when

where

what

Note to the teacher: Use with "Deliciously Descriptive" on page 147.

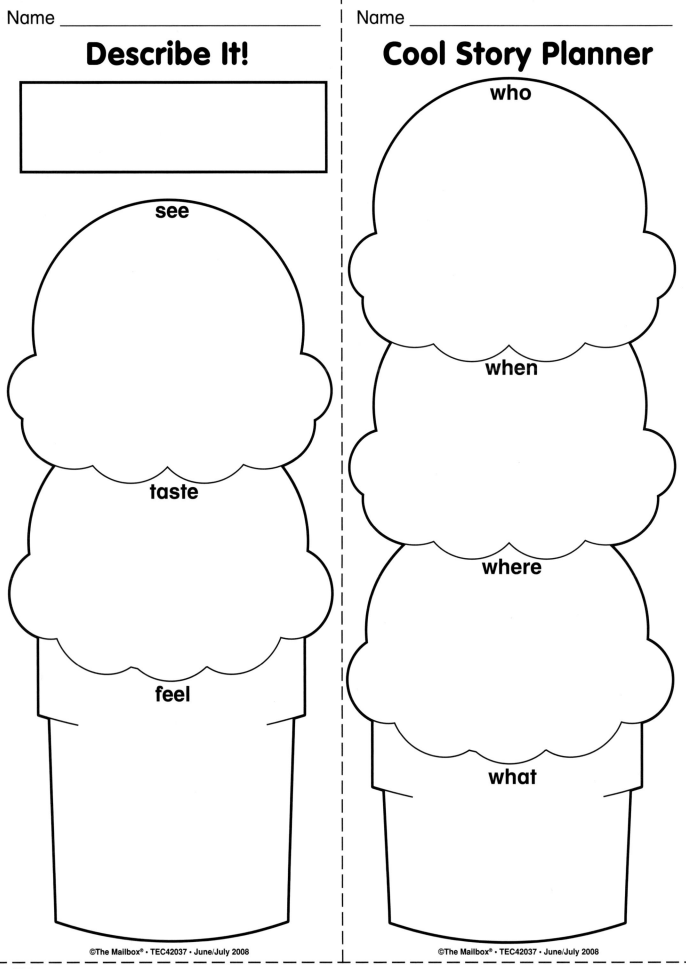

LITERACY UNITS

All Aboard With Consonants!

These easy-to-adapt ideas are specially engineered to increase students' letter knowledge and phonics skills.

ideas contributed by Angie Kutzer, Garrett Elementary, Mebane, NC

On the Right Track

Letter knowledge or letter-sound associations

Use one or both versions of this magnetic board activity to deliver just-right skills practice. To prepare, draw on the board a column of train engines. Or post on the board copies of a train engine card from page 158. Draw a track for each engine. Label the last engine with a star and label each of the other engines with a different consonant. Place several corresponding magnetic letters in a container and then add randomly chosen letters to make a class supply.

For a letter knowledge version, a child takes a letter at random. If it is a featured letter, he names it and puts it on the corresponding track. If it is not a featured letter, he places it on the track with the starred engine.

For a letter-sound association version, a student takes a letter at random and names it. If it is a featured consonant, he names a word that begins with that letter and then places it on the appropriate track. If it is not a featured consonant, he simply puts it on the track with the starred engine.

Clickety-clack. Clickety-clack.
Listen to the letter train going down the track.
[/s/-/s/-/s/, /s/-/s/-/s/].
Listen to the letter train going down the track!

Chug, Chug, Chant!

Letter-sound associations

Deliver loads of skill reinforcement in a jiffy! Write a different consonant on each of several train engine cards (patterns on page 158). Next, hold up a card. Lead students in the chant shown as you pantomime the train engine moving on a track. Then set aside the card. Repeat the chant as described with the remaining cards. **For more advanced students,** instead of setting aside each train engine after the chant, place the engines in separate rows of a pocket chart. Glue clip art of objects whose names begin with featured consonants on blank cards to make train cars. Then have students sort the train cars into the appropriate rows of the chart. Which train will get all of its cars first?

Link Up!
Letter-sound associations

After students can identify several consonants and the corresponding sounds, try this kid-pleasing activity. Divide a class supply of index cards into three equal groups. Program each group of cards with a different consonant, writing one letter per card. Randomly distribute the cards to students and ask each youngster to conceal her letter by holding her card to her chest.

Next, say, "All aboard!" At this signal, each youngster walks around the classroom as she says the sound associated with her letter. When she finds a classmate saying the same sound, she stands behind her and puts her free hand on the youngster's shoulder to begin forming a train. Students continue joining youngsters with the same sound as described to form three trains. After each youngster is aboard a train, say, "Put on the brakes!" Have students stand in place and reveal their letters. Then check the letter-perfect cargo!

Missing Cargo
Initial or final consonants

The locomotives at this center carry short-vowel words. Make several colorful copies of the train workmat on page 158. Glue a picture of a different consonant-vowel-consonant word on each engine. Then write part of the word on the train cars, writing one letter per car and leaving a blank car for either the initial or final consonant. Set out the workmats and a supply of letter manipulatives. To complete the activity, a child names the pictures and completes the words with the correct letters. **For more advanced students,** have each youngster write the words he completes.

Railway Lines
Letter formation

This idea is just the ticket for promoting proper handwriting. Display a copy of page 159 on an overhead projector. Point out to students that the big puff of smoke is at the top line, the smokestack is at the dashed line, and the train wheels are on the track. Refer to these parts of the illustrations as you model how to write familiar consonants. For example, explain that an uppercase *C* starts just below the smoke line and "sits" on the track. Whether you have students write individual letters or entire words, they will be full steam ahead to first-class writing!

Train Cards
Use with "On the Right Track" and "Chug, Chug, Chant!" on page 156.

Train Workmat
Use with "Missing Cargo" on page 157.

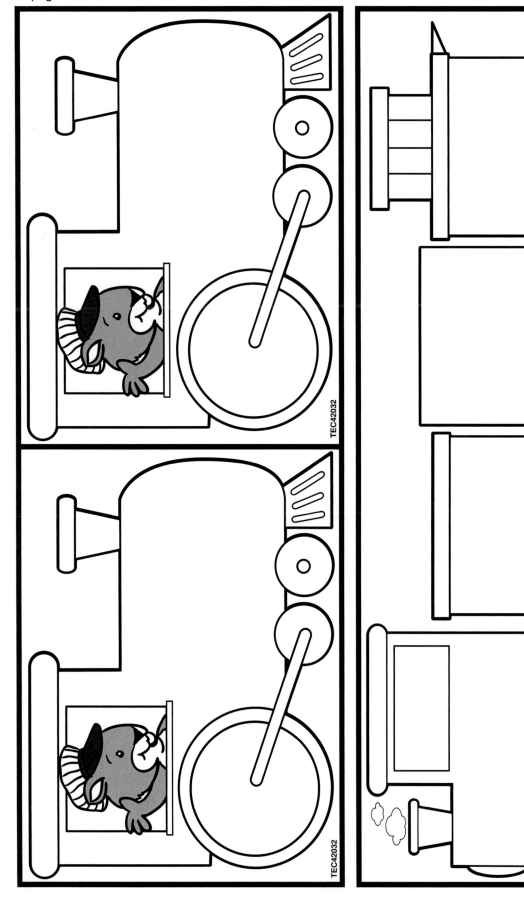

©The Mailbox® • TEC42032 • Aug./Sept. 2007

Note to the teacher: Use with "Railway Lines" on page 157.

Wild About High-Frequency Words

Use this menagerie of activities with any words, anytime of the year! It's a surefire step toward developing fluent readers.

Word Birds

These fine-feathered friends are perfect for an on-the-spot word review. Use the parrot pattern on page 162 to make several birds of various colors. Program each bird with a different high-frequency word. Display the birds around your classroom. Have students search for designated words with imaginary binoculars and then describe the corresponding birds. Or invite students to "bird-watch" for a few minutes and silently read the words they see. Then ask volunteers to point out different birds and name the corresponding words. Plan similar bird-watching experiences periodically to keep students' reading skills sharp, and replace or add birds after you introduce different words to students.

Cindy Barber, Fredonia, WI

Find the Cards!

A variation of the "Going on a Bear Hunt" chant sets the stage for this activity. To prepare, make a class supply of high-frequency word cards. Make three more sets of cards with the same words, making each set a different color.

To begin, establish a steady clapping rhythm. Say the first chant shown, pausing for students to echo each line. Then take the cards and students outdoors or to a large unoccupied room such as the school gym. Next, distribute one set of cards to students. As students practice reading the words, scatter the remaining cards nearby. Then ask each youngster to find the three cards with the same word that is on his card. Once a child finds the cards, he sits in a designated location and reads his cards to any other seated classmates. Lead students in the second chant to wrap up the search. **For a more challenging version,** give each child a list of five words. Arrange for him to find one card for each word.

Begin
We're going on a word hunt.
We're going to have lots of fun.
What an exciting day!
We're so glad.

End
We just went on a word hunt.
Reading words was lots of fun.
What an exciting day!
We love reading!

Sapna Datta, English Estates Elementary, Fern Park, FL

Read, Find, and Write!

After students are familiar with this partner game, they can take it home and play it with their families. Have each student color a copy of page 163, cut apart the word and picture cards, and then put the cards in a resealable plastic bag. Give each youngster a game marker and a sheet of paper. To play, each twosome uses one board and one set of cards. The players put the cards in a disposable cup, and each player puts her marker on a space with an arrow.

To play, Player 1 takes a card at random. If it has a word, she reads it aloud, moves in a clockwise direction to the first space with the word, and then writes the word. If the card has a picture, she advances to a chosen word space, reads the word, and then writes it. Player 2 takes a turn in the same manner. Alternate play continues as time allows, with the players reusing the cards as needed. Then the players read their lists to one another.

A Bright Approach

To individualize reading practice, give each youngster a list of high-frequency words appropriate for his skill level. (Copy different lists on different colors of paper for easy management.) Have each student read his list to you. Then place highlighter tape on any words with which the child needs practice. After he masters a highlighted word, invite him to remove the tape that covers it!

Caryn Kim, Beechtree Elementary, Falls Church, VA

Covered!

Whether you use this game for partners or small groups, it's sure to be a hit! Each player needs an equal number of high-frequency word cards. (Players may use either the same or different words.) Each twosome or group also needs a number cube. Cover the 5 and 6 with masking tape. Then write "1" on one taped side and "2" on the other taped side.

Each player spreads out her cards faceup in front of her. To take a turn, a player rolls the number cube. She reads the corresponding number of her cards and turns them facedown. The players alternate turns as described. Once a player turns over all her cards, she calls out, "Covered!" Play continues until each player's cards are facedown.

adapted from an idea by Katie Zuehlke
Bendix Elementary
Annandale, MN

Parrot Pattern
Use with "Word Birds" on page 160.

TEC42033

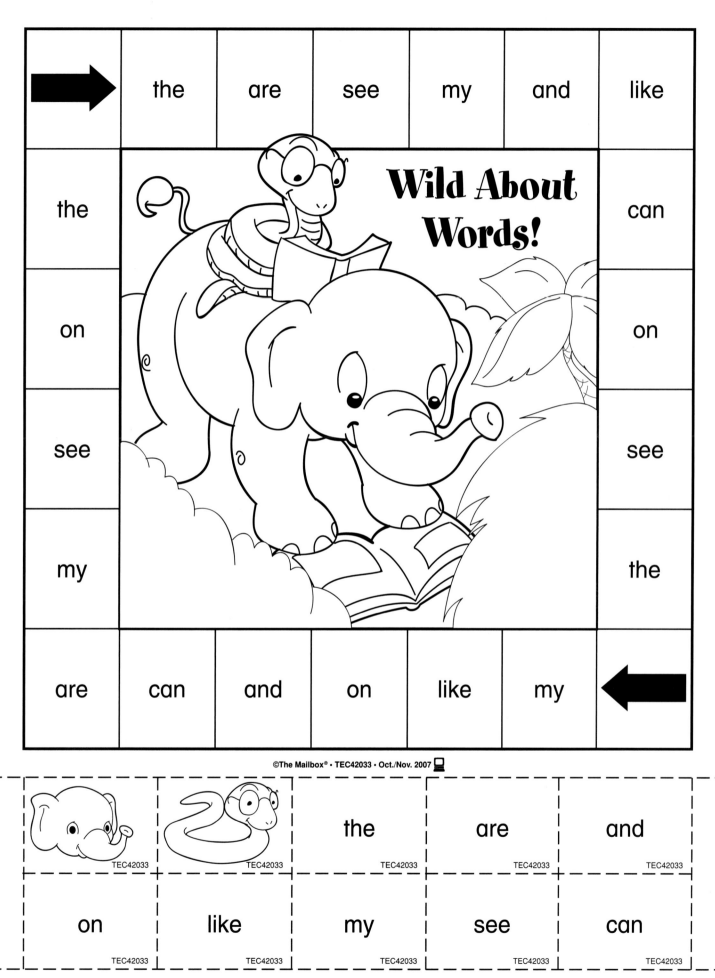

Wild About Words!

the	are	see	my	and	like

the		can
on		on
see		see
my		the

| are | can | and | on | like | my |

		the	are	and
TEC42033	TEC42033	TEC42033	TEC42033	TEC42033
on	like	my	see	can
TEC42033	TEC42033	TEC42033	TEC42033	TEC42033

Note to the teacher: Use with "Read, Find, and Write!" on page 161.

Having a Ball With Onsets and Rimes

Use these fun-filled activities to get students into the swing of hearing the sounds in words!

Sliding Together
Blending sounds

Give wordplay new meaning with this kid-pleasing workmat. Instruct each child to color and cut out a copy of the slide workmat and picture cards on page 166. To begin, secretly choose one of the pictures and say the first and last parts of its name (onset and rime). Have each student say the word and hold up his corresponding card. Next, ask each student to repeat the two parts of the word as he moves the card up the ladder. Then instruct him to say the whole word as he moves the card down the slide. Continue with the other cards in the same manner. No doubt students will be eager to give each animal several turns on the slide!

Stephanie Affinito, Glens Falls, NY

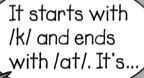

It starts with /k/ and ends with /at/. It's...

/d/–/og/

Dog!

Partner Practice
Segmenting words, blending sounds

Here's a quick review that students can do on their own while you're working with a small group. Pair students and give each twosome a copy of the picture cards on page 166. Ask each twosome to cut out its cards. To begin, the partners spread the cards out faceup. Partner 1 secretly chooses one of the pictures and says the first and last part of its name (onset and rime). Partner 2 says the whole word and takes the corresponding card. Then the partners switch roles. The activity continues as described, with the partners alternating roles, until no cards are left in play.

Stephanie Affinito

Three in a Row

Blending sounds or segmenting words

The gameboard and cards on page 167 can be used for two different games! Give each child a copy of the page. Ask her to cut out the cards and glue one card in each gameboard section. (Have her discard the extra card.) Then choose an option below.

Blending Lotto: Cut apart a copy of the picture cards on page 167 to use as caller cards. Give students game markers. To begin, take a card and segment the corresponding word into its onset and rime. Have students say the word. Then instruct each student who has the picture to place a game marker on it. Continue as described until one or more students marks three pictures in a horizontal, vertical, or diagonal row. **For more advanced students,** instead of orally segmenting each word, write the words on the board using different colors of markers for the onsets and rimes and have students read the words.

Segmenting Tic-Tac-Toe: Pair students and give them different game markers. Have one player in each twosome set aside her gameboard and cards. To take a turn, a player names a picture and then segments the onset and rime. She names the picture again and puts a game marker on it. Players take turns until the game is declared a draw or one player claims three pictures in a horizontal, vertical, or diagonal row.

adapted from an idea by Stephanie Affinito, Glens Falls, NY

A Change in Tune

Forming new words

Help students connect sounds and letters with this toe-tapping activity. Write the word *can* on the board, using markers of different colors for the onset and rime. After students read the word, lead them in the song below. Then ask a volunteer to change the word as the song suggests. Explore different verses as described.

(sung to the tune of "The Farmer in the Dell")

Let's look at the word [*can*].
Let's look at the word [*can*].
Tell me now what should we do
To turn it into [*pan*]?

Ada Goren, Winston-Salem, NC

165

Slide Workmat

Use with "Sliding Together" on page 164.

Super Sound Slide

©The Mailbox® • TEC42033 • Oct./Nov. 2007

Picture Cards

Use with "Sliding Together" and "Partner Practice" on page 164.

TEC42033

TEC42033

TEC42033

TEC42033

TEC42033

TEC42033

TEC42033

TEC42033

TEC42033

TEC42033

©The Mailbox® • TEC42033 • Oct./Nov. 2007

Monkey Business

©The Mailbox® • TEC42033 • Oct./Nov. 2007

Note to the teacher: Use with "Three in a Row" on page 165.

167

In the Word Family Neighborhood

Students are sure to feel right at home with these literacy-boosting ideas. After all, you can use the activities with any word families!

Introductions

Forming words

This approach to introducing word families results in a handy reading and writing reference! To teach students a word family, label the roof of a large house cutout with the rime. Post the house on a magnetic board and use magnetic letters to spell the rime beside the house. Nearby, place several magnetic letters that form words with the rime.

To begin, say, "Let's meet the [*-ap*] family!" Then ask a student to introduce the class to a designated word by forming it with the magnetic letters. Write the word on the house and then have a different student form another [*-ap*] word. Continue as described until you list a desired number of words. After you make houses for several different rimes, connect them with a metal ring to make a book. It's a perfect tool for quick reviews!

Debbie Reinhardt, Glenn L. Sisco School, Kinnelon, NJ

Round and Round

Blending onsets and rimes

For this unique center idea, place one foam cup in another foam cup. Then label the cups, as shown, with a rime and onsets that form words with the rime. Label additional cups in the same manner to reinforce different rimes. Place the cups at a center stocked with paper. To complete the activity, a youngster takes a set of cups. She turns the inner cup to form words with the onsets and rime, reads the words, and writes them on a sheet of paper. Then she reads her completed list. **For more advanced students,** include onsets that do not form real words, and have students distinguish between the real and nonsense words.

BillieJo Mustonen, Thornebrooke Elementary, Ocoee, FL

On the Map

Writing word families

Use this display idea for a fun review of several rimes. To begin, give each youngster a copy of an outline of a house. Have him write on the house an assigned rime and words that contain the rime. Then ask him to add crayon details to the house and cut it out. Next, have students help you illustrate a length of paper with roads and scenic details to make a background. Guide students to group the houses on the background as desired and then glue them in place. Add corresponding signs, such as "Long *e* Street" and "Short *i* Hill." Then display the neighborly mural on a wall.

Victoria Merkel
American School of Durango
Durango, Durango, Mexico

A Full House

Writing and using word families

Here's a cute way for students to keep a record of familiar rimes. For each student, staple several copies of the booklet page on page 170 between two house-shaped covers. To complete his booklet, a youngster illustrates the front cover and signs his name. He writes on each page an assigned rime and words that have the rime. Then he writes sentences with the words.

Elizabeth Foret, Waterford Elementary, Orlando, FL

Home, Sweet Home!

Sorting by rimes

To prepare this partner center, title two sheets of paper with different rimes to make game mats. Make eight or more word cards for each rime. Color and cut out two copies of the house game pieces on page 171. Place each set of game pieces in a separate resealable plastic bag.

To begin, two students scramble the cards and stack them facedown. Each youngster takes a mat and a set of game pieces. To take a turn, a player draws the top card and reads the word. If the word has her assigned rime, she places a game piece on her mat. If the word does not have the rime, she puts the card in a discard pile. The players take turns, reusing the cards as needed, until one player finishes building her house and calls out, "Home, sweet home!"

adapted from an idea by Rebecka Spence, Greensboro, NC

Booklet Page
Use with "A Full House" on page 169.

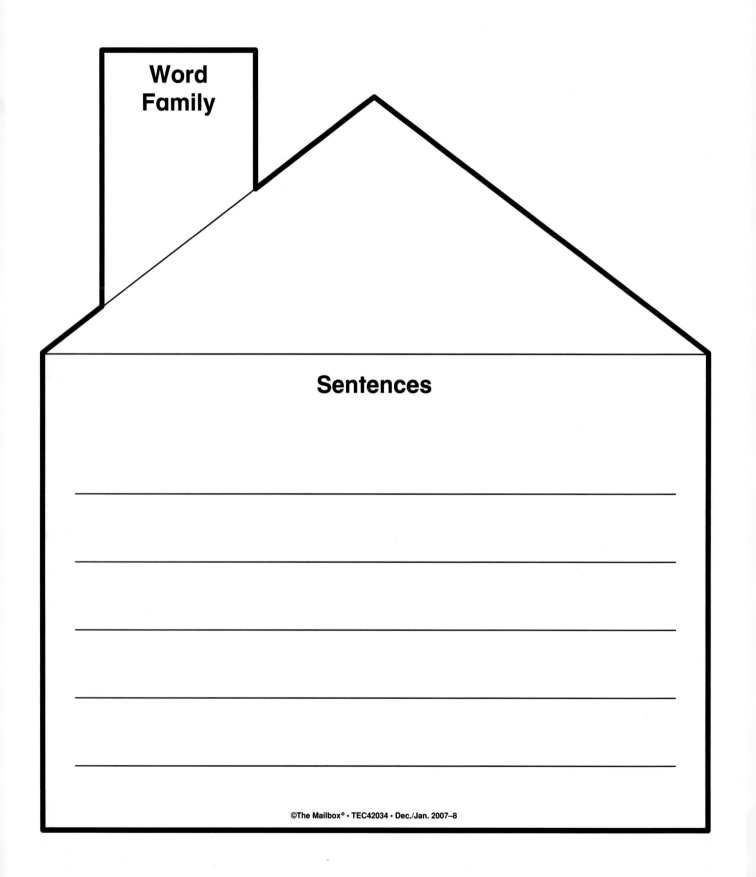

Word Family

Sentences

Booklet Page
Use with "A Full House" on page 169.

TEC42034

TEC42034

TEC42034

TEC42034

TEC42034

TEC42034

TEC42034

Name _____

172

Moving Day

✂ Cut. Glue. Read.

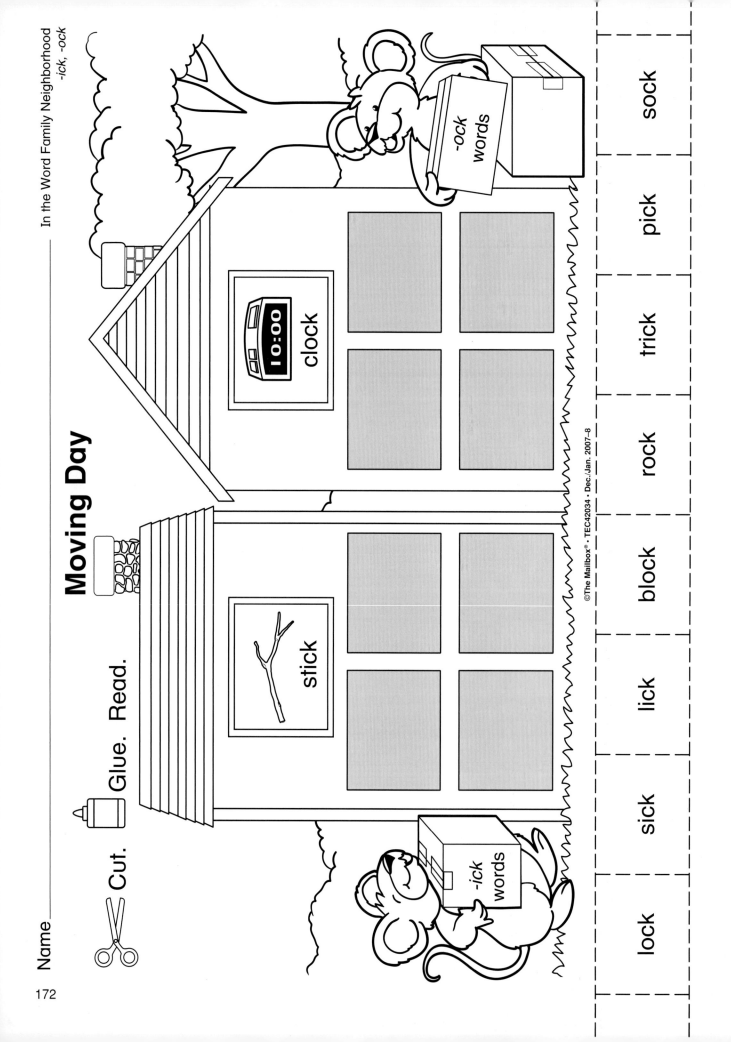

clock

stick

-ock words

-ick words

lock	sick	lick	block	rock	trick	pick	sock

"PURR-FECT" for POCKET CHARTS

This collection of literacy ideas is tailor-made for hands-on skills practice!

Centered on Names

What's in a name? Plenty of skill-boosting opportunities! Write each child's first name on a separate sentence strip. Choose an option below. Familiarize students with the activity and then offer it as a learning center choice.

Concepts about print: Display in a pocket chart column headings like the ones shown that describe the number of letters in students' names. Instruct students to place each name below the correct heading. **For more advanced students,** after the names are sorted, have each youngster list each group of names on a paper with labeled columns.

Letter knowledge: Write a chosen letter, the word *yes,* and the word *no* on separate blank cards. Put the letter card in the top row of a pocket chart. Put the yes and no cards in the row below it to create column headings. Instruct students to place each youngster's name below the appropriate heading to show whether it has the featured letter.

Molly Lynch, Arundel School, San Carlos, CA

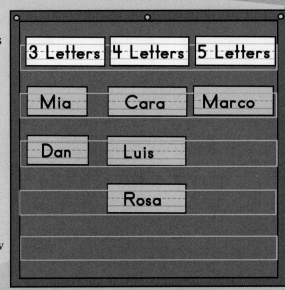

Rhyme Time
Tracking print, matching words

This nursery rhyme activity has so much potential for skill reinforcement that you'll want to use it over a few days. To prepare, display in a pocket chart a nursery rhyme on white sentence strips. Write the same nursery rhyme on colorful sentence strips and then cut the strips between the words.

To begin, lead students in reading the displayed rhyme. After youngsters are familiar with it, hold up one of the colorful words. Guide youngsters to find the same word in the pocket chart, read it, and then place the colorful word over it. (If the word occurs in the rhyme more than once, invite youngsters to display all of the matching words as described.) Continue with the remaining words in the same manner. The rhyme will change color right before students' eyes!

Amanda Thompson
Our Lady of Lourdes School
Omaha, NE

From Words to Sentences
Reading sentences

Here's a simple way to build on students' reading skills throughout each week. Put a few recently learned words in the top row of a pocket chart. In another row, arrange word cards to form a sentence that includes one or more of the words. (Substitute pictures for challenging nouns.) After students read the words, ask volunteers to take turns reading the sentence. Revisit the sentence with students on the following days. Once youngsters are familiar with the sentence, expand it with a color word or another grade-appropriate addition. Repeat the activity each week with different words, increasing the number of sentences as students' skills progress.

Cathie Noble, New Life Christian Preschool and Kindergarten, Poland, OH

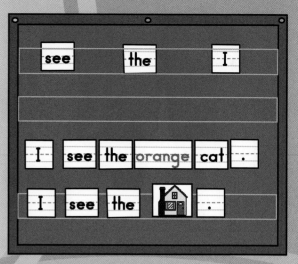

Perfect Pizza
Predictable text, color words

For this two-part activity, write the sentences on page 176 on sentence strips, using the corresponding colors for the color words. Display the sentences in a pocket chart below the title "Make a Pizza!" After students read the sentences a few times, give each child a copy of page 176. Help him draw a line under each color word with the corresponding color of crayon. Then instruct him to cut out the booklet pages and stack them in order. Staple the stack between two 3" x 7" paper strips as shown. Have the youngster complete the booklet with a title and cover illustration.

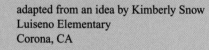

adapted from an idea by Kimberly Snow
Luiseno Elementary
Corona, CA

Scrambled Letters
Spelling

To prepare this short *a* activity, color a copy of the picture cards on page 175 and back them with tagboard. On the back of each card, write the name of the corresponding picture. Write the letters for each word on separate cards, using cards of a different color for each word. Display selected pictures in a pocket chart. Place beside each picture the corresponding letters in random order. To complete the activity, students unscramble the letters and then turn the pictures over to check their work. **For a reading version,** make word cards instead of letter cards. Ask students to match the words to the pictures.

Kathleen Reddy, Tampa Palms Elementary, Tampa, FL

TEC42032

TEC42032

TEC42032

TEC42032

TEC42032

TEC42032

TEC42032

TEC42032

TEC42032

TEC42032

TEC42032

TEC42032

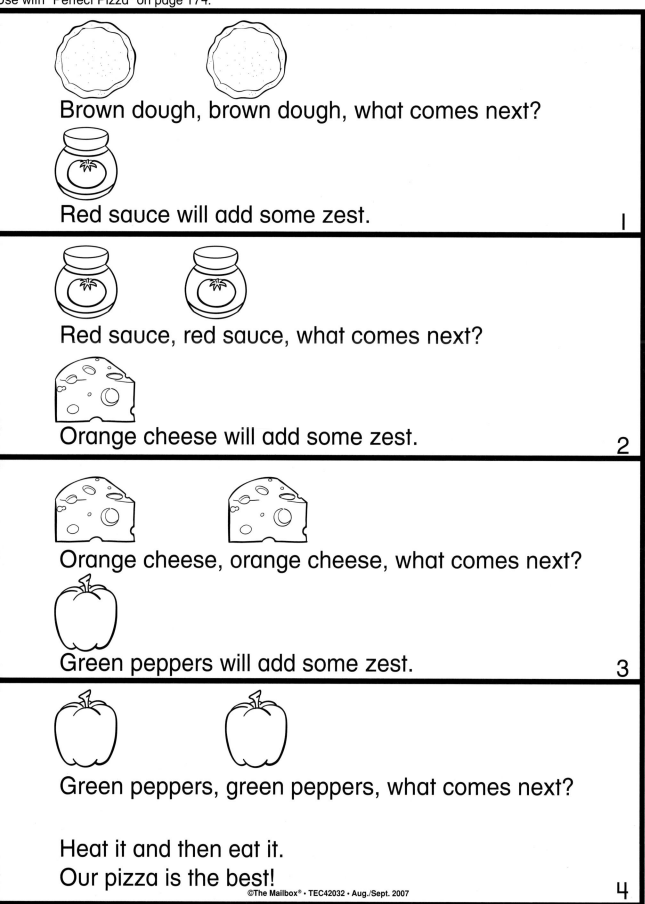

Brown dough, brown dough, what comes next?

Red sauce will add some zest.

1

Red sauce, red sauce, what comes next?

Orange cheese will add some zest.

2

Orange cheese, orange cheese, what comes next?

Green peppers will add some zest.

3

Green peppers, green peppers, what comes next?

Heat it and then eat it.
Our pizza is the best!

4

Extra! Extra! Write All About It!

Have your young writers report on the latest student, classroom, and school news with these simple ideas.

ideas contributed by Jane Glass, Green Year Round Elementary, Raleigh, NC

Photo Opportunity

Writing captions

This display idea not only tells the news, but it also shows it! Share selected newspaper photos with students and read aloud the captions. Point out that the captions convey important, specific details about the photos. Then show students several photos of class activities or school sights. Have them dictate captions for you to write or pair students and ask each twosome to write a caption for a different photo. To showcase the photos, decorate the top part of a bulletin board to look like a newspaper masthead. Then arrange the photos and captions below the masthead as desired.

This is Teddy and Barry and their snowman. They made the snowman during recess.

Things We Noticed

new projects outside the office

kids singing

really long cafeteria line

parents having lunch with the kids

On the Beat

Generating writing ideas

Here's an easy way to help your cub reporters brainstorm writing topics. Whenever you take your class someplace in the school, such as the cafeteria or media center, ask them to pay close attention to what they observe in the hallway and at the destination. After you and the youngsters return to the classroom, list students' observations on chart paper. When it's time to write, they'll have lots of inspiration!

News Sources

Generating writing ideas

Use this tip to ensure that students always have something to write about. Give each youngster a copy of the topic list on page 179. Have him keep it in his journal or another convenient location, and he'll never be at a loss for writing ideas!

Good News!

Writing about familiar events

This skill-boosting idea doubles as a way to promote home-school communication. Have each child write the name of the school, the date, and her name on a copy of page 180. Then have her write about a positive school experience or event. For example, she might write about using a computer, doing well on a spelling test, or visiting a book fair. Remind her to write a title in the provided space and illustrate her work. No doubt she'll be eager to share her news bulletin with her family!

Weekly Highlights

Writing about familiar events

Every school day is newsworthy with this class book! Each day of the school week, designate a different category of school news, such as classroom news, recess news, or art news. Write student-generated sentences about each topic on a separate sheet of chart paper, inviting youngsters to help with the writing as appropriate. Then have students add illustrations. At the week's end, bind the papers into a book titled "Our News This Week." Compile similar books throughout the year to create an ongoing record of your students' school experiences.

PAL Report

Using a prewriting strategy

For this interview idea, see the report form on page 179 and choose an option below.

Classroom visitor: Invite a school staff member to tell your class about his school-related activities and things he likes, such as his favorite foods and animals. Write the information on an overhead transparency of the report form. Later, write sentences with the information as a class.

Teacher interview: Instruct each youngster to write your name on a copy of the report form. As you share the indicated information, have each youngster write it on his form. Then ask him to write relevant sentences on provided paper.

Partner activity: Pair students. Have each student complete a copy of the report form with information about his partner. Then instruct him to write about the classmate.

Name _____

What Can I Write About?

bus

recess

lunch

music

computer

books

physical education

art

©The Mailbox® • TEC42034 • Dec./Jan. 2007–8

Name _____

PAL Report Form

Person

Activities

Likes

©The Mailbox® • TEC42034 • Dec./Jan. 2007–8

Good News Gazette

_____ _____
school   date

Reported by _____

Title: _____

_____

- -

_____

- -

_____

- -

_____

- - - - - - - - - - - - - - - - - - -

_____

- - - - - - - - - - - - - - - - - - -

_____

Note to the teacher: Use with "Good News!" on page 178.

High-Flying Phonics

Send students' skills soaring with these versatile ideas!

ideas contributed by Katie Zuehlke
Bendix Elementary, Annandale, MN

Wishing for Wind
Initial consonants or consonant blends

The goal of this small-group game is to collect bows for kites. Cut a supply of 1" x 3" rectangles to make bows. Draw a sad face on each of a few bows. Decide whether to make the game for consonants or consonant blends. Then write a consonant or blend on each blank bow. (You may write the same programming on more than one bow.) Put all the bows in a container. Give each group member a 6" x 9" construction paper kite without bows.

To take a turn, a youngster takes a bow. If it has a sad face, she says, "It's not windy!" and puts the bow aside. If the bow has a consonant or blend, she identifies it, names a word that begins with that consonant or blend, and then puts the bow on her kite string. Players take turns as described until the container is empty. Then they compare how many bows each kite has.

It's not windy!

s

r

b

In the Clouds
Initial consonants or consonant digraphs

Reproducible spinners and game mats make this idea a winner! To prepare for a small group, choose an option below. Color and cut out a copy of the appropriate spinner pattern. Then attach a paper clip to it with a brad. Give each player a game mat and several cotton balls (clouds). To take a turn, a player spins the spinner and then names the corresponding consonant or digraph. Next, he finds a matching kite on his game mat. He identifies the corresponding word and puts a cloud on it. (If no matching kites are unmarked, his turn is over.) The players take turns in the same manner as time allows or until all the kites are hidden by clouds!

For initial consonants: See the "Search and Say!" spinner pattern on page 183 and the corresponding game mat on page 184.

For consonant digraphs: See the "Search and Read!" spinner pattern on page 183 and the corresponding game mat on page 184.

Kite Categories

Sorting words

This independent activity keeps students on the move! Choose two or more word-sort categories, such as different word families or long *e* words and short *e* words. Program several kite cutouts with corresponding words, writing one word per kite. Display the kites around the room. Make student copies of a chart that has columns titled with the word-sort categories, and set out clipboards. To complete the activity, a youngster puts a chart on a clipboard and walks around the room looking for kites. When she finds one, she reads the corresponding word and writes it on the chart. After the chart is complete, she reads each group of words.

Long *e*	Short *e*
green	pet
tree	hen
me	wet

me

green

wet

Changing Words

Onsets and rimes

It's a breeze to give students blending practice with this kite booklet! To make one, make a few construction paper diamonds. Cut all but one of the diamonds in half vertically. Then staple the diamond halves on the intact diamond and attach a string as shown. Next, write a chosen rime on the right half of the booklet backing. Write an onset on each page and on the left half of the backing. Use the booklet with reading groups for quick reviews or have students practice reading the words on their own. When the booklet is not in use, post it on a wall for a colorful, skill-boosting decoration!

k ing

Puzzling!

Onsets and rimes

Since this hands-on activity is self-contained, it's perfect for a learning center. To prepare, glue an envelope facedown on the back of a construction paper kite without bows. (Do not glue the envelope flap.) Use an option below and the bow patterns on page 183 to make several bows. Then cut the bows in half and put them in the envelope. To complete the activity, a student assembles the bows on the kite string and reads the resulting words.

Easier version: Make bows of different colors. Write on each bow a word with the same rime, writing the onset on the left half of the bow and the rime on the right half.

More advanced version: Program identical bows, as shown, with words that have different rimes.

tr ut

r ug

n uck

Spinner Patterns
Use with "In the Clouds" on page 181.

Bow Patterns
Use with "Puzzling!" on page 182.

Search and Say!

k   t

h   s

TEC42035

Search and Read!

ch   sh

th

TEC42035

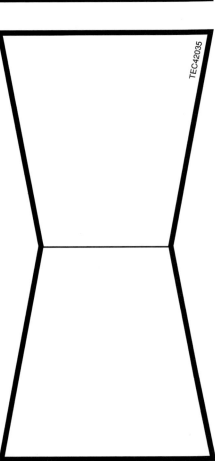

TEC42035

TEC42035

Search and Say!

Search and Read!

this   shell   that

shop   chip   they   chick

Note to the teacher: Use with "In the Clouds" on page 181.

Happily Ever After Comprehension

Use these enchanting skill-based ideas with your choice of fairy tales!

Poof! You're Little Red Riding Hood.

Poof!
Answering questions

Looking for a way to give read-alouds a magical touch? Try this engaging idea! Make a magic wand by decorating a dowel with a star cutout and arts-and-crafts supplies, such as ribbon, glitter glue, and sequins. Begin reading aloud a chosen fairy tale. Then pause, wave the wand at a student, and say, "Poof! You're [character's name]." Ask the youngster a character-related question, such as, "How do you feel?" or "What might you do next?" After the youngster responds, continue reading, pausing at each of several points in the story to use the wand and ask a question as described. It's a charming way to get students into the story!

Crown Creations
Story details

Students are sure to feel like royalty with this story-recall idea. In advance, cut the top edge of a sentence strip, as shown, for each student. To begin, read aloud a fairy tale with royal characters, such as a king and a queen. Then give each youngster a prepared sentence strip and a label with the book title. Size the strip to his head and instruct him to attach the label to the back of the strip. Have him illustrate the labeled side of the strip with story details. Then tape the ends of the strip together with the artwork to the outside to make a crown. After students complete their work, call on them, saying the word *Prince* or *Princess* before their names. Invite each student to tell the class how his artwork relates to the story.

For more advanced students, ask each youngster to write on his strip the title of a chosen fairy tale. Then have him illustrate a few story events in chronological order.

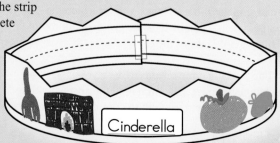

Cinderella

Mary Davis, Keokuk Christian Academy, Keokuk, IA

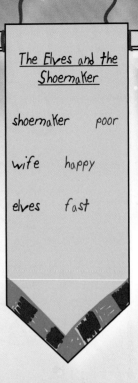

The Elves and the
Shoemaker

shoemaker   poor

wife   happy

elves   fast

Cast of Characters
Identifying and describing characters

To begin this fairy-tale follow-up, give each student a 4½" x 12" piece of paper and have him cut one end of it into a point. Instruct him to position the paper vertically with the point at the bottom. Next, ask him to label the paper with the book title. Have him list the characters with a marker of one color and use a different-colored marker to write a describing word for each character. To complete his project, invite the youngster to add crayon details and then have him tape a craft stick to the back of his project. Then help him tie a length of yarn to the stick to make a hanger. Showcase students' resulting banners with the title "Fairy-Tale Folks."

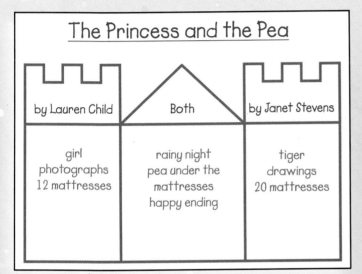

Story Similarities
Text-to-text connections

This variation of a Venn diagram is fit for a king! Share two versions of a chosen fairy tale with students. Then draw on a large sheet of paper a castle like the one shown. Write the title of the story above the castle. Title the middle section of the castle "Both" and label a separate section of the castle for each book. Then ask students to name various story details and identify the sections in which they belong. Write the information on the poster. After the poster is complete, ask students which book they prefer and why.

Tale Talk
Story elements or making connections

Keep these spinners near your storytime area for quick and easy comprehension checks. To prepare, color and cut out a copy of each spinner pattern on page 187. Use a brad to attach a paper clip to each spinner.

For story elements, a youngster chooses the round spinner and reads the word on which the spinner lands. Then he tells the group about the corresponding part of the story.

For making connections, have a youngster use the banner spinner. Help him read the corresponding sentence starter and ask him to complete the sentence.

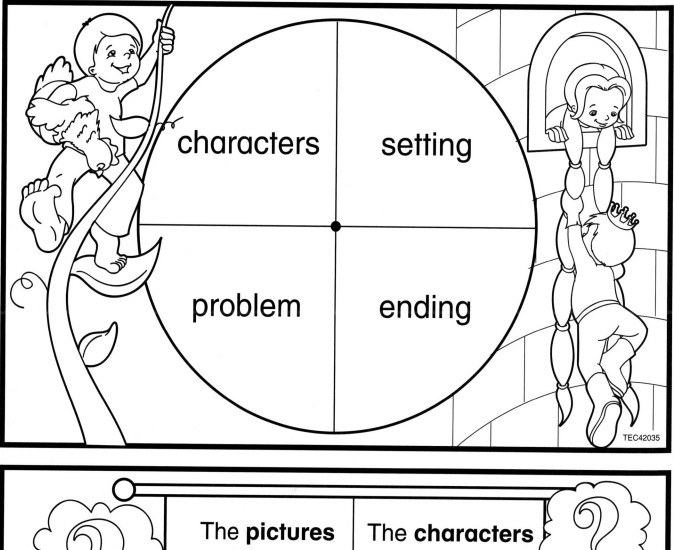

characters | setting

problem | ending

TEC42035

The **pictures** make me think of…

The **characters** make me think of…

The **book** makes me think of…

The **ending** makes me think of…

TEC42035

Aflutter Over Words

ideas contributed by Ada Goren
Winston-Salem, NC

Butterfly Buddies
Compound words

For this class activity, post a large, simple illustration of a flower in an open area of your classroom. Make a supply of like-colored butterfly cards so there is one card for every two students (pattern on page 190). Write a compound word on each card, writing the first part of the word on the left wing and the second part of the word on the right wing. Then cut each card in half.

To begin, give each child a card half. Next, have each student walk around the room looking for the classmate who has the matching card half. When she finds him, the two youngsters say the compound word that their words form. Then they "fly" to the flower and sit together. After all the students are at the flower, ask each twosome to announce its compound word. List the words on the flower to make a "scent-sational" word reference!

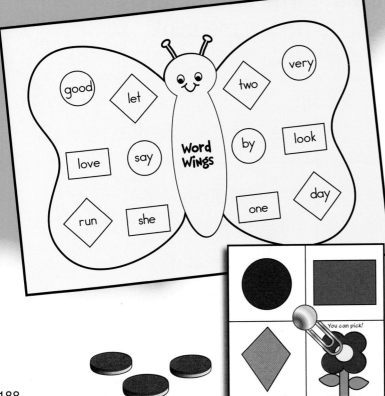

Shaped for Readers
Word recognition

This quick game can be used with any words! To prepare for a small group, color and cut out a copy of the spinner pattern on page 190. Attach a paper clip with a brad. Make one copy of page 191 and write a word on each shape. Then give each child a copy of the paper and 11 game markers.

To take a turn, a youngster spins the spinner. If it lands on a shape, he finds a matching shape on his butterfly, reads the corresponding word, and puts a game marker on it. (If no matching shapes are unmarked, his turn is over.) If the spinner lands on the flower, the child may read any word and then mark the shape. Players take turns as described until one player marks all the words on one wing.

Find the Flowers!
Skill review

The goal of this small-group game is to get all the butterflies in the flower garden. To prepare, make an equal number of butterfly and flower cards (patterns on page 190). Program the cards as described below. To begin, students arrange the flower cards facedown in the center of the group. Then they evenly divide the butterfly cards among themselves. To take a turn, a player flips over a flower card. If she has a matching butterfly, she sets it on the flower. If she does not have a matching butterfly, she turns the flower card back over. The players take turns as described until all the butterflies are on the correct flowers.

Letter-sound associations: Write a letter on each butterfly. Program the flowers with pictures whose names begin with the chosen letters.
Word recognition: Write a word on each flower. Program the butterflies with the same words, writing one word per butterfly.
Contractions: Write a contraction on each flower. Write each pair of corresponding words on a separate butterfly.

Which Wing?
Sorting words

Whether students sort word families, words with digraphs, or other types of words, this butterfly chart is sure to make learning fun! Display a laminated poster-size butterfly within student reach. Use a wipe-off marker to title each wing with a chosen word category. Then have students use reusable adhesive to post word cards on the correct wings.

Colorful Mix-Up
Spelling

Use the butterfly puzzle pattern on page 190 for these learning center options.

Easier version: Make several picture cards for three-letter words. (Old phonics workbooks are good sources for pictures.) Write each word on the back of its card. Also write each word on a copy of the puzzle pattern, writing one letter per section. Then cut the puzzles apart. A student chooses a picture, assembles a puzzle to spell the corresponding word, and then flips the picture card to check his work.

More advanced version: Write a three-letter word on each of three like-colored copies of the puzzle pattern, writing one letter per section. Cut the puzzles apart. Instruct youngsters to assemble the puzzles and write the words they form.

189

Butterfly Card

Use with "Butterfly Buddies" on page 188 and "Find the Flowers!" on page 189.

TEC42036

Flower Card

Use with "Find the Flowers!" on page 189.

TEC42036

Butterfly Puzzle Pattern

Use with "Colorful Mix-Up" on page 189.

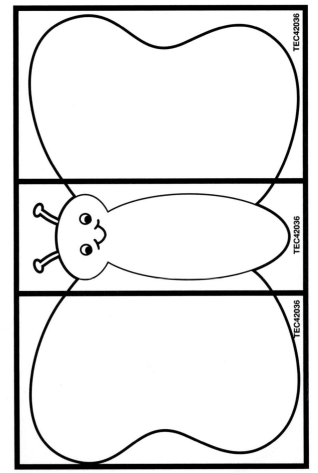

TEC42036

TEC42036

Spinner Pattern

Use with "Shaped for Readers" on page 188.

You can pick!

TEC42036

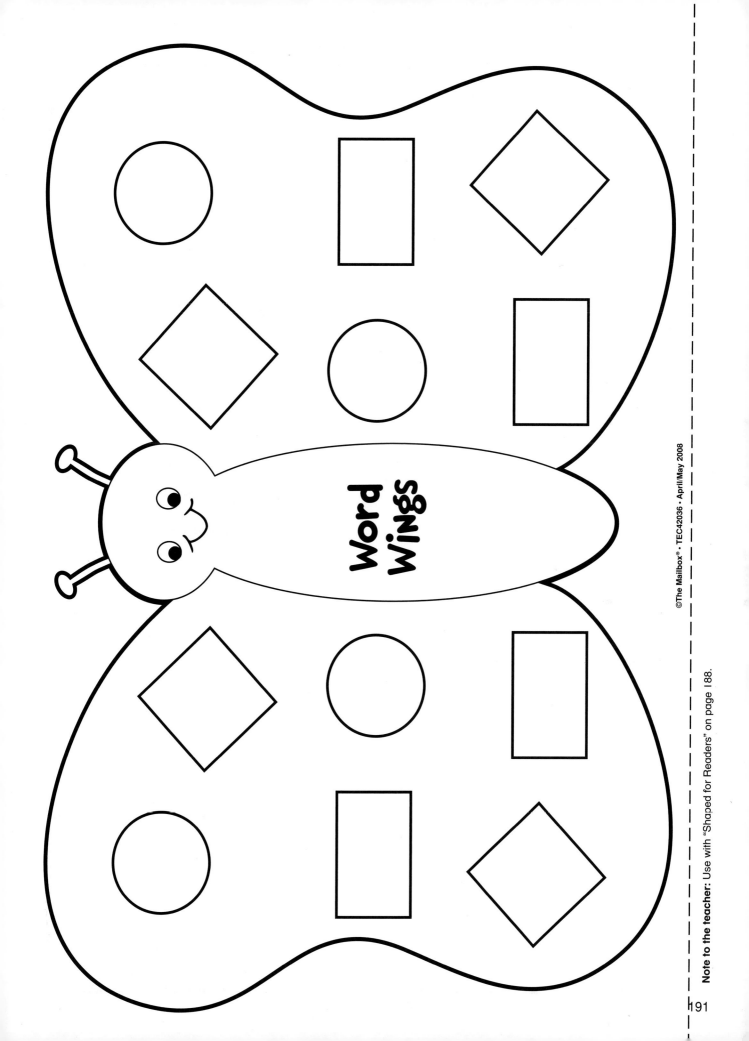

Word
Wings

Note to the teacher: Use with "Shaped for Readers" on page 188.

Making a Splash With Reading and Writing

Help your students leap ahead in literacy with these "toad-ally" terrific ideas!

ideas contributed by Courtney C. Pate
Burlington, NC

Fly Feast

Reading and writing words

Students "catch" flies during this small-group game! Copy the fly cards from page 194 to make a supply of three different colors of cards. Cut out the cards and then write a chosen word on the back of each card. Color a copy of the spinner from page 194, making the fly sections the same colors as the cards. Then cut out the spinner and attach a paper clip to it with a brad. Have each player write her name on a copy of the lily pad pattern on page 195. Ask the players to spread out the cards word side down.

To take a turn, a player spins the spinner. If it lands on a fly section, she takes a card of the same color. She reads the word, uses it in a sentence, and then writes it on her lily pad. (If there are no cards of the same color in play, her turn is over.) If the spinner lands on the "Buzz! Buzz!" section, she takes any two cards and continues her turn as described. The players take turns until no cards remain in play.

Pond Pairs

Compound words

For this energizing activity, make one copy of both frog cards from page 194 for every two students. Program each pair of cards with a compound word as shown. Then cut out the cards. To begin, designate a large open area as the pond. Give each youngster a card. Then have each student hop around the pond, looking for the classmate whose word forms a compound word with his word. When he finds him, the two youngsters say, "Ribbit!" Then they sit together. After all the students are sitting, ask each twosome to announce its compound word. **For a center variation**, color the programmed cards. Have students correctly pair the cards and write the compound words on provided paper.

Froggy Friend
Publishing writing

This paper topper adds an adorable touch to any writing! After a child edits her writing, give her a five-inch green semicircle and two green frog feet (pattern on page 195). Ask her to attach two paper reinforcements to the semicircle as shown to make eyes. Have her draw a mouth. Then instruct her to glue the head to the back of her work and the feet to the top of her work as shown.

All About Frogs

SPLASH!

Name Freddy

Making a Splash With Reading and Writing
Writing

How to Play Leapfrog

1 Get two pepul.

2 One prsn gets dn on the grn.

3 The othr prsn leps ovr him.
Thay kep going this way.

"Ribbiting" Writing
Writing sentences or how-to directions

Choose an option below and have each child complete a copy of page 196 as described. After he checks that each sentence begins with a capital letter and ends with the appropriate punctuation, invite him to color each corresponding illustration.

Sentences: List student-generated frog words on a poster-size lily pad. Then ask each child to title his paper "Frogs." Encourage him to refer to the list as he writes a frog-themed sentence beside each illustration.

How-to directions: Invite students to demonstrate how to play leapfrog. Next, have each child title his paper as shown. Then instruct him to write "1" on the first lily pad and write the first step in playing the game. Ask him to label and write the remaining steps in the same manner, using additional copies of the page if needed.

Hop to It!
Contractions

A frog pointer adds a twist to this pocket chart activity! To make a pointer, color and cut out a copy of the frog pattern on page 195 and then attach it to one end of a ruler. Display the sentence shown in a pocket chart. Also display similar sentences that have different pronouns in place of the word *I*. Write the corresponding contractions on separate cards. To begin, point to the first sentence and have students hop once for each word as they read the sentence. Next, replace *I will* with *I'll*. Instruct students to hop as they read the revised sentence. Explore the remaining sentences and contractions in the same manner. It's a great way to show that contractions shorten sentences!

I'll

I will hop.

Spinner Pattern and Fly Cards
Use with "Fly Feast" on page 192.

Frog Cards
Use with "Pond Pairs" on page 192.

Lily Pad Pattern
Use with "Fly Feast" on page 192.

_____'s
Lily Pad List

TEC42037

Frog Pattern
Use with "Hop to It!" on page 193.

Frog Foot Pattern
Use with "Froggy Friend" on page 193.

TEC42037

TEC42037

Name

©The Mailbox® • TEC42037 • June/July 2008

Note to the teacher: Use with "'Ribbiting' Writing" on page 193.

LITERATURE UNITS

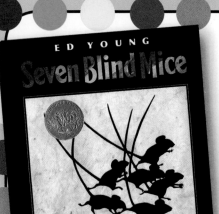

Seven Blind Mice

By Ed Young

When seven blind mice encounter a strange Something, they wonder what it is. Each of the first six mice explores a different part of the thing and reaches a different conclusion. It's not until the seventh mouse examines the thing from end to end that the mice find out what it really is!

ideas by Katie Zuehlke, Bendix Elementary, Annandale, MN

One by One
Ordinal numbers

Use this story participation idea to reinforce the order in which the curious rodents approach the mysterious thing. To prepare, cut out one large construction paper semicircle in each of the seven mouse colors. Decorate each semicircle as shown with a mouse face, two construction paper ears, and a yarn tail. Hand each mouse to a different student. Then begin reading the story aloud. When you read that the red mouse goes to investigate the thing, ask the student with the red mouse to stand in front of the group. As you continue the story, have each remaining student with a mouse join the first student at the appropriate point in the story so that the props are displayed in order. At the end of the story, name the ordinal numbers in random order and have youngsters identify the corresponding mice.

For reinforcement, label each mouse with the appropriate ordinal number. Place the mice and book at a center. Invite students to revisit the story and correctly sequence the mice.

Clever Comparisons
Vocabulary development

There's a big difference between being a snake and being as supple as a snake! Read the story aloud. Then discuss with students the comparisons that the white mouse makes and the corresponding illustrations that show what the colorful mice imagine. No doubt students will delight in realizing how the colorful mice reach the wrong conclusions!

For more advanced students, later guide youngsters to name comparisons that describe themselves, such as *as busy as bees* and *as hungry as bears*. Create a class book of the comparisons titled "We Are…" and conclude the book with a class photo.

We are as busy as bees.

Puzzling Parts
Main idea of the story

This display idea helps students relate to the challenge that the mice have: identifying something by exploring just one part. For each student, cut out two identical construction paper shapes. (The shapes can be regular or irregular.) Give each youngster a piece of paper that you have folded in half and labeled with the question shown. Next, have the youngster glue one shape to the front of the paper. Instruct her to glue the other shape inside and incorporate it into an illustration. Then help her write a caption that identifies her completed artwork. Post students' folded papers on a wall and title the display "Puzzling Parts." Students will be eager to put their guessing skills to the test!

What is it?

It is a flower.

Look Around!
Color words

Each of the first six mice imagines that the strange Something is the same color as the mouse is. Encourage students to explore all six colors with this follow-up activity. Give each child crayons and a copy of page 200. Help him read each color word and color its crayon to match. Then instruct him to find one classroom item of each featured color and illustrate it below the appropriate crayon. After each youngster completes his paper, have students tell the class about their colorful finds. **For more advanced students,** ask each youngster to label his illustrations.

Name __Raj__

Seven Blind Mice
Color words

Colors in the Classroom

Read.
Color.
Draw.

| red | green | yellow |
| purple | orange | blue |

Daily Words
Days of the week

After students are familiar with the day-by-day story structure, divide a large vertical strip of paper into seven sections to make a game mat. Label the sections with the days of the week in order as shown. Place the game mat and a beanbag on the floor. Nearby, post a blank graph with a column for each day of the week.

Next, ask a student to stand facing the mat and toss the beanbag onto it. To help students identify the day on which the beanbag landed, have students name the days as you point to each word from the beginning of the mat to the section with the beanbag. Once students correctly identify the word, color the appropriate space on the graph. Continue in the same manner as time allows or until one entire column of the graph is colored.

Saturday
Friday
Thursday
Wednesday
Tuesday
Monday
Sunday

Seven Blind Mice
Color words

Colors in the Classroom

Read.

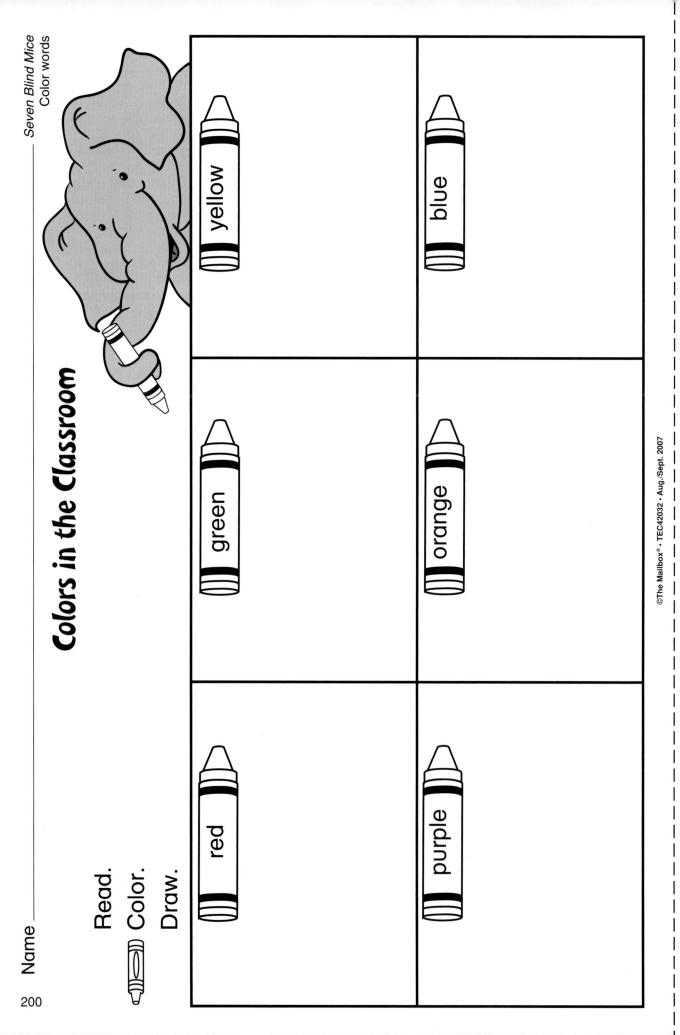

Color.

Draw.

red	green	yellow
purple	orange	blue

Note to the teacher: Use with "Look Around!" on page 199.

The Pick of the Crop

A bushel of learning fun is packed into these literature activities!

ideas contributed by Laurie K. Gibbons
Huntsville, AL

The Apple Pie Tree

Written by Zoe Hall
Illustrated by Shari Halpern
Two sisters observe the seasonal changes in an apple tree and eagerly anticipate making a pie.

The Apple Pie Tree
BY Zoe Hall
ILLUSTRATED BY
Shari Halpern

Look Inside!
Responding to literature

What's the girls' favorite part of an apple pie? It's the apples! And hidden in this pie project is your students' favorite part of the story. After you read the book aloud, give each youngster a large, sturdy paper plate without fluted edges. Also give him an equal-size white construction paper circle. Next, instruct each student to place his plate on a work surface, curved side up. Ask him to color the rim brown and draw fork pricks so that the plate resembles a piecrust. Then have him paint the plate light brown with watercolor paint. While the paint dries, instruct him to color and cut out a copy of the pie label on page 203. Have him glue it near the top of the paper circle and then illustrate and/or write about his favorite part of the story. Staple the plate to the top of the circle to assemble the one-of-a-kind pie.

PKn apls

Fruit Favorites
Writing

The two sisters clearly like apple pie. Is it tops among your students too? To find out, familiarize students with the poem below and then invite volunteers to answer the question. Next, give each child a white apple cutout like the one shown. Ask her to illustrate it with her favorite apple food. Have her write a caption or dictate a caption for you to write. Then instruct her to glue the white cutout on a slightly larger red apple cutout. Ask her to glue a stem and leaf in place and then write her name on the leaf. Display students' completed projects with the poem. **For more advanced students,** give each youngster a copy of the poem and have her circle the words *apple* and *apples* each time they appear.

Sarah

I like candy apples.

Red apples, green apples, yellow apples—yeah!
Apple crisp, applesauce, apple pie—hooray!
Apple butter, apple muffins, candy apples—sweet.
With so many yummy choices, what's your favorite one to eat?

The Seasons of Arnold's Apple Tree

By Gail Gibbons

Throughout the year, a young boy enjoys his secret place and the apple tree that grows there.

From Spring to Winter

Science

With this booklet project, students can imagine observing a tree's seasonal changes just as Arnold does. For each student, staple four six-inch blue construction paper squares to a 6" x 9" blue construction paper rectangle as shown to make a booklet. Also make a copy of the booklet labels, a brown copy of the tree trunk pattern, and a green copy of the treetop pattern on page 203.

To begin, each child glues the trunk on his last booklet page so that the bottom edges are aligned. Next, he writes his name on the treetop and glues it to the cover. Then he cuts apart his labels and glues one near the top of each page, beginning with spring and continuing in seasonal order. Over the next few days, give him a green treetop for each of his first three booklet pages. (Use a copy of the treetop pattern on page 203 as a tracer.) To complete the pages, he illustrates separate treetops with the following: pink blossoms for spring, green leaves for summer, and red apples for fall. He glues the treetops to the appropriate pages. Then he glues pieces of torn white paper (snow) to the branches on the winter page. The completed booklet will be a reminder of both the story and the seasonal changes!

Tree Tune

Language, science

This song recaps many of the seasonal changes that Arnold observes.

(sung to the tune of the first verse of "My Bonnie Lies Over the Ocean")

In springtime the apple tree is blooming.
The smell of blossoms fills the air.
In springtime the apple tree is blooming.
Pink blossoms burst everywhere!

In summer the apple tree is shady,
And Arnold can play down below.
In summer the apple tree is shady
As green leaves and apples grow!

In autumn the apple tree is crowded
With shiny fruit hanging down.
In autumn the apple tree is crowded;
A yummier sight can't be found!

In winter the apple tree is resting.
Its branches are empty and bare.
In winter the apple tree is resting,
Waiting for spring to warm the air!

Pie Label
Use with "Look Inside!" on page 201.

This is my favorite part of *The Apple Pie Tree.*

TEC42032

Treetop and Tree Trunk Patterns
Use with "From Spring to Winter" on page 202.

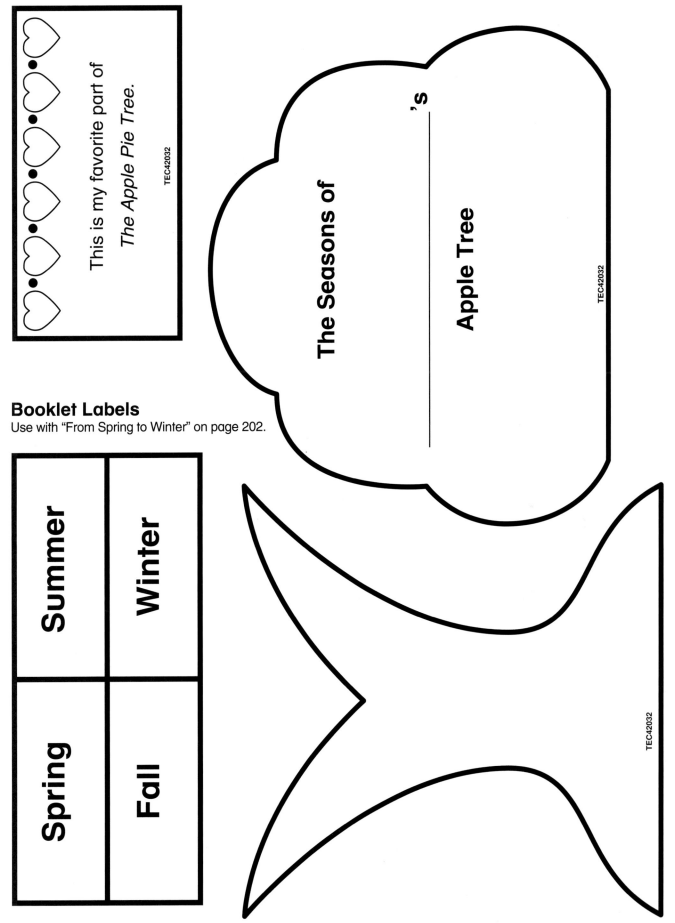

The Seasons of

'_s_

Apple Tree

TEC42032

TEC42032

Booklet Labels
Use with "From Spring to Winter" on page 202.

Summer	Winter
Spring	Fall

Which Season?

 Cut. Glue on the correct tree.

Color each treetop to match the season.

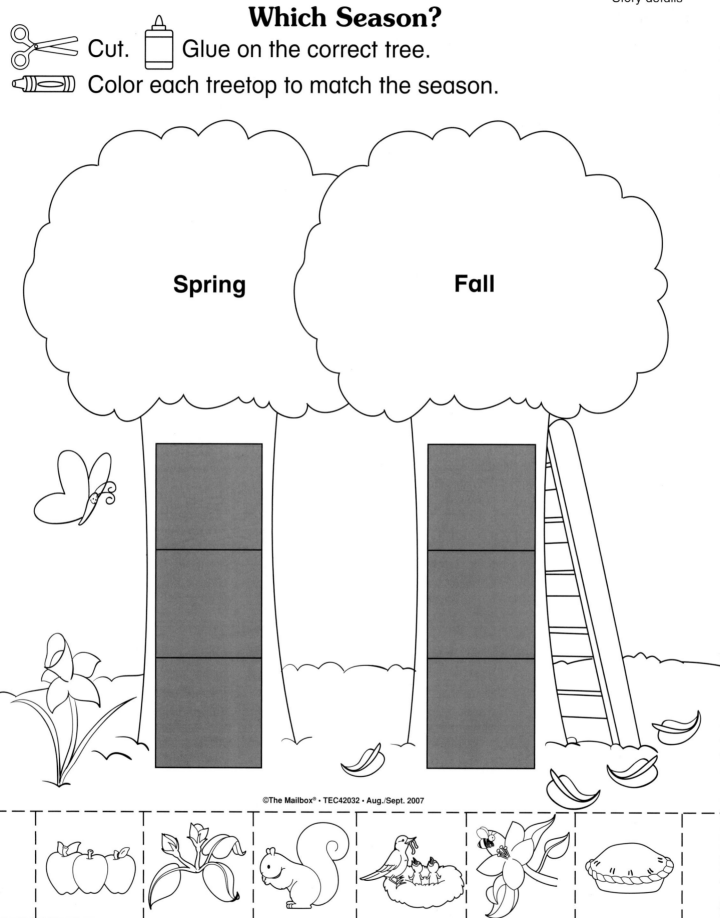

Spring

Fall

Note to the teacher: After students are familiar with *The Apple Pie Tree* by Zoe Hall, have each youngster complete a copy of this page.

Barn Dance!

Written by Bill Martin Jr. and John Archambault
Illustrated by Ted Rand
In this entrancing, rhythmic tale, a young boy hears a fiddle playing late one moonlit night. He creeps out of his house and follows the sounds to an incredible hoedown.

ideas contributed by Margie Rogers
Colfax Elementary
Colfax, NC

Find a Partner!
Rhyming

After seeing the fun that the boy and animals have dancing, no doubt your students will be eager to kick up their heels! Copy the picture cards on page 207 on paper of one color and the picture cards on page 208 on paper of a different color to make one card per student. Cut out the cards. To begin, divide the class in half. Instruct the students in each half to line up side by side and face the other group, leaving a few feet between the two groups. Next, give one set of cards to each group. (If you do not use all the cards, make sure that each card you hand out has a matching rhyming card.)

Next, ask the first youngster in one line to name the picture on her card. Have the student with the corresponding rhyming card hold it up and name the picture. Instruct the two youngsters to step forward and dance to the end of the lines. Then invite the next student in the first line to name the picture on her card. Continue as described until all the students partner up and dance down the lines.

Quilted Memories
Captions

Use this display idea to showcase memorable hoedown sights. After you read the story aloud, revisit the last page with students and point out the boy's contented expression. Invite students to name hoedown details that the boy might recall fondly. Next, ask each youngster to illustrate a grin-inducing hoedown sight on an eight-inch white square. Have him write a caption or dictate a caption for you to write. Then instruct him to glue the square on a slightly larger colorful square and draw stitch marks around it. After students complete their work, arrange the squares on a hallway wall so that they resemble a quilt.

Look Inside!
Identifying or describing characters
What is in the barn? That's the topic of this follow-up activity! For each student, place a 6" x 9" piece of paper on a 9" x 12" sheet of paper with the bottom edges aligned and then staple it on both sides. Trim the 9" x 12" paper to make a barn roof. Carefully cut the 6" x 9" paper in half to make barn doors. After each youngster adds desired crayon details to her barn, use an option below to have students complete the activity.

Easier version: Ask each youngster to make illustrations of several characters and then glue them in her barn. Encourage her to take the barn home and refer to it as she tells her family about the story.

More advanced version: Have each youngster make an illustration of a secretly chosen character and glue it in her barn. Help her write clues about the character and then read them to the class. After students guess the animal, have the youngster open the barn to reveal the answer.

I get dizzy.
I fall.
I am pink.

Amazing Night
Writing
Help students write about the story with a picture-perfect word bank. To make a word bank, color and cut out a copy of the picture cards on page 207. Glue them on a sheet of chart paper titled as shown. Label each card with the corresponding word. Then display the resulting poster. When students write about the story, invite them to refer to the poster for story details and spelling help.

On the Farm
Identifying the setting, characters, and events
What better way to set the stage for story discussions and retellings than with a mural? In advance, post a barn on a bulletin board backed with black paper. To begin, have students identify when and where the story takes place. Guide them to name setting details such as the moon, trees, and house. List the details on a sheet of chart paper. Then write a student-generated list of characters. Next, assign each student either part of the setting or a character. Have him illustrate it on provided paper and cut it out. After you arrange students' illustrations on the bulletin board, enlist students' help to summarize the main story events on sentence strips. Then post the strips near the mural.

Picture Cards

Use with "Find a Partner!" on page 205 and "Amazing Night" on page 206.

TEC42033

TEC42033

TEC42033

TEC42033

TEC42033

TEC42033

TEC42033

TEC42033

TEC42033

TEC42033

TEC42033

TEC42033

Picture Cards

Use with "Find a Partner!" on page 205.

TEC42033

TEC42033

TEC42033

TEC42033

TEC42033

TEC42033

TEC42033

TEC42033

TEC42033

TEC42033

TEC42033

TEC42033

Harold and the Purple Crayon

by Crockett Johnson

In this captivating classic, a young boy creates a series of imaginative adventures with the help of a big purple crayon.

Comprehension With Crayons
Visualizing

What better way to increase students' understanding of the story than by having them picture it? Read the title aloud and explain that Harold brings the story to life with drawings. Then give each child a purple crayon and a paper divided into four sections. Next, read aloud the first several pages of the story without showing students the illustrations. During the reading, pause at four preselected points for each youngster to draw in a different section of his paper what he visualizes. After students compare the book illustrations with what they pictured, show them the remaining illustrations as you finish reading the story.

Nancy Dietrich, Harris Elementary, St. Charles, MO

That's What Happened!
Cause and effect

Once Harold decides to take a walk, one thing leads to another! After students are familiar with the story, flag an illustration of each of the following: the tree, picnic, and balloon. Show students each illustration and ask them to recall what causes Harold to draw it. For more practice identifying cause-and-effect relationships, have each youngster complete a copy of page 210.

Julie Hays, Maryville, TN

Story Sketches
Responding to literature

Invite students to create colorful adventures, just as Harold does! Have each youngster illustrate a person cutout so that it resembles her. Next, place a class supply of crayons in a container. Instruct each student to take a crayon at random. Then ask her to make a paper crayon of the same color for her cutout to hold. Instruct her to glue the paper crayon to the cutout and glue the cutout to a large sheet of white paper. Have her draw an illustration modeled on the book and then help her add a caption. Showcase students' work with large crayon cutouts and the title "Kids and Crayons."

Julie Hays

Kendra wanted to fly, so she made an airplane.

Colorful Connections

Use a purple crayon.

Draw a line from each effect to its cause.

Note to the teacher: Use with "That's What Happened!" on page 209. **For more advanced students,** have each child choose a pair of pictures after completing the activity. Then instruct her to write what happened and what caused it to happen.

Two Tales With a Twist

From their intriguing beginnings to their surprise endings, these clever selections by Keiko Kasza are sure to tickle your students' funny bones!

ideas by Diane L. Tondreau-Flohr, Kent City Elementary, Kent City, MI

My Lucky Day

by Keiko Kasza

A daring pig outsmarts a fox in this humorous award-winning book.

Quick Thinking?
Analyzing characters

Promote critical thinking with this idea for before, during, and after reading. Before you read the story aloud, show students the front cover and tell them that the story is about a pig and a fox. Write the names of the two animals on the board. Then poll students to find out how many of them predict the pig is smarter and how many of them predict the fox is smarter. Write the information on the board. Encourage students to continue thinking about the question as you read the story aloud. At the end of the story, poll students again and ask youngsters to explain their thinking. Follow up with the questions below for more thought-provoking discussion.

- Is it smart for the pig to go to the bear's house? Why or why not?
- How else could the story end? Which character would be smarter then?

According to the Plan
Sequencing story events

This pig booklet is an adorable tool for recapping the story. Give each youngster a pink copy of page 213. Review the events represented by the illustrations. Then have each youngster cut out the pages, cover, and label. Instruct her to sequence the pages by the order of the events and write the corresponding numbers in the boxes. Help her stack the pages in order. Then place the cover on the stack and staple the entire stack to the center of a 6½-inch pink circle as shown.

To complete the booklet, instruct her to draw two eyes and a smile. Ask her to cut two ears from pink scrap paper. Then have her glue the ears and label to the back of the booklet. Encourage her to take the booklet home and refer to it as she tells her family about the grin-inducing story.

211

The Wolf's Chicken Stew

by Keiko Kasza

When a greedy wolf tries to fatten up a chicken for dinner, things don't go as he plans.

From Uncle Wolf
Counting to 100 by ones or skip-counting

After the chicks show the wolf how much they appreciate his baking, the wolf plans to make another batch of 100 goodies. To explore this quantity, make a chick pocket for each student by stapling an eight-inch yellow semicircle to an eight-inch yellow circle as shown. Instruct each youngster to fold a four-inch orange square in half diagonally and then glue it to the top of his pocket to make a beak. Have him draw two eyes and tape a craft feather to the back of his chick. Then choose an option below.

For counting by ones, have students sit in a circle with their chicks. Evenly distribute 100 round counters (cookies) to students. Then go around the circle, having the youngsters "feed" their chicks the cookies one by one as the group keeps count.

For skip-counting, give each youngster a copy of several circles (cookies) that you have numbered with a desired skip-counting sequence. Have him cut out the cookies. Then instruct him to "feed" the cookies to his chick in numerical order as he says the corresponding numbers.

10   20   30   40   50   70   10   0

Sasha will make yummy cupcakes for the chicks.

Scrumptious!
Using describing words

What other yummy treats would the chicks like? As students share their ideas, guide them to name adjectives that describe the foods. Then have each youngster complete a copy of the sentence frame shown, glue it to a sheet of paper, and illustrate it. Bind students' mouthwatering work into a book titled "More Scrumptious Treats." **For a math variation,** help youngsters determine how many treats they each need to make in order for the class to make 100 treats in all. Have each youngster make a page with the appropriate number of treats.

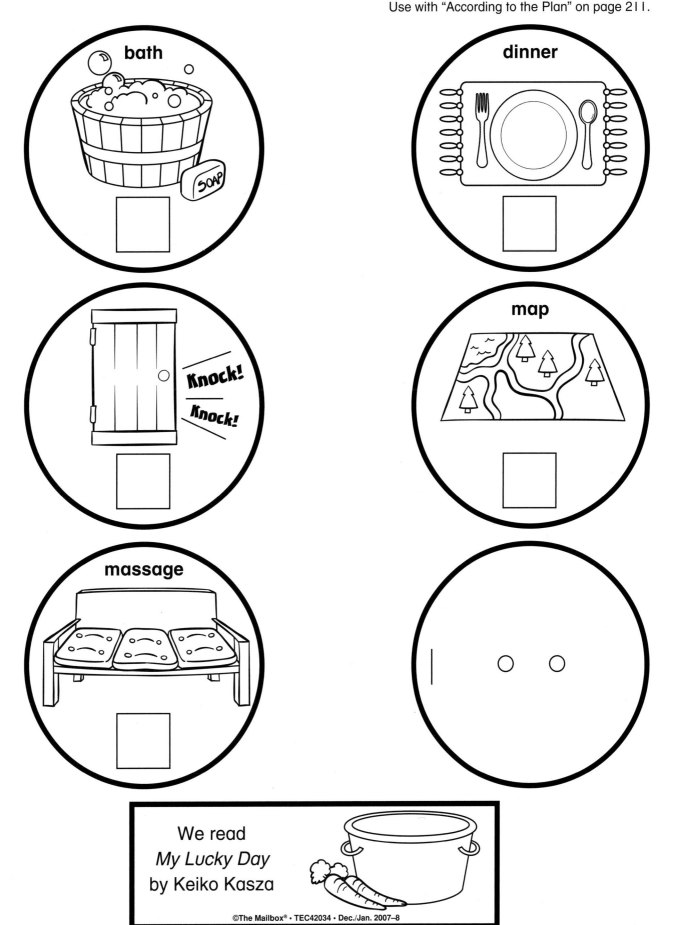

bath

dinner

Knock!
Knock!

map

massage

We read
My Lucky Day
by Keiko Kasza

Gingerbread Baby

By Jan Brett

In this wintry version of the traditional tale, a troublesome gingerbread baby leads a crowd on a spirited chase. In the end, a young boy secretly figures out a solution that's pleasing to everyone, including the mischievous cookie!

ideas contributed by Ada Goren
Winston-Salem, NC

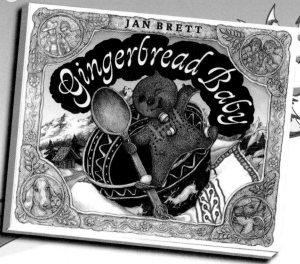

In Pursuit
Making predictions

Matti doesn't join in the chase, but he has a plan for catching the Gingerbread Baby. Will it work? Read aloud the story to the point where Matti vows to catch the Gingerbread Baby. Draw a T chart on a sheet of chart paper. To make column headings, post two gingerbread cookies—one labeled "Yes" and one labeled "No." (See the pattern on page 216.) Then poll students to determine how many youngsters predict Matti will catch the Gingerbread Baby and how many predict Matti will not catch him. Write the corresponding numbers on the chart.

Next, finish reading the story, pausing midway to poll students again and ask them to share their thinking. If students do not mention the clues in the border illustrations, direct their attention to them. At the end of the story, compare students' predictions with the actual story events. Did anyone guess Matti's plan?

> Why do you think Matti keeps his plan a secret?

why

Recipe for Understanding
Asking and answering questions

Increase students' comprehension with this tempting approach to questioning. Make several construction paper gingerbread cookies (pattern on page 216). Label the cookies with various question words, writing one word per cookie. (You may write the same word on more than one cookie.) Place the cookies facedown in a cookie tin.

After students are familiar with the story, have a youngster take a cookie at random and read the word aloud. Then ask students a story-related question with the word. Once a child appropriately answers the question, invite a different student to take a cookie. Continue as described until the cookie tin is empty. **For a more advanced version,** have students come up with the questions.

Missing!
Story problem and solution

With this follow-up idea, students imagine luring the Gingerbread Baby just as Matti does! Explain to students that the story inspired you to bake some gingerbread men. Take out a lidded, opaque container suitable for holding baked goods. Then open it and notice with mock surprise that it is empty. Comment that it reminds you of Matti's problem. Have students explain his problem and how he solves it by making a home for the runaway cookie. Then use the instructions below to help each youngster make a gingerbread house. Later, when students are not in the room, put a small gingerbread man cookie behind the door of each youngster's house for a sweet surprise.

Gingerbread House Instructions

Make a class supply of eight-inch brown construction paper houses. Cut a door in each house, cutting each door on three sides and folding it back as shown. Make a copy of the candy patterns on page 216 for each student. Then have each youngster follow the steps below. **For more advanced students,** provide house tracers and instruct each youngster to make his own house.

Steps:
1. Color and cut out the candy patterns.
2. Glue the candy on a house. Add any desired crayon decorations.
3. Glue the house on a sheet of colorful paper, being sure not to glue the door.

Gingerbread Baby by Jan Brett
and
The Gingerbread Boy by Paul Galdone

Story Similarities
Compare and contrast

No doubt the book reminds your students of other gingerbread tales. Read aloud another version of the traditional tale, and encourage students to notice how it is like *Gingerbread Baby* and how it is different. Then give each youngster a booklet with two brown covers and two white pages. Have her title one page "Same" and one page "Different." Then ask her to compare and contrast the stories on the corresponding booklet pages. After she completes her writing, give her a cover label with the titles of the two books. Have her glue the label on the front cover. Then invite her to decorate the cover with white paint details that resemble frosting.

Gingerbread Cookie Pattern
Use with "In Pursuit" and "Recipe for Understanding" on page 214.

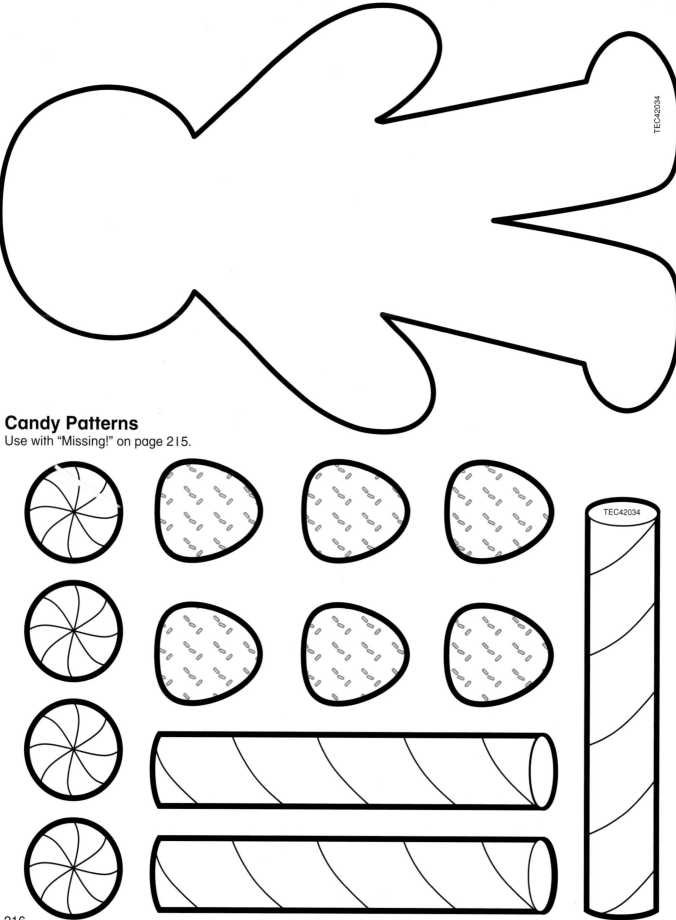

Candy Patterns
Use with "Missing!" on page 215.

A Seuss Spectacular

What better way to celebrate reading than by sharing Dr. Seuss's zany tales? With these book ideas, there's sure to be learning fun for everyone!

Big A, Little *a*
Beginning sounds

It's as easy as A, B, C to inspire young writers with this alliteration activity! In advance, program the top part of a sheet of paper as shown and then copy the paper to make a class supply. Write a chosen letter in the blanks of each copy. To begin, read aloud *Dr. Seuss's ABC*. Then have each child complete a programmed paper as described below. To showcase students' Seuss-style work, post the papers in alphabetical order with the title "Letter-Perfect Papers."

Easier version: Ask each youngster to list and illustrate words that begin with the assigned letter.

More advanced version: Help each student write a silly alliterative sentence that features the assigned letter. Then ask her to illustrate her work.

Beth Weaver and Melissa Hinkle, Benhaven Elementary, Olivia, NC

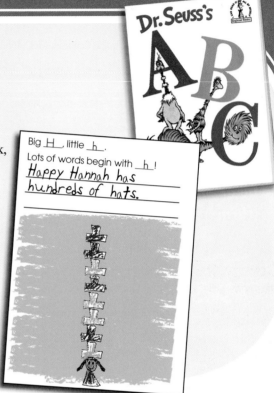

Big H, little h.
Lots of words begin with h!
Happy Hannah has hundreds of hats.

Something Fishy!
Graphing

Add a colorful twist to math with *One Fish, Two Fish, Red Fish, Blue Fish*. Read the book aloud and then give each child a copy of page 219. Have him color the fish so there is at least one fish of each featured color. Next, ask him to cut out the fish, sort them by color, and complete the graph. Then have him color the watery scene below the graph and glue the fish in the water. After each child completes his work, invite two students at a time to show their graphs to the group and help youngsters compare the graphs. **For a snacktime variation,** give each child 12 assorted Goldfish Colors crackers. Ask him to color the fish on his paper to match the crackers. Once he completes the graph and illustration as described above, invite him to eat the crackers!

Jill Davis, Kendall-Whittier Elementary, Tulsa, OK

Creature Combinations
Responding to literature
Spark your young author-illustrators' imaginations with this follow-up to *Horton Hatches the Egg*. First, review the characteristics of the baby elephant-bird. Then give each youngster a paper divided into three sections as shown. In each top section, instruct each child to illustrate and label a different type of animal. In the bottom section, have her illustrate and label a made-up creature that has characteristics of both animals. Afterward, invite her to describe her one-of-a-kind creature orally or in writing.

Andrea Hoerig, Mohawk Local Schools, McCutchenville, OH

duck   rabbit

dabbit

About Dabbits
A dabbit has long ears. It has yellow fethrs and a fuzee tal. It can swim. It can hop too!

Yum!
Snack
Here's a prereading activity for *Green Eggs and Ham* that's sure to hit the spot! Post a T chart with the first column titled "Before Tasting" and the second column titled "After Tasting." Write in the first column students' predictions about how green eggs taste. Next, have each youngster spread a spoonful of whipped topping on a plate and then top it with a scoop of lime sherbet to make a green egg. After each youngster samples his egg, ask students whether their opinions about green eggs have changed. Add their comments to the chart. When you read the book, students are sure to relate to the experience of trying new foods!

Shana Kinnison, Northside Elementary
Nebraska City, NE

There's a goat...

...in the boat!

A Game With Aim
Rhyming
No doubt this beanbag game will remind your students of the Cat in the Hat and his playful tricks. To prepare, cover a large clean and empty can with red and white paper as shown. Then secure the bottom of the can to a white circle to make a hat. To begin, place the hat on the floor. Have a youngster hold a beanbag and stand a designated distance from the hat. Next, lead students in chanting, "Ready, set, aim. Let's play the Cat in the Hat game!" Say the first part of a rhyme and have the youngster complete it. Then ask the group to repeat the entire rhyme and encourage the youngster to toss the beanbag into the hat. Continue as described to give each youngster a turn.

Lucille Iscaro, P. S. 257, Bronx, NY

Name _____

Smiley Swimmers

Listen for directions.

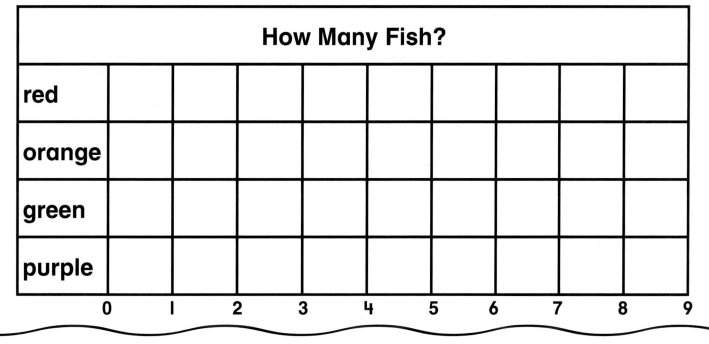

How Many Fish?									
red									
orange									
green									
purple									
	0	1	2	3	4	5	6	7	8	9

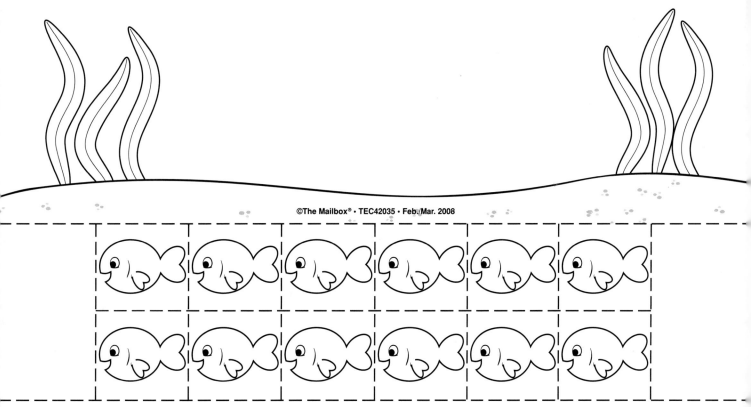

©The Mailbox® • TEC42035 • Feb./Mar. 2008

Note to the teacher: Use with "Something Fishy!" on page 217.

Tops & Bottoms

Adapted and illustrated by Janet Stevens

While Bear lazes on his porch, Hare makes a business deal with him: Hare does all the gardening while Bear sleeps, and they divide the crops equally. What's the catch? Hare tricks Bear into taking the least useful parts of the crops!

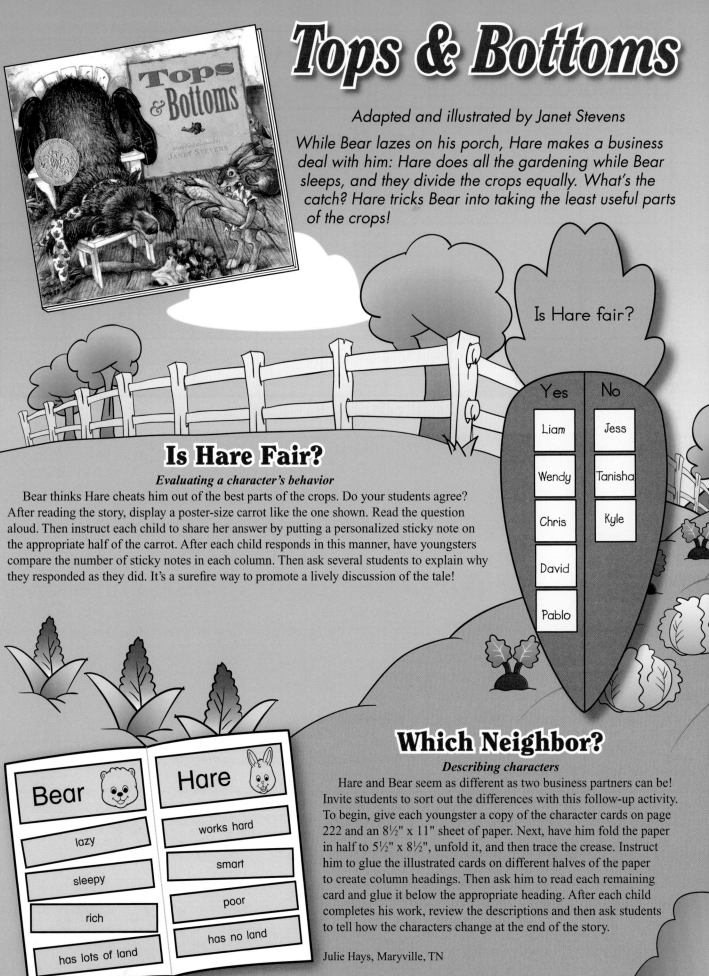

Is Hare Fair?

Evaluating a character's behavior

Bear thinks Hare cheats him out of the best parts of the crops. Do your students agree? After reading the story, display a poster-size carrot like the one shown. Read the question aloud. Then instruct each child to share her answer by putting a personalized sticky note on the appropriate half of the carrot. After each child responds in this manner, have youngsters compare the number of sticky notes in each column. Then ask several students to explain why they responded as they did. It's a surefire way to promote a lively discussion of the tale!

Which Neighbor?

Describing characters

Hare and Bear seem as different as two business partners can be! Invite students to sort out the differences with this follow-up activity. To begin, give each youngster a copy of the character cards on page 222 and an 8½" x 11" sheet of paper. Next, have him fold the paper in half to 5½" x 8½", unfold it, and then trace the crease. Instruct him to glue the illustrated cards on different halves of the paper to create column headings. Then ask him to read each remaining card and glue it below the appropriate heading. After each child completes his work, review the descriptions and then ask students to tell how the characters change at the end of the story.

Julie Hays, Maryville, TN

220

A Life Lesson

Identifying a story's main message

Here's a fun way for students to explore why Bear decides to change his ways. Give each child a 2½" x 7" white paper strip, an eight-inch brown circle, and a five-inch brown circle. To begin, each youngster cuts one end of the white strip into a point to make a tie. She writes on the tie what Bear learns and then glues the tie to the large brown circle. Next, she draws a face on the small brown circle and glues the head in place. Then she cuts ears, arms, and legs from brown paper scraps and glues them to her project. To showcase students' completed work, post the bears on a board along with student-made vegetables and the title "The 'Bear' Facts."

adapted from an idea by Julie Hays, Maryville, TN

Bear lrnd that he shd not be laze.

Plant Parts

carrot: root

radish: root

beet: root

lettuce: leaf

broccoli: flower bud

celery: stem

corn: seed

At the Veggie Stand

Parts of plants

After students are familiar with the story, pair science and snacktime with this simple idea. Bring to school some dip and story-related vegetable snacks, such as carrot sticks, celery sticks, and small pieces of broccoli. As youngsters sample each type of vegetable, encourage them to recall whether Hare refers to it as a top, bottom, or middle. Then guide them to identify the corresponding plant parts. (See the list on this page.) It's a delicious approach to science vocabulary!

Julie Hays

Carrot Crop

Antonyms

With this center activity, students don't separate tops and bottoms as Hare does; they put them together! Color and cut out several copies of the carrot cards on page 222. Program each pair of cards with an antonym word pair so there is one word on each carrot top and carrot. Then choose an option below.

Center activity: A student correctly pairs the cards and then writes each resulting word pair on a sheet of paper.

Partner game: Two students arrange the cards facedown. They play as in the traditional game of Concentration, matching antonym word pairs.

up

down

awake

asleep

sad

glad

221

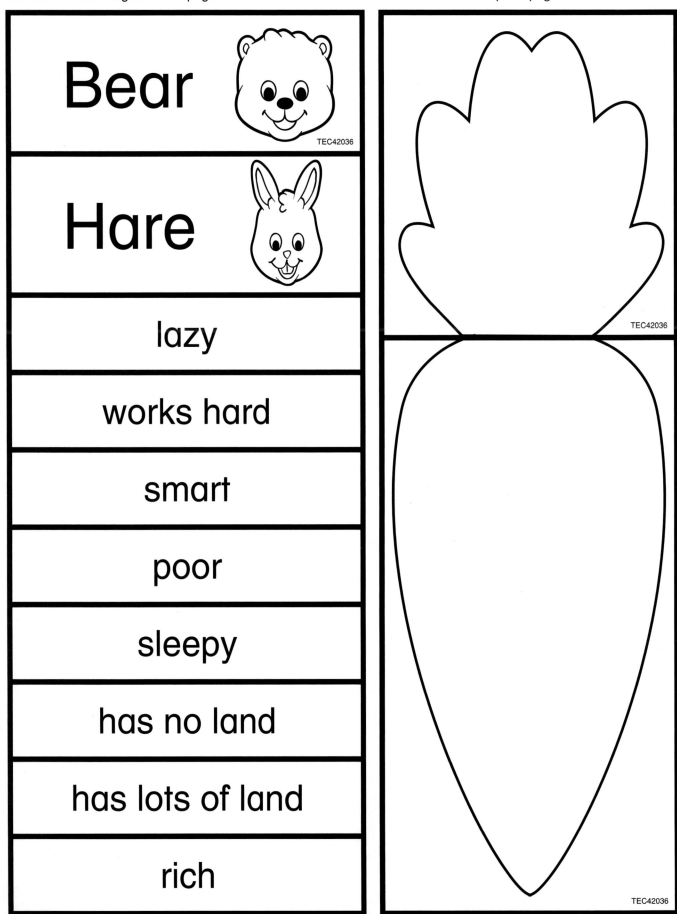

Bear

Hare

lazy

works hard

smart

poor

sleepy

has no land

has lots of land

rich

TEC42036

TEC42036

MATH UNITS

Calendar Time Math

These quick and easy ideas are something to smile about!
Not only are they simple to incorporate into your calendar
routine, but they're also sure to boost students' math skills.

☼ AUGUST ☼

Sunday	Monday	Tuesday	Wednesday	Thursday	Friday	Saturday
			1	2	3	4
5	6	7	8	9	10	11
12	13	14	15	16	17	18
19	20	21	22	23	24	25
26	27	28	29	30	31	

Mystery Number
Number sense

What do you need for this version of I Spy? Just
a calendar! At least several days into a month, give
students one or more clues about a date on the calendar.
For example, you might say, "I spy the number nine" or,
"I spy the number that is one more than eight." After a
student points out the correct date, present a clue about a
different date to continue.

Kristen Egge, Lincoln Learning Center, Willmar, MN

Day by Day
Yesterday, today, and tomorrow

Start the day with a cheerful tune! After students
identify the day's date, ask them to name the current
day, the day it was yesterday, and the day it will be
tomorrow. Then lead them in the song below.

(sung to the tune of "Are You Sleeping?")

Today is [Tuesday]. Today is [Tuesday].
[August 21], [August 21].
Yesterday was [Monday].
Tomorrow will be [Wednesday].
Hip hip hooray! What a day!

Laura Disharoon, Kellogg Elementary, Chula Vista, CA

Daily Highlight
Number recognition, number patterns

Here's a skill-boosting way to keep track of the first
100 days of school. Display a poster-size hundred chart
near your classroom calendar. Designate highlighters of
three different colors for coloring the chart—one color
for each number that ends with a five, a different color for
each number that ends with a zero, and another color for
the remaining numbers. Each day, ask a student to use the
appropriate highlighter to color the square that corresponds
with the number of days school has been in session. Once a
few rows of the chart have been colored, guide students to
identify the number patterns.

After the chart is completely colored on the 100th day of
school, write randomly selected numbers on small individual
sticky notes. Direct students to identify the numbers and
place them on the matching numbers on the chart. It's a
terrific strategy for reinforcing number sense!

Cathy Allmaras, Oberon Elementary, Oberon, ND

I see a pattern!

Hundred Chart

1	2	3	4	5	6	7	8	9	10
11	12	13	14	15	16	17	18	19	20
21	22	23	24	25	26	27	28	29	30
31	32	33	34	35	36	37			40
41	42	43	44	45	46	47	48		
51	52	53	54	55	56	57	58	59	60
61	62	63	64	65	66	67	68	69	70
71	72	73	74	75	76	77	78	79	80
81	82	83	84	85	86	87	88	89	90
91	92	93	94	95	96	97	98	99	100

How Handy!
Number patterns

As this colorful display grows, so do students' number skills. Each month, make one construction paper hand for every five days of school, alternating left and right hands. (Use a different color for each month.)

On the first day of school, post a left-hand cutout and write the number 1 on the first finger. On the second day of school, write the number 2 on the second finger, and so on until all five fingers are numbered. Then write the number 5 on the palm and circle it. The next school day, post another cutout. Continue as described, labeling the palms by fives and arranging the cutouts to form a rainbow if desired. If a new month begins before you number all the fingers on a cutout, cover the remaining fingers with the appropriate color of paper. The colors make it easy to compare the number of school days in each month, and the hands are a great skip-counting tool!

Becky Mallatt, LaPine Elementary, LaPine, OR

"Sum" Trains
Beginning addition

Plan to do this hands-on activity on days with dates equal to grade-appropriate sums. On a chosen day, pair students. After students identify the date, give each twosome a train with the corresponding number of Unifix cubes. Have the partners count their cubes and then divide them into two trains. Instruct the students in one pair to tell how many cubes they have in each train. Then use the numbers to write an addition sentence on a whiteboard or an easel. Continue as described with different addition combinations. Later in the year, invite students to take your role and write the number sentences.

Debbie Patrick, State College, PA

Page-a-Day Book
Number recognition, number words

Try this supersimple idea the first full month of school. In advance, get a spiral-bound set of large index cards. On the first school day of the month, write the number 1 and the word *one* on the first card. On each following day of school that month, read the previously labeled pages with students and then complete the next blank page with the appropriate number and number word. For reinforcement, have youngsters identify selected numbers. Or cover chosen numbers and ask them to read the number words. Students might even notice the number patterns!

Jamie Perry, I. W. and Eleanor Hyde Elementary
League City, TX

225

Fun With Numbers

Increase students' number sense with these "pet-acular" ideas.

ideas contributed by Ada Goren
Winston-Salem, NC

Seeing Spots

This adorable doggy workmat can be used in two different ways! Have each student color a copy of page 228. Then choose an option below.

Modeling numbers: Give each child six round counters (spots). Have one youngster roll a large number die and name the number rolled. Ask each youngster to put that many spots on his dog. To continue, instruct students to clear their mats and invite a different student to roll the die.

Addition combinations: Give each youngster a sheet of paper and a disposable cup containing several two-sided counters. Ask each student to pour out the counters (spots) on his dog. Instruct him to count how many spots there are of each color and write the corresponding addition combination. Have students model and write different addition combinations in the same manner.

Dinnertime!

WAGS

Number Dog, Number Dog, who gave you the bone?

Ten!

Bone Mystery
Number identification

Whether your students are boning up on numbers to ten or higher numbers, this game is sure to please. To prepare, make a large tagboard bone. Gather a class supply of blank cards and write a familiar number on each card. (If you repeat some numbers, write them with different-colored markers to distinguish them.)

To play one round, designate a student as Number Dog. Have her sit in a chair with her back to the group. Give each remaining student a number card to hold in clear view. Next, silently give a cardholder the bone and have her quietly put it behind the dog. After the youngster returns to her place, lead the group in asking the question shown. At this signal, the dog turns and faces the group. To guess the answer, she names the number a student is holding or names that student. (If she cannot identify the number, name it for reinforcement.) Once the dog identifies the correct student or makes three incorrect guesses and you reveal the answer, have the group name the numbers on all the cards.

Hungry Dogs
Comparing sets

Are there enough bones for these dogs? Students use one-to-one correspondence to find out! Make a supply of dog cards and bone cards. (See page 229.) Give each child in a small group a resealable plastic bag containing several dog cards and a different number of bone cards, varying the amounts in each bag. Have each child pair the dogs and bones, count them, and tell whether there are more dogs or bones. Then instruct him to return the cards to the bag. Ask students to trade bags for more "bone-a fide" math practice!

Pooch Pals

Invite students to wear dog headbands during these partner activities. To make one, attach two paper dog ears to a sentence strip headband. For each option below, have each student cut out a copy of the bone cards on page 229.

Comparing sets: Each partner, in turn, rolls a die and takes that many bones. The youngsters determine who has more bones, and that child says, "Bowwow!" If the partners have an equal number of bones, both children say the word. The children return the bones and continue in the same manner as time allows.

Addition: Each partner needs a copy of the recording sheet on page 229. Each partner rolls a die and sets out that many bones. Then the partners each write an addition sentence with the two numbers. They count the bones to check the sum. They continue as described to complete their recording sheets.

Name **Trevor** Fun With Numbers Recording sheet

How Many Bones?

$3 + 2 = 5$
$6 + 1 = 7$
$4 + 2 = 6$
$4 + 3 = 7$
$2 + 2 = 4$

Dog Tales
Modeling addition

Since this story-problem activity is self-contained, it's perfect for math practice over several days. For each child, fold up the bottom of a vertical 6" x 9" sheet of paper about 3½ inches and staple the sides. Then trim the top of the paper to resemble the roof of a doghouse. Instruct each student to label her doghouse as shown and illustrate it. Have her color and cut out several dog cards (patterns on page 229). Next, direct youngsters to model an addition story such as the one shown. Then write the corresponding number sentence on the board with student input. Explore different problems as described, having youngsters store their dogs in the doghouses when they are not in use.

My Math Dogs

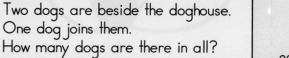

Two dogs are beside the doghouse.
One dog joins them.
How many dogs are there in all?

A Crop of Fresh Math Ideas

Harvest a variety of skill reinforcement with these pumpkin activities!

Fast-Growing Pumpkins

Counting or counting on to add

For counting, draw several large circles on the board. Write a different number in each circle. Then ask students to take turns drawing one or two pumpkins in the circles, cautioning them that the number of pumpkins in the circles should not exceed the designated numbers. Periodically have students stop and determine how many more pumpkins are needed. Continue as described until each circle has the correct number of pumpkins.

For counting on to add, draw a large circle on the board and label it with a number from 6 to 9. Write an addition problem using the number as the first addend and 1, 2, or 3 as the second addend. To solve the problem, have a volunteer draw one or more pumpkins to correspond with the second addend. Guide students to count on from the greater addend, using the illustration as a visual cue. Then ask the volunteer to write the answer.

Angie Kutzer, Garrett Elementary, Mebane, NC

Start at eight. Nine, ten.

8 + 2 = 10

The Right Heights

Using nonstandard units

To cultivate students' measurement skills, make several pumpkin cutouts of various shapes and sizes. Letter the pumpkins for easy identification and then post them at the bottom of a wall. Set out recording sheets and connecting cubes. When a student visits the pumpkin patch, he determines how tall each pumpkin is to the nearest whole cube and writes the measurements on a recording sheet. **For more advanced students,** write on one pumpkin how many cubes tall it is to give students a measurement benchmark. Ask each student to estimate the height of each remaining pumpkin before he measures it.

Angie Kutzer

Recording Sheet

A. about __1__ cubes tall

B. about ____ cubes tall

C. about ____ cubes tall

D. about ____ cubes tall

232

Ripe for the Picking?

Graphing

Students will be eager to find out what the results of this activity will be! Give each student a copy of page 234. Have her color the happy side of the two-sided pumpkin orange and the sad side green. Ask her to cut out the pumpkin, fold it in half, and then glue it together. Next, the youngster stands, holds the pumpkin by the stem, and then lets it fall. She colors a space on the graph to show which side of the pumpkin is faceup. She continues in the same manner until she colors ten spaces. Then she tells about the graph, using words such as *more, less,* and *equal to.*

Angie Kutzer, Garrett Elementary, Mebane, NC

Great Games

Addition Trail Game: Color a copy of page 235. Make a pumpkin spinner like the one shown. Have each player put a game marker on Start. To take a turn, a player rolls two dice and announces the sum of the numbers he rolled. Then he spins the spinner, advances the corresponding number of spaces, and follows any instructions in the space where he lands. The players take turns as described until one player reaches Finish.

Number Lotto: Make a few copies of page 236. Program each gameboard space with a number, making each board unique. Then make matching caller's cards. Have each student color a copy of a programmed page and cut out the game markers. Then play the game like lotto until one or more students marks four in a row. **For more advanced students,** instead of calling the numbers to mark, describe them with the words *before, after,* and *between.*

adapted from an idea by Yolanda Arnold, Hudson School, Birmingham, AL

Toss and Total!

Addition sentences or math stories

For this group activity, cut out the centers from two plastic lids such as the covers of margarine containers. Keep the resulting rings and discard the centers. Draw pumpkins or adhere pumpkin stickers all over a large piece of paper, varying the amount of space between the pumpkins. Place the paper on the floor. Next, have two students toss the rings on the paper and then announce how many pumpkins are in each ring. Ask youngsters to write an addition sentence or tell a math story with the two numbers. Continue in the same manner to give each youngster a turn tossing a ring.

Angie Kutzer

Ripe for the Picking?

Listen for directions.

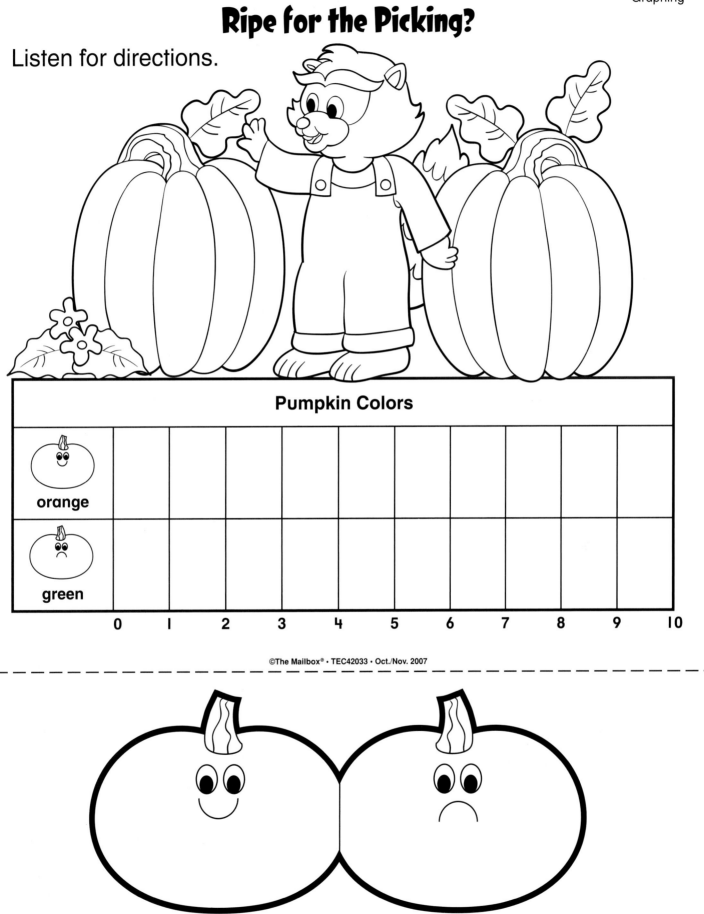

Pumpkin Colors

	0	1	2	3	4	5	6	7	8	9	10
orange											
green											

Note to the teacher: Use with "Ripe for the Picking?" on page 233.

Pete's Pumpkin Farm

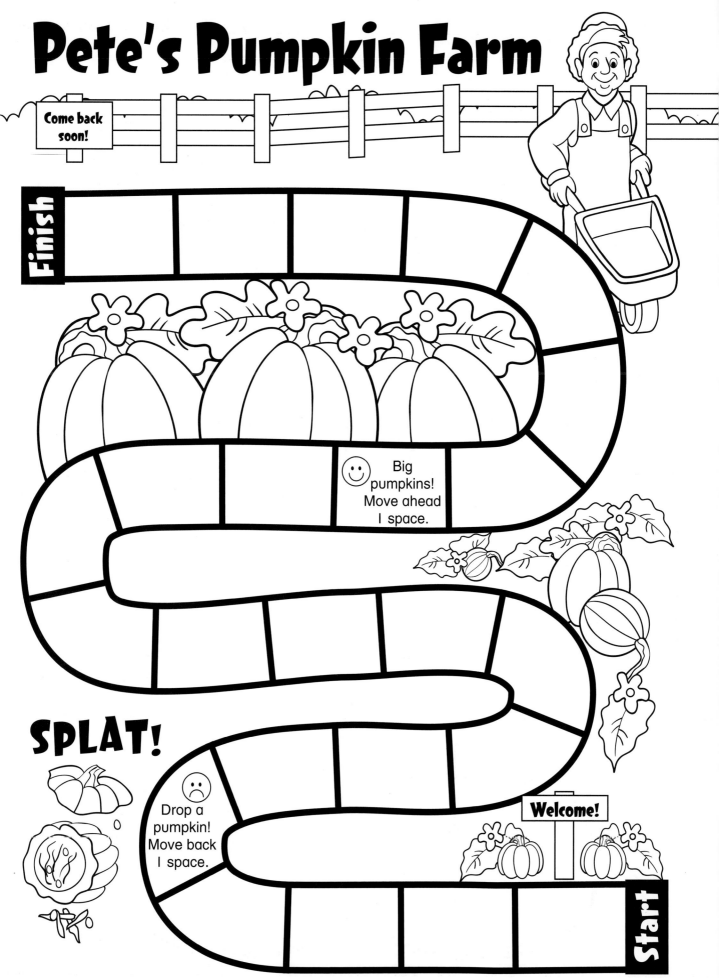

Come back soon!

Finish

Big pumpkins! Move ahead 1 space.

SPLAT!

Drop a pumpkin! Move back 1 space.

Welcome!

Start

Pumpkin Lotto

©The Mailbox® • TEC42033 • Oct./Nov. 2007

TEC42033
TEC42033
TEC42033
TEC42033
TEC42033
TEC42033
TEC42033
TEC42033
TEC42033
TEC42033
TEC42033
TEC42033

Getting a Jump on
SUBTRACTION

Students are bound to leap ahead in math with these surefire ideas!

Frogs on a Log

Jump-start these activities with the traditional song "Five Little Speckled Frogs."

Understanding subtraction: Repeat the song with students, having them act it out with five green cubes and a log cutout. Pause after each verse to tell the corresponding subtraction story.

Writing subtraction sentences: Have each youngster write the appropriate subtraction sentences on a copy of page 239. After he colors, cuts out, and sequences the pages, staple them between two covers. Then have the youngster title and sign the resulting booklet.

Kathy Ginn, Jeffersonville Elementary, Jeffersonville, OH

Five Frogs
by Kyle

Twelve fish were swimming.
We caught four fish.
Eight fish are left.

Fishy Facts

Attach a paper clip to each of several fish cutouts. Place a yarn circle on the floor to make a pond. To make a fishing pole, attach a string to one end of a ruler and then attach a magnet to the free end of the string. Use the ideas below to have students fish for math facts!

Understanding subtraction: Spread out the fish in the pond and have students stand around the pond. Pass the fishing pole to a youngster. Next, set a timer for a chosen amount of time and say, "Go fishing!" At this signal, the youngster catches a fish and then passes the pole to the next student. After this child catches a fish, she passes the pole to the next student, and so on. When the time is up, help students tell a relevant subtraction story.

Creating and solving subtraction problems: Number 12 fish from 1 to 12 and then arrange them facedown in the pond. Have each of two students catch a fish. Ask the group to create a subtraction problem with the corresponding numbers and then solve it.

Laura Wanke, Pecatonica Elementary, Pecatonica, IL

237

Topped With Pepperoni

Subtraction combinations

For mouthwatering math practice, have each youngster color a white paper plate so that it resembles a cheese pizza. Give him a chosen number of red circles (pepperoni slices) to put on his pizza. Then instruct him to model and write all the subtraction combinations for that number. **For an easier activity,** tell students subtraction stories to solve with their pepperoni.

adapted from an idea by Laura Wanke, Pecatonica Elementary
Pecatonica, IL

$$9 - 8 = 1$$
$$9 - 3 = 6$$
$$9 - 4 = 5$$

$$12 - 0 = 12$$
$$12 - 3 = 9$$
$$12 - 5 = 7$$

Spill and Write

Subtraction combinations

Divide students into small groups for this hands-on activity. Then give each group a sheet of paper and a disposable cup containing an equal number of two-sided counters. (This is the number that students will subtract from.)

In each group, a student spills the counters from the cup. Then she says a corresponding subtraction sentence. For example, if five yellow sides and seven red sides are faceup, she says either, "Twelve minus five equals seven," or, "Twelve minus seven equals five." A youngster writes the subtraction sentence on the group's paper if it is not already listed. Then the students return the counters to the cup. Students continue as described until time is up or they write all the subtraction combinations. To follow up, make an organized list of all the combinations as a class.

Angie Kutzer, Garrett Elementary
Mebane, NC

On the Line

Counting back to subtract

To play this partner game, each pair of students needs a number line from 1 to 12, a sheet of paper, two game pawns, and a number cube with the numbers 1–3. (For easy preparation, use masking tape to cover the numbers 4–6 on a number cube and then renumber those sides.) To begin, the partners place their pawns on the number line at the number 12. To take a turn, a player rolls the cube. He counts back as he moves his pawn accordingly. Then he writes the corresponding subtraction sentence. Players take turns as described. The game is over after both players land exactly on 1. (If a player rolls a number that would result in moving past 1, he does not move and his turn is over.)

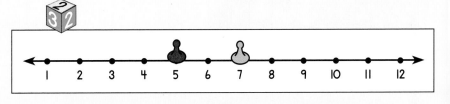

The reproducible on page 240 was written by Angie Kutzer, Garrett Elementary, Mebane, NC.

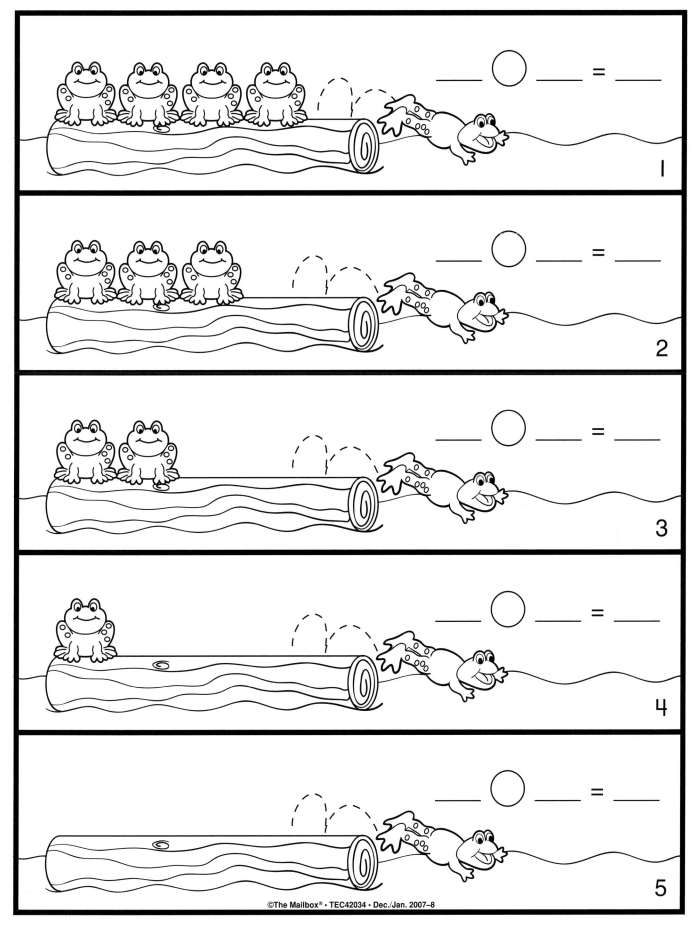

In the Stars

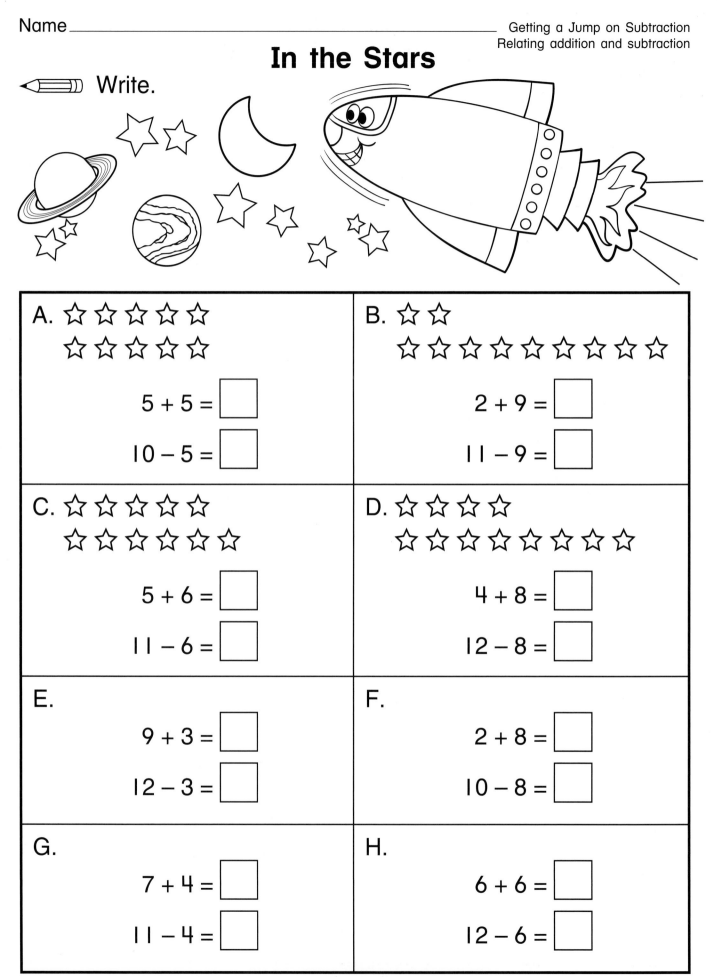

Write.

A. ☆ ☆ ☆ ☆ ☆
☆ ☆ ☆ ☆ ☆

$5 + 5 = \boxed{}$

$10 - 5 = \boxed{}$

B. ☆ ☆
☆ ☆ ☆ ☆ ☆ ☆ ☆ ☆ ☆

$2 + 9 = \boxed{}$

$11 - 9 = \boxed{}$

C. ☆ ☆ ☆ ☆ ☆
☆ ☆ ☆ ☆ ☆ ☆

$5 + 6 = \boxed{}$

$11 - 6 = \boxed{}$

D. ☆ ☆ ☆ ☆
☆ ☆ ☆ ☆ ☆ ☆ ☆ ☆

$4 + 8 = \boxed{}$

$12 - 8 = \boxed{}$

E.

$9 + 3 = \boxed{}$

$12 - 3 = \boxed{}$

F.

$2 + 8 = \boxed{}$

$10 - 8 = \boxed{}$

G.

$7 + 4 = \boxed{}$

$11 - 4 = \boxed{}$

H.

$6 + 6 = \boxed{}$

$12 - 6 = \boxed{}$

Name_____

By Leaps and Bounds

Subtract.

Use the number line to help you.

Mighty Jumpers

1 2 3 4 5 6 7 8 9 10 11 12

A. $\begin{array}{r} 12 \\ -\ 3 \\ \hline \end{array}$	B. $\begin{array}{r} 9 \\ -\ 1 \\ \hline \end{array}$	C. $\begin{array}{r} 8 \\ -\ 2 \\ \hline \end{array}$	D. $\begin{array}{r} 10 \\ -\ 3 \\ \hline \end{array}$	E. $\begin{array}{r} 11 \\ -\ 1 \\ \hline \end{array}$
F. $\begin{array}{r} 8 \\ -\ 1 \\ \hline \end{array}$	G. $\begin{array}{r} 12 \\ -\ 2 \\ \hline \end{array}$	H. $\begin{array}{r} 10 \\ -\ 1 \\ \hline \end{array}$	I. $\begin{array}{r} 9 \\ -\ 2 \\ \hline \end{array}$	J. $\begin{array}{r} 8 \\ -\ 3 \\ \hline \end{array}$
K. $\begin{array}{r} 11 \\ -\ 3 \\ \hline \end{array}$	L. $\begin{array}{r} 12 \\ -\ 1 \\ \hline \end{array}$	M. $\begin{array}{r} 11 \\ -\ 2 \\ \hline \end{array}$	N. $\begin{array}{r} 10 \\ -\ 2 \\ \hline \end{array}$	O. $\begin{array}{r} 9 \\ -\ 3 \\ \hline \end{array}$

Three Cheers for the 100th Day!

Math Mascot

Counting by tens

How many spots does this cute pooch have? Why, 100, of course! Gather three empty boxes: two for the dog's body and one for its head. Cover the boxes with white paper. Then secure the boxes in a stack with the largest box on the bottom. Glue two black ears and four white paws to the boxes. Then use markers to illustrate a dog face and add paw details.

Next, determine how many spots each child should make in order for the class to make 100 spots in all. Have each child cut out the designated number of spots from black paper. Then help the youngsters group the spots in sets of ten to check that they have the correct amount. After students count the sets by tens and add or subtract spots if needed, have them glue the spots to the dog. The resulting dalmatian will be an adorable reminder of teamwork and the 100th day of school!

Teresa Swenson, Kirkwood Elementary, Coralville, IA

100 Steps
Line Leader: Dottie

Step by Step

Comparing units of measure

When you and your class walk to the cafeteria or another daily destination, why not incorporate some math? Several days before the 100th day of school, ask students to silently count their steps on the way to a chosen destination as you and the line leader softly keep count. Once you reach 100, have the class stop. Post a sign similar to the one shown to mark the distance of 100 steps from your classroom. Then continue with students to the destination. Repeat the activity over the next several days with different line leaders. On the 100th day of school, revisit the signs with students and compare their locations. Guide students to realize that since the units of measure (footsteps) vary, the distances vary too.

Barb Bieger, Pocalla Springs Elementary, Sumter, SC

242

Counting on Streamers

Writing numbers to 100

Invite students to create festive decorations with this skill-boosting partner activity! A day or two before the 100th day of school, give each twosome a length of adding machine tape and two different-colored markers. Instruct the students to write the numbers from 1 to 100 by tens so that the colors alternate. To differentiate the activity, instruct selected pairs of students to write the numbers by ones, twos, or fives. Display the completed streamers on the big day as desired.

Randi Austin, Gasconade C-4 Elementary, Falcon, MO

| 10 | 20 | 30 | 40 | 50 | 60 | 70 | 80 | 90 | 100 |

| 5 | 10 | 15 | 20 | 25 | 30 | 35 | 40 | 45 | 50 | 55 | 60 | 65 | 70 |

| 2 | 4 | 6 | 8 | 10 | 12 | 14 | 16 | 18 | 20 | 22 | 24 | 26 | 28 | 30 |

Growing Candle

Counting by fives

This party treat is a sweet math tool! Have each youngster color and cut out a copy of the cupcake and number strip patterns on page 244. Instruct him to glue the number strip patterns together in numerical order. Then ask him to cut a flame from yellow paper and glue it at the top of the strip so the strip resembles a candle. Slit the cupcake on the dashed lines and then help the young-ster thread the candle through the openings. Have him count to 100 by fives as he slowly pulls the candle up and reveals the corresponding numbers. **For more advanced students,** mask several numbers on a copy of the number strips. Give each youngster a copy and have him write the missing numbers before he completes the project.

adapted from an idea by Diane L. Flohr
Orchard Trails Elementary, Kent City, MI

Changing the Lineup

Modeling 100

To introduce this literature-based idea, ask students to imagine being at the end of a line of 100 people. Then read aloud *One Hundred Hungry Ants* by Elinor J. Pinczes. Next, have students connect 100 Unifix cubes to represent the line of ants. Reread the story up to the point where the littlest ant proposes that the ants make two lines of 50 ants. Instruct students to rearrange the cubes to represent the ants' new lines. Then read the rest of the story, pausing each time the ants adjust their lines to have students rearrange the cubes accordingly. It's a great way to deepen students' understanding of the concept of 100!

Peggy Wright, Waverly Elementary, Waverly, TN

We need ten rows of ten cubes.

243

Cupcake and Number Strip Patterns

Use with "Growing Candle" on page 243.

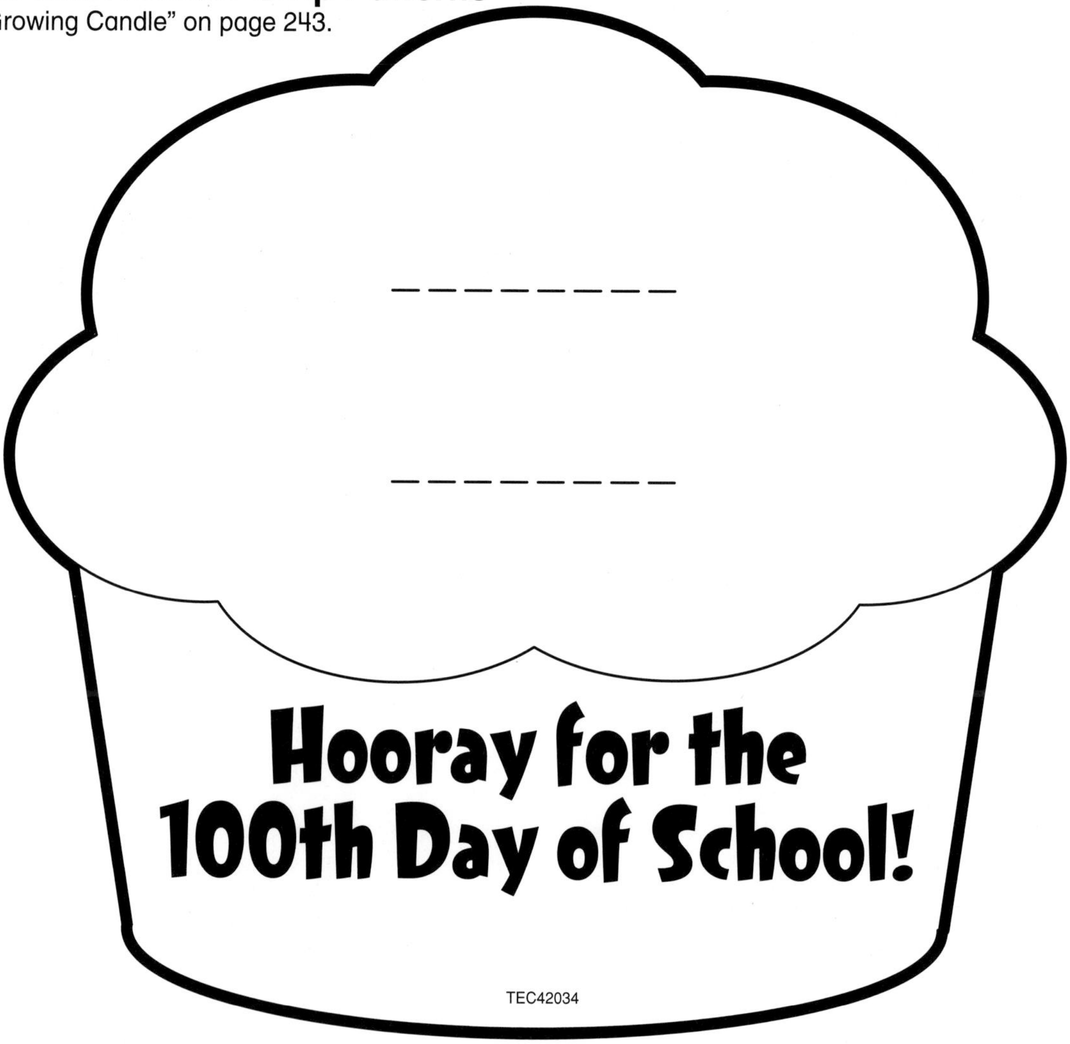

_ _ _ _ _ _ _ _

_ _ _ _ _ _ _ _

Hooray for the 100th Day of School!

TEC42034

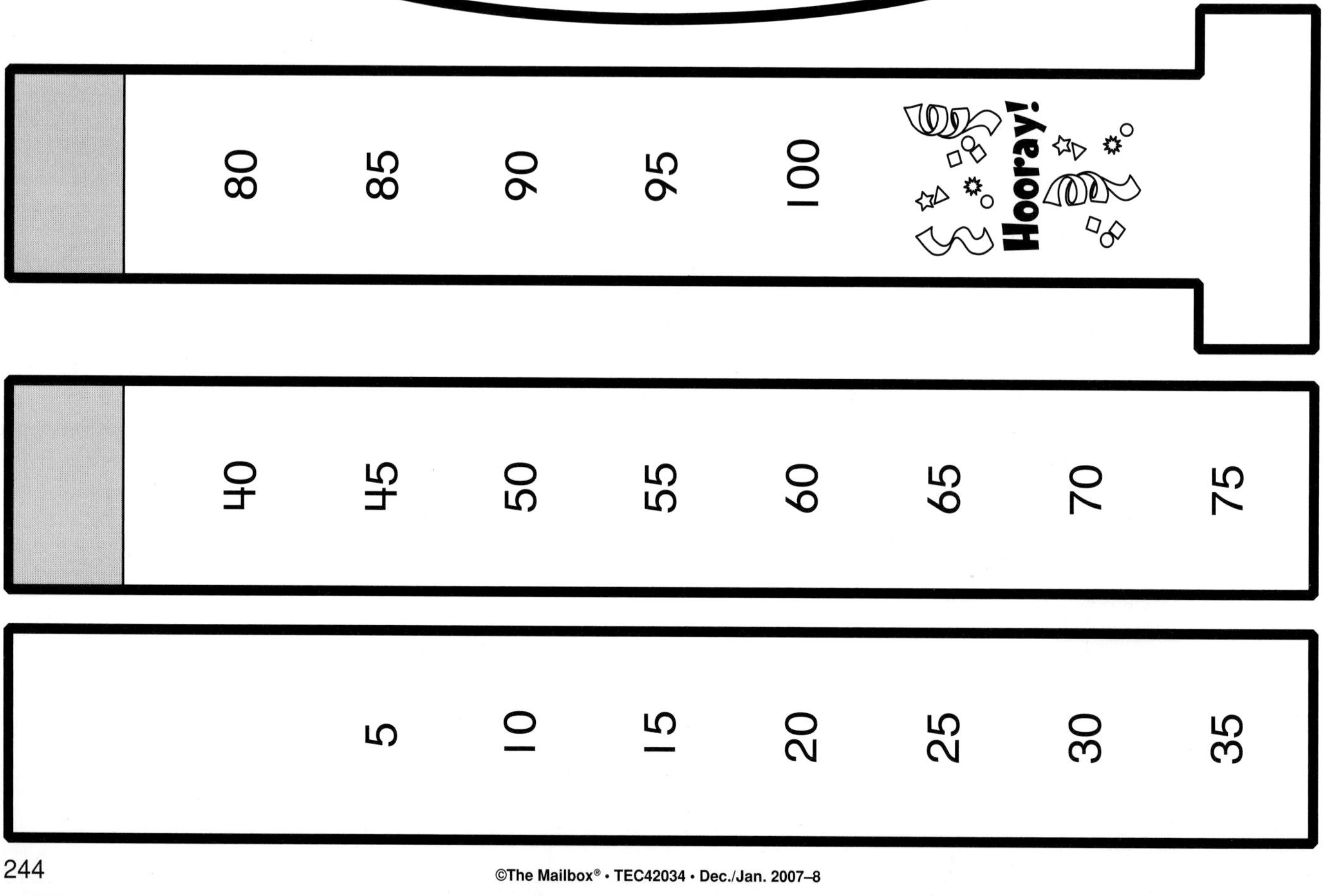

| 80 | 85 | 90 | 95 | 100 | Hooray! |

| 40 | 45 | 50 | 55 | 60 | 65 | 70 | 75 |

| 5 | 10 | 15 | 20 | 25 | 30 | 35 |

"Paws-itively" Pleasing Math Ideas

Kitty Facts
Adding sets or addition facts

Each option below results in projects that are "purr-fect" to display! To prepare, have each student color and cut out a copy of the cat and bow patterns on page 247. Then give him 12 narrow paper strips (whiskers).

Adding sets: Have each student put a designated number of whiskers on each side of his cat's nose. Ask students to determine how many whiskers each cat has in all. Then instruct each youngster to draw an X on the corresponding number on his cat. After students explore different sums in the same manner, have each child glue two sets of whiskers on his cat, write the corresponding sum on his bow, and glue the bow to the cat.

Addition facts: For this partner activity, one student rolls two number cubes. He says the corresponding addition fact. Then he finds the sum on his cat and draws an X on it if it is not already marked. His partner takes a turn in the same manner. Alternate play continues as time allows or until one student marks all the numbers. Then each youngster glues whiskers on his cat to illustrate a chosen addition fact. He writes the fact on his bow and glues the bow to the cat.

Diane L. Tondreau-Flohr, Kent City Elementary, Kent City, MI

There are seven whiskers in all!

Fetch and Find!
Number order

Students bone up on the concepts of before and after with this idea. Write a different number on each of several bone cutouts and then draw a line before and after each number as shown. Write each corresponding number on a separate blank card. Put the bones and cards at a center stocked with paper. When a youngster visits the center, she spreads out the cards. She takes a bone and completes the number sequence with the appropriate cards. Then she writes the three numbers in order on a sheet of paper. She completes and writes different number sequences in the same manner.

dog	■	■	■	■	■		
cat	▨	▨	▨	▨	▨	▨	

Dog or Cat?
Data analysis, probability

Here's a "pet-acular" look at more and less likely outcomes. Post a blank graph with two rows, one labeled "dog" and one labeled "cat." Label two sides of a small empty tissue box "dog" and four sides of the box "cat." To begin, ask students to predict whether they will roll one word more often or whether they will roll the words an equal number of times. Then have students take turns rolling the box, reading the word on top, and coloring the graph accordingly. After students roll the box several times and record the results, have them read the graph. Then guide youngsters to understand why they were more likely to roll the word *cat*.

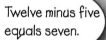

Twelve minus five equals seven.

Bony Solutions
Addition or subtraction

For these hands-on activities, give each student a copy of the workmat on page 248 and 12 small craft sticks (bones).

Addition: Have a youngster roll a die. Instruct each student to put the corresponding number of bones on his fish. Invite a child to roll the die to determine how many bones each student should add to his fish. Then write the matching number sentence on the board with student input.

Subtraction: Pair students and give each twosome several counters. Have each child put the same number of bones (6 to 12) on his fish. To play one round, each player, in turn, rolls a die, takes the corresponding number of bones from his fish, and says the matching subtraction fact. The player with more bones remaining on his fish takes a counter. (If the players have an equal number of bones, they each take a counter.) Then the players put the bones back on the fish. After students play several rounds, the player with more counters wins.

Diane L. Tondreau-Flohr, Kent City Elementary, Kent City, MI

The reproducible on page 249 was written by Diane L. Tondreau-Flohr.

Bony Solutions

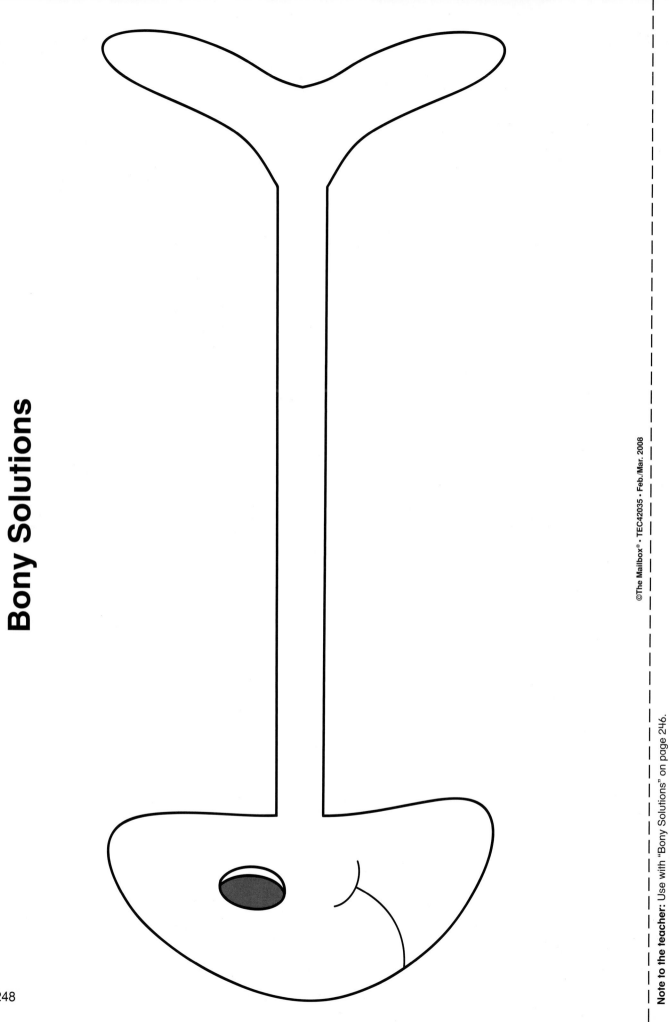

©The Mailbox® • TEC42035 • Feb./Mar. 2008

Note to the teacher: Use with "Bony Solutions" on page 246.

Wishing for Fish

X out fish to solve the problems.

Write.

3 – 2 = _____

4 – 1 = _____

5 – 3 = _____

4 – 2 = _____

6 – 3 = _____

6 – 4 = _____

5 – 2 = _____

4 – 3 = _____

Size It Up

Use these fun-filled ideas to deliver practice with capacity and weight in a big way!

Math to Go
Ordering by capacity

What's a surefire way to spark students' interest in measuring? Use props from local fast-food restaurants! Collect from different restaurants clean and empty cups of various sizes. Divide students into small groups and give each group a few different-size cups. Ask the students in each group to order their cups from the cup that can hold the least to the cup that can hold the most. After the group members are satisfied with the order of the cups, give them a supply of math cubes or other manipulatives that they can use to fill each cup, in turn. Ask the youngsters in each group to compare the quantities of manipulatives that the cups can hold and make any needed corrections in their cup lineup. For more fast-food math, have each group trade its cups with another group and repeat the activity.

adapted from an idea by Jennifer Kresicki
Perquimans Central School
Winfall, NC

Made to Measure
Estimating capacity

For this guess-and-check activity, put at a center two different-size measuring cups and a supply of manipulatives, such as math cubes, uncooked pasta, or pom-poms. Also set out a class supply of recording sheets similar to the one shown. To complete the activity, a student estimates how many manipulatives will fit in the smaller measuring cup. After she writes her estimate on a recording sheet, she determines how many manipulatives the cup can hold and records the quantity on the recording sheet. Next, she uses the measurement from the first cup to make a reasonable estimate of how many manipulatives the larger measuring cup can hold. She records the estimate. Then she determines and records the actual quantity.

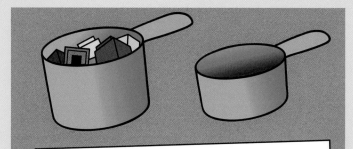

Name _Ella_

Recording Sheet

Cups	Guess	Check
$\frac{1}{2}$	6 cubes	9 cubes
1	16 cubes	18 cubes

Lots to Lift!

Comparing objects by weight

This partner game gives students practice using the words *light* and *heavy*. Divide an 8½" x 11" sheet of paper into two columns. Label one column "Light" and the other column "Heavy." Cut out the cards on a copy of page 252 and glue each card in the appropriate column of the prepared paper. Then make one copy of the paper for every two students to use as an answer key. Have each child color a copy of page 252, cut out the cards, and then write his initials on the back of each card.

To begin, two players put their cards in a container. Then one player takes a card at random. If he gets an "Oops!" card, he puts the card aside and his turn is over. If he gets a picture card, he names the pictured object and identifies it as being light or heavy, checking the answer key if needed. If he does not already have that picture on his mat, he puts the card on an appropriate box. If he already has the picture, he returns the card to the container. His partner takes a turn in the same manner. Alternate play continues until one player has eight cards on his mat.

Balancing Pasta

Weighing with nonstandard units

Two kinds of pasta and a pan balance are the main ingredients for these center activities.

Easier version: Set out a pan balance and two different-size varieties of pasta. Invite students to compare the weights of different sets of pasta. For example, students may determine whether five pieces of rigatoni are heavier or lighter than five pieces of macaroni.

More advanced version: Place at a center student copies of the recording sheet on page 253, a pencil, two crayons, and a supply of butterfly pasta and shell pasta. To complete the activity, a student estimates how many pieces of butterfly pasta equal the weight of a pencil. She writes her estimate. Then she determines the actual number and writes it. She completes the rest of the recording sheet in a similar manner.

Lidelle Corey, Chicod School, Greenville, NC   251

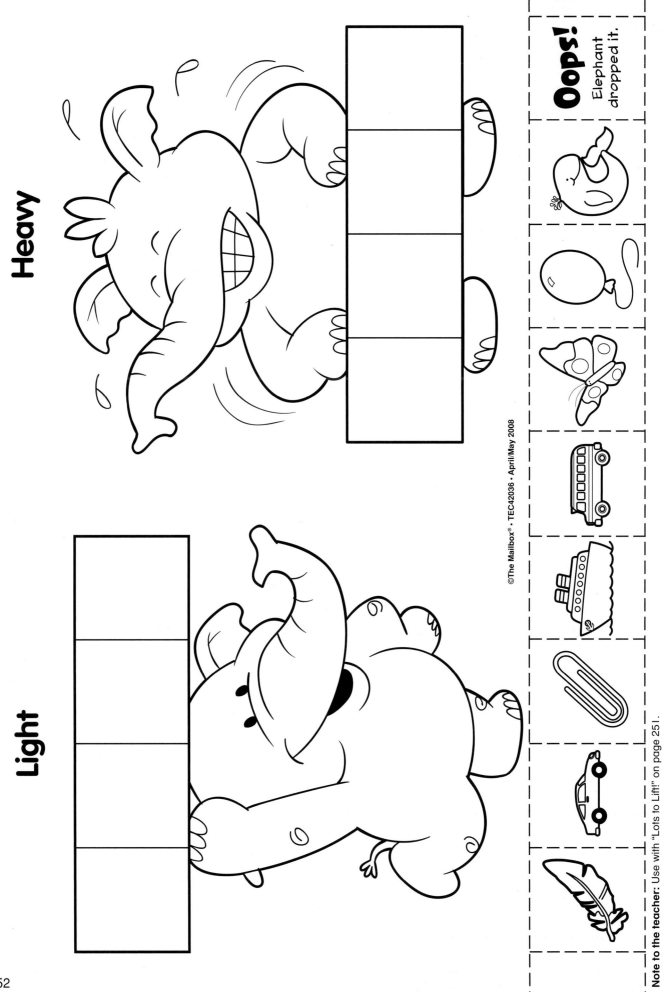

Heavy

Light

Oops! Elephant dropped it.

Note to the teacher: Use with "Lots to Lift!" on page 251.

Balance the Scale!

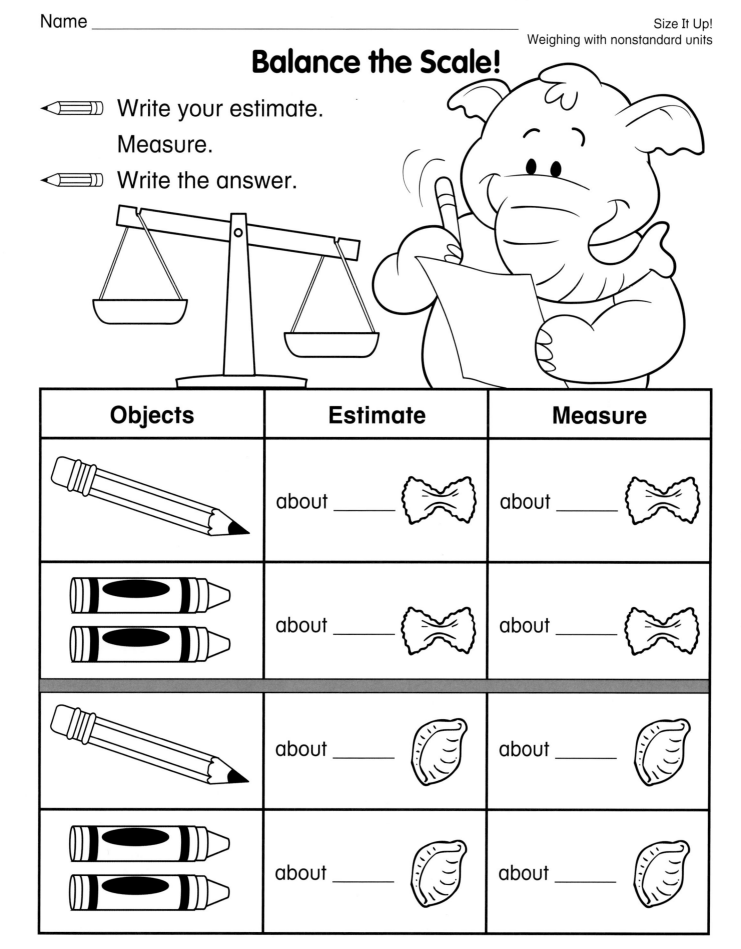

✏️ Write your estimate.

Measure.

✏️ Write the answer.

Objects	Estimate	Measure
(pencil)	about _____ (bowtie pasta)	about _____ (bowtie pasta)
(two crayons)	about _____ (bowtie pasta)	about _____ (bowtie pasta)
(pencil)	about _____ (shell pasta)	about _____ (shell pasta)
(two crayons)	about _____ (shell pasta)	about _____ (shell pasta)

Note to the teacher: Use with "Balancing Pasta" on page 251.

253

GRADE A
Number Patterns

Twenty-five!

High-Five Fun
Counting by fives

Counting orally: Divide students into two equal groups. Have the students in each group stand side by side facing the other group. Explain that students standing directly across from one another are partners. Then lead students in counting by fives as they give their partners high fives!

Problem solving: Ask students, "How many fingers do [three] students have altogether?" Then ask the designated number of youngsters to hold up their hands. Have students skip-count the youngsters' fingers to confirm the correct answer.

Bernadette Todaro, Grand Island, NY

Money Math
Counting by fives and tens

Help youngsters make "cents" of skip-counting with this transition tip. When students are waiting in line or moving from one activity to another, ask them to count by dimes (tens) or nickels (fives). Youngsters will soon understand the connection between the coin values and skip-counting!

Hilarie Hutt, Summit School, Summit, SD

Clap and Count!
Skip-counting

For this spirited chant, divide the class into two groups. Instruct the groups to stand facing one another. Then have the groups clap a steady beat as they say the chant. Ask the groups to switch roles or chant about fives or tens for more energizing math practice!

Group 1: We can count by [twos]; it's true. We can count by [twos]. Can you?
Group 2: [2, 4, 6, 8, 10, 12.] Yeah, [twos]!

Heather E. Graley
Grace Christian School
Blacklick, OH

Have a Ball!
Skip-counting

Use this fast-paced game for counting by twos, fives, or tens. Hold a beach ball as you sit with students in a circle. Announce the number to which you want students to skip-count. Then say the first few numbers of a skip-counting sequence. Next, pass the ball to a student beside you. Have him say the next number in the sequence and then pass the ball to the next student. Continue around the circle in this manner until a student says the designated number. Ask that child to change places with another child. Then begin a new skip-counting sequence!

Jennifer Troise
Ruth C. Kinney Elementary
Islip Terrace, NY

Odd	Even
11	6
5	
9	

Paired Pom-Poms
Odd and even numbers

For this partner activity, each twosome needs a plastic ice cube tray, two dice, a supply of pom-poms, and a recording sheet like the one shown. The two students sit across from one another and horizontally position the tray between them. To begin, each student rolls a die and takes the corresponding number of pom-poms. Then each youngster begins at the same end of the tray and puts her pom-poms in separate sections on her side. After the students count all the pom-poms, they determine whether the total number is odd or even and write it on the recording sheet. The youngsters empty the tray and roll the dice to continue.

Terrific Treetops
Odd and even numbers

To prepare this file-folder center, label two leafless tree cutouts as shown. Then glue each tree on a different half of an open file folder. Number a supply of leaf cutouts, beginning with a chosen number. Glue to the back of the folder an envelope for storing the leaves. Then choose an option below.

Easier version: Code the back of the leaves for self-checking. A student spreads out the leaves faceup and then sorts them on the trees. He flips the leaves to check his work.

More advanced version: A student puts each leaf on the correct tree. Then he arranges one group of leaves in numerical order and writes the number sequence on provided paper.

Hope Denicola, Jackson Avenue School, Mineola, NY

Chicken Coop Counting

How many eggs are in each group of nests?
Count by fives.

✏ Write.

There are _____ eggs in all.

There are _____ eggs in all.

Ready to Hatch

Count by twos.
Write the numbers.

Can you find a number pattern?

2 ___ 6 ___ 10

12 14 ___ 18 ___

22 ___ 26 ___ 30

32 ___ ___ 38 ___

42 44 ___ ___ ___

Spotting Geometry

Count on skill reinforcement to take shape with these hands-on math activities.

Sort and Draw!

Solid figures

Since this center activity uses real-life objects, it's sure to be a favorite among your students! Collect several objects that are various solid figures, such as spheres, cubes, rectangular prisms, cones, and cylinders. For example, you might gather assorted sizes of balls and boxes, kitchen funnels, cone-shaped paper cups, cardboard tubes, and cylindrical containers. Place the objects at a center stocked with paper and crayons. When a student visits the center, he sorts the objects by shape. Then he draws a chosen group of objects and titles his paper with the name of the corresponding solid figure.

Suzanne Moore, Tucson, AZ

Five in a Row

Solid figures

A combination of luck and strategy make this partner game a winner. To prepare for two students, cut out a colorful copy of the spinner from page 260. Then use a brad to attach a paper clip to the spinner. Give each of the two youngsters a copy of the gameboard on page 260 and counters to use as game markers.

To take a turn, a player spins the spinner. If the spinner lands on a figure, she names it and marks one corresponding figure on her board. (If no corresponding figure is unmarked, her turn is over.) If the spinner lands on "Free Space," she names and marks a figure of her choice. The players take turns as described until one player marks all the figures on one horizontal or vertical side of her board. Then that player calls out, "Five in a row!"

Lovely Ladybug
Symmetry

This adorable math idea doubles as an art project. To begin, ask each child to fold a seven-inch red circle in half and then unfold it. Have him paint a few black dots to the left of the fold line. Next, instruct him to refold the circle, press the halves of the circle together, and then unfold the circle. After the paint has dried, instruct him to cut the circle on the fold line to make two wings. Have him glue together a four-inch black circle and a seven-inch black circle to make a ladybug head and body. Then help him use a brad to attach the wings to the body as shown.

Lynn Creede Mode, Benton Heights Elementary, Monroe, NC

Down the Line
Symmetry

These supersimple folding projects are a no-fail approach to exploring lines of symmetry.

Kaleidoscope: Set out three shallow containers of water that you have tinted different colors. Instruct each student to fold a coffee filter to make a pie-shaped wedge. Instruct her to dip each corner of the filter, in turn, into a different container of water. Have her allow the filter to dry and then unfold it. It is a colorful way to show her that some things have more than one line of symmetry!

Through the year: To make a figure listed below, instruct each child to fold a paper rectangle in half. Have her draw or write on the fold as described and help her punch a hole if indicated. Then ask her to cut out the figure. After she unfolds the paper, ask her to trace the line of symmetry and embellish the figure if desired.

Butterfly: Write a large letter *B* on the fold.

Heart: Write a large "2" on the fold. (Cut only on the curve.)

Tree: Draw a right triangle on the fold.

Jack-o'-lantern: Draw a half circle on the fold. Draw half a nose and half a mouth on the fold. Punch a hole away from the fold to make the eyes.

Ellen Javernick
Loveland, CO

259

Gameboard and Spinner Pattern

Use with "Five in a Row" on page 258.

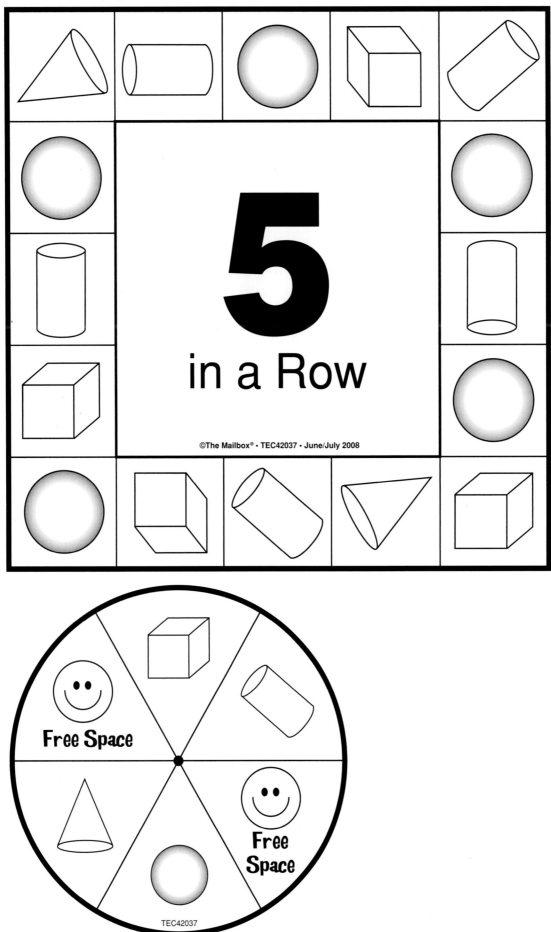

5 in a Row

TEC42037

Free Space

Free Space

Name _____

Shape Shopper

✂ Cut. 🪣 Glue to match.

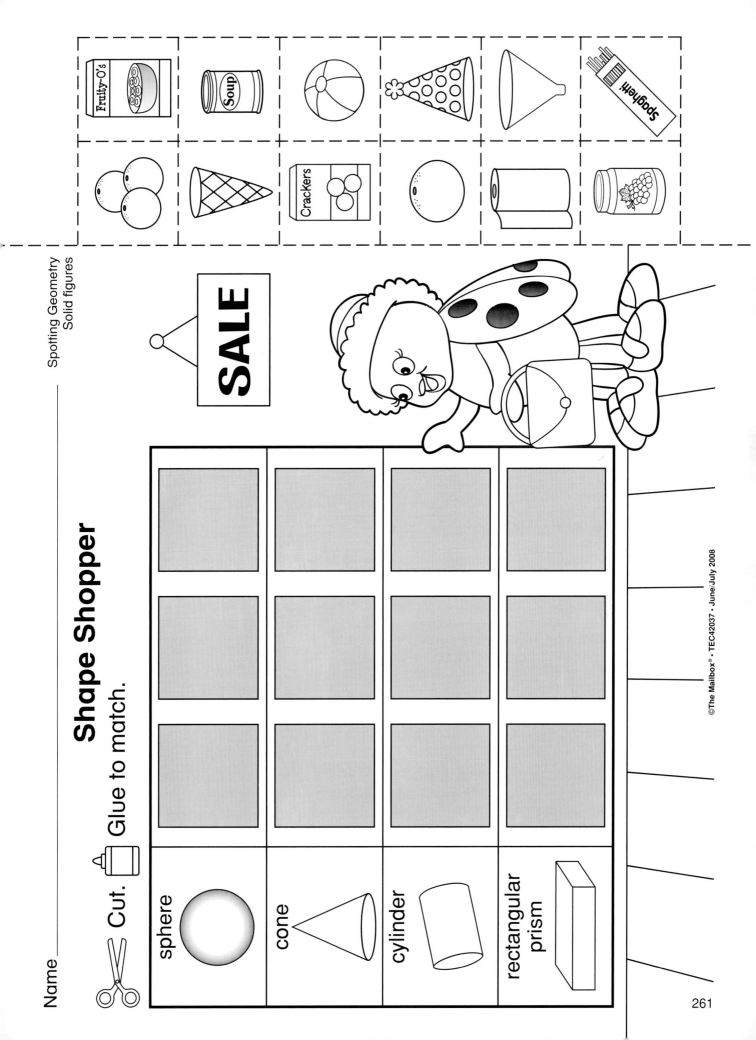

sphere			
cone			
cylinder			
rectangular prism			

SALE

Fruity-O's

Soup

Crackers

Spaghetti

261

Hooked on Math Games

Fill the Bucket!

Skip-counting

Reel in practice with counting by twos, fives, or tens!
Get a small plastic bucket. Have students sit in a circle
and give each student a colorful fish card (patterns on
page 264). Instruct each youngster to put his card in
front of him on the floor. Tell students whether they
will count by twos, fives, or tens and announce a target
number such as 50 or 100. Then hand the bucket to a
student.

Next, ask students to pass the bucket around the
circle as they skip-count, saying one number each time a
different student takes the bucket. When the youngsters
reach the designated number, have the student holding
the bucket put his card in the bucket, pass the bucket
to the next youngster, and then move out of the circle.
To resume play, ask all the students to begin the skip-
counting sequence again. Continue play for a desired
number of rounds.

Diane L. Tondreau-Flohr
Kent City Elementary
Kent City, MI

They're Keepers!

Comparing numbers

To prepare this partner game, make an even number of fish cards (patterns on page 264). Write
a different number on each fish and then place the cards number-side down on a pond cutout.
Give each player a large disposable cup (bucket). To begin, each player takes a card. The players
compare the corresponding numbers. Then the player with the greater number puts both cards
in her cup. Play continues as described with the remaining cards. Then the players compare how
many fish they have in their cups. **For an easier version,** make a number line like the one shown
and have the players put two cards below the corresponding numbers to compare them.

Diane L. Tondreau-Flohr

"Sum" Buckets

Addition

For this small-group activity, draw a bucket on each of several blank cards. Label each bucket with a different sum. Program separate fish cutouts with corresponding addition combinations, writing or illustrating one combination per fish. Arrange the bucket cards in a pocket chart and spread out the fish facedown nearby. Assign each bucket to a student. To take a turn, a student takes a fish and identifies the corresponding addition combination. If the sum matches the number on her bucket, she puts it behind the bucket. If it does not match, she returns the fish to the pond. Students take turns as described until all the fish are sorted. Then each youngster reviews the different addition combinations in her bucket.

Lots to Catch

Beginning addition or subtraction facts

Pair students for these colorful fishing games! Give each twosome crayons and one copy of the gameboard on page 264. Then choose an option below. Have the partners take turns as described for the allotted time or until they "catch" all the fish.

Beginning addition: Partner 1 rolls two dice and announces the corresponding sum. Partner 2 colors the number of fish equal to the sum. Then the partners switch roles.

Subtraction facts to 10: Partner 1 rolls one number cube and then subtracts the number she rolled from ten. Partner 2 colors the number of fish equal to the difference. Then the partners switch roles.

Diane L. Tondreau-Flohr, Kent City Elementary, Kent City, MI

Something Fishy

Addition facts to 18

Here's a totally fishy approach to writing number sentences! Use masking tape to cover the numbers 1, 2, 3, 4, and 5 on two number cubes. Write the numbers 6, 7, 8, and 9 on separate blank sides of each cube, repeating a chosen number. Place the cubes, crayons, and student copies of page 265 at a center. When a student visits the center, he rolls the cubes. He writes on his paper an addition sentence with the numbers rolled. Then he colors the fish with the sum if it is not already colored. He continues as described until he completes the number sentences. Then he writes in the blank at the bottom of the paper how many fish he colored.

adapted from an idea by Diane L. Tondreau-Flohr

263

Fish Cards

Use with "Fill the Bucket!" and "They're Keepers!" on page 262.

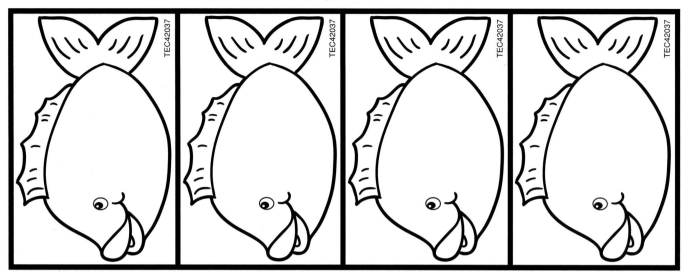

Gameboard

Use with "Lots to Catch" on page 263.

Lots to Catch

Name _____

Something Fishy

Follow your teacher's directions.

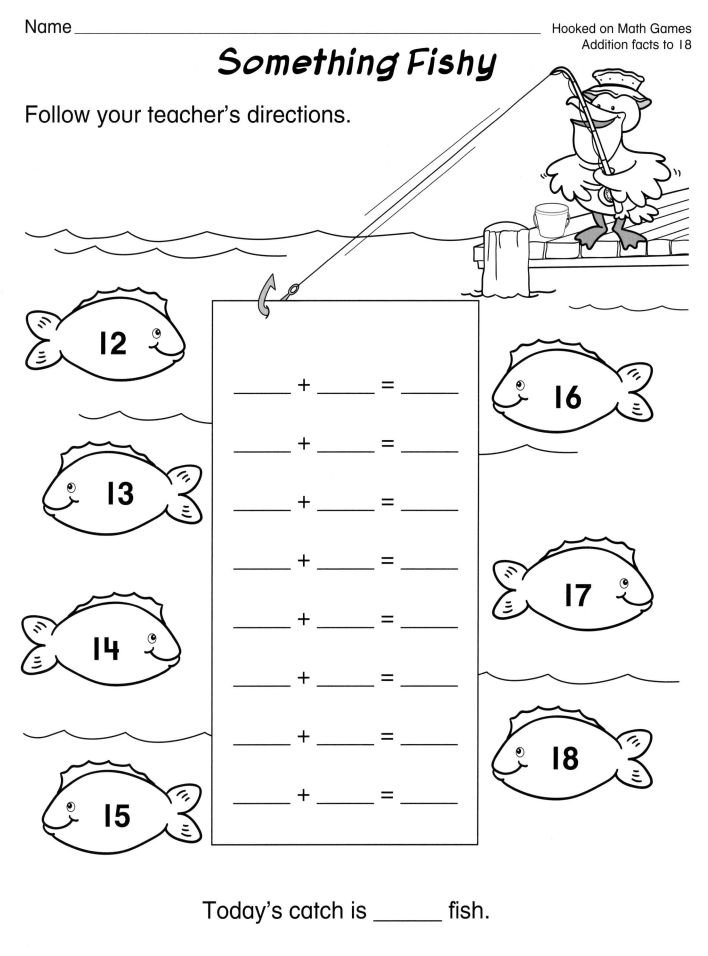

_____ + _____ = _____

_____ + _____ = _____

_____ + _____ = _____

_____ + _____ = _____

_____ + _____ = _____

_____ + _____ = _____

_____ + _____ = _____

_____ + _____ = _____

Today's catch is _____ fish.

Note to the teacher: Use with "Something Fishy" on page 263.

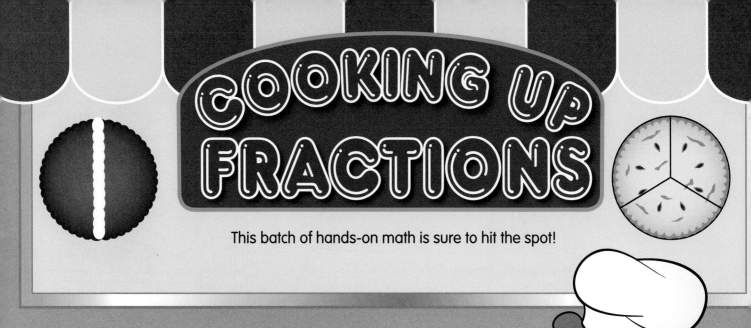

COOKING UP FRACTIONS

This batch of hands-on math is sure to hit the spot!

Fresh From the Oven!
Identifying fractional parts

For this sorting activity, make a supply of round, square, or rectangular craft foam cookies and gather a few paper plates. Use an option below for programming. Then spread the cookies on a cookie tray. Put the tray, the labeled plates, and a spatula at a center. To complete the activity, a student uses the spatula to put each cookie on the correct plate.

Easier version: Use a permanent marker to divide some cookies into equal parts and the rest of them into unequal parts. Label a paper plate "Equal" and another paper plate "Not Equal." Code each plate with a happy or sad face to help young readers.

More advanced version: Use a permanent marker to divide the cookies into halves, thirds, and quarters. Write each different fraction on a separate paper plate.

Courtney Pate
Burlington, NC

It's one-third chocolate!

Chocolate and Vanilla
Describing fractional parts

Unifix cubes are all you need for this flavorful idea! Connect one brown cube to one, two, or three white cubes. Invite students to imagine that the cubes are a cake that is part chocolate (brown) and part vanilla (white). Ask students whether they think the cake is divided equally and to explain why. Then guide students to identify the fraction for the part of the cake that is chocolate. Model a few different fractions in the same manner and have students identify them.

For reinforcement, divide students into small groups and give each group cubes of two different colors. Then announce different fractions for students to model.

Randi Austin
Lebanon, MO

Cookie Puzzles

Exploring fractions

To prepare this center activity, make several identical construction paper circles (cookies). Use a marker to trace them on a foil-covered cookie tray. Then cut some cookies into halves, some cookies into thirds, and some cookies into fourths. Have students assemble the cookies on the tray so that each cookie has equal parts.

Mary Davis
Keokuk Christian Academy
Keokuk, IA

Busy Bakers

Dividing shapes

Students make cookies to order with this imaginative activity. Program each of several recipe cards with a grade-appropriate fraction concept, such as halves or four equal parts. (More than one card may have the same concept.) Place the cards and a cookie tray at a center along with a rolling pin, round cookie cutters, plastic knives, play dough or clay, and small sticky notes.

To complete the activity, a student makes a play dough or clay cookie and sets it on the tray. He puts a recipe card beside the cookie and divides the cookie to match. He makes and divides additional cookies as described. Then he writes his name on a sticky note and puts it near the cookies.

Courtney Pate
Burlington, NC

Racing for Dessert!

Identifying fractions

Who can make pies more quickly? That's what students find out with this partner activity! To prepare, make four copies of the game mat and one copy of the game cards on page 268. Cut out the game cards and put them in a container. Cut out two mats and set them aside. On each of the two remaining mats, color the pie divided in half one color, the pie divided into thirds a different color, and the pie divided into fourths another color. Then cut out the pieces of each pie.

To begin, the players sort the pie pieces by color and each player takes a mat. Next, Player 1 draws a card. If it is a Baker's Bonus card, she puts a chosen piece of pie on her mat. If it is a fraction card, she reads it. Then, if there is a corresponding blank space on her mat, she puts a matching piece of pie on it. After she sets the card aside, Player 2 takes a turn as described. Alternate play continues, with the players reusing the cards as needed, until one player assembles all her pies and says, "Dessert is ready!"

267

Game Mat and Game Cards

Use with "Racing for Dessert!" on page 267.

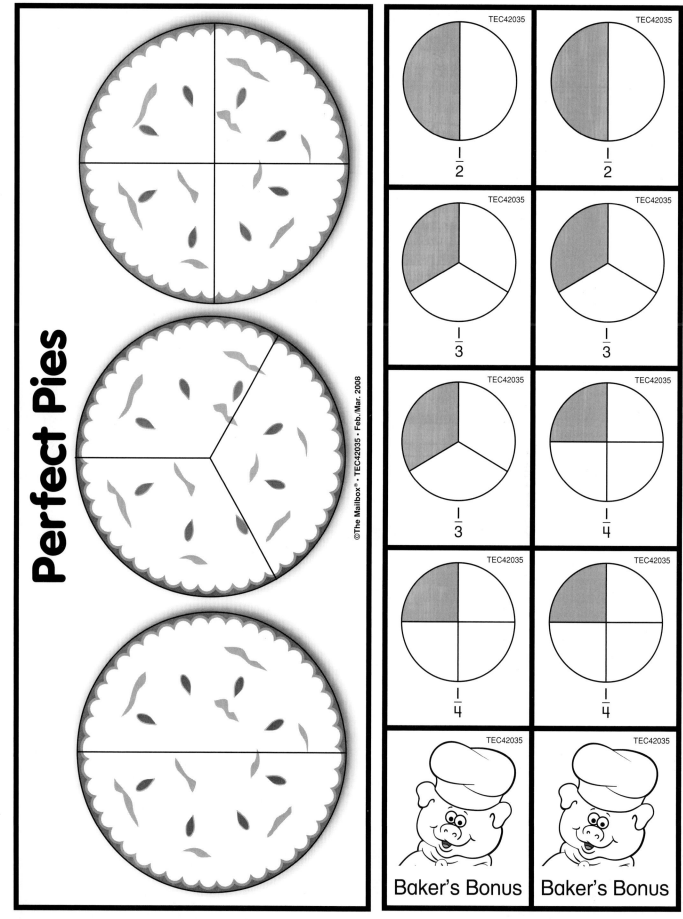

Perfect Pies

TEC42035

TEC42035
$\frac{1}{2}$

TEC42035
$\frac{1}{2}$

TEC42035
$\frac{1}{3}$

TEC42035
$\frac{1}{3}$

TEC42035
$\frac{1}{3}$

TEC42035
$\frac{1}{4}$

TEC42035
$\frac{1}{4}$

TEC42035
$\frac{1}{4}$

TEC42035
Baker's Bonus

TEC42035
Baker's Bonus

©The Mailbox® · TEC42035 · Feb./Mar. 2008

SCIENCE AND
SOCIAL STUDIES UNITS

Exploring With Five Senses

Take students on a sensory expedition with these science activities. They'll be amazed at what they discover by following their noses (and eyes, ears, hands, and tongues)!

"Sense-sational" Sing-Along

The actions that accompany this familiar tune are sure to make it a favorite among your students. After singing the song once with students, repeat it five more times, replacing each sense word, in turn, with a corresponding motion. For example, during the first repetition point to your eyes instead of singing the word *see*. During the second repetition, point to your eyes and then point to your ears instead of singing the words *see* and *hear*. No doubt you'll hear students' giggles by the end of the song!

Sandy Guilmette
Knightsville Elementary
Summerville, SC

(sung to the tune of "Bingo")

We use five senses every day to
  help us learn and play!
See, hear, smell, touch, taste.
See, hear, smell, touch, taste.
See, hear, smell, touch, taste.
We use senses every day.

Wow!

Look Closely!

With this observation activity, students see things from a fresh perspective. To begin, take youngsters on a nature walk. Ask each child to find one item to take back to the classroom for closer observation. After you return to the classroom, have each child draw a line down the center of a sheet of paper. Instruct him to look at his object carefully and draw it on the left half of his paper. Next, invite him to look at the item with a magnifying glass and draw his observations on the right half of the paper. Then ask him to compare his drawings.

For a more in-depth exploration, give each youngster a paper divided into three sections. Also provide students with access to a magnifying glass and a microscope. Instruct each student to draw in separate sections of his paper what he sees when he looks at the object unaided and when he observes it with each science tool.

Carrie Sturges
McCordsville, IN

270

Secret Sounds

What's the key to this guessing game? It's careful listening! Ask each student to bring to school an item from home that makes a noise. Encourage youngsters to keep the items secret from their classmates for the time being. After each student brings in an item, have each child meet with you (or a classroom volunteer) individually and show you her item without letting her classmates see or hear it. Make a recording of the youngster introducing herself and then making a sound with the item. Once each student's sound is recorded, play the recording for the entire class. Pause the recording after each sound for students to try to identify it and to have the youngster who made the sound reveal the noisemaker.

Tammy Lutz
George E. Green Elementary
Bad Axe, MI

Brrrring!

Handy Words

Promote the use of descriptive words with this texture activity. Set out items of various textures. Give each child a large construction paper hand and then instruct him to glue several different items to it. Ask him to write (or dictate for you to write) near each item a word that describes the corresponding texture. It's a surefire way to increase students' vocabularies as well as their observation skills!

Jessica Johner, Hillsborough Elementary
Hillsborough, NJ

smooth
bumpy
rough
soft
hard

Science Bargain

A visit to a grocery store is a treat for all five senses! Arrange for a class tour of a local grocery store. During the tour, take photos to help students remember the details of the experience and to use as writing prompts. Also ask youngsters to make various sensory observations. For example, have them observe the colors and shapes of different packages, the aromas in the bakery department, the flavors of any foods they sample, and how they feel in the frozen food section. Before you leave the store, encourage youngsters to close their eyes and focus on what they hear.

When you return to the classroom, list students' observations on a chart with a separate column for each sense. Youngsters are bound to agree that a store has more than what meets the eye!

Laura Prymak
Ettrick Elementary
Chesterfield, VA

I smelled cinnamon bread at the store!

Bakery

271

Simply "MAP-nificent"!

ideas contributed by Laurie K. Gibbons
Huntsville, AL

Land Ho!

Identifying land and water on maps

For this variation of Pin the Tail on the Donkey, post a large country or world map within students' reach. Point out that water and land are represented with different colors and guide youngsters to identify bodies of water, such as rivers, lakes, and oceans. Then have each child illustrate a boat on a small blank card and write his initials on the back of it. Collect the illustrated cards.

Next, take a card at random. Put reusable adhesive on the back of the card and then pass the card to its owner. Invite him to wear a blindfold or close his eyes. Then ask him to put the boat on the map. Once the boat is posted, have the youngster look at it and tell whether it is on land or water. Then ask a different student to "launch" his boat in the same manner. On each of the next few days, clear the map and have several different youngsters post their boats as described until the entire fleet has been displayed. **For more advanced students,** ask youngsters to use cardinal directions to describe the boats' positions on the map.

My boat is on land!

City Slickers

Using cardinal directions

Invite students to make a citywide search with this three-dimensional map. To prepare, gather several empty boxes. Remove the lids or push the box flaps inward and then set the boxes open-side down. With students' help, decorate the boxes to resemble various city buildings. Make a map with the boxes and set out a toy car. Then secretly place a small toy animal under a box. To help students find the animal, use cardinal directions to give students step-by-step directions and have youngsters take turns "driving" the car as directed. Once the car is at the last destination, ask a child to lift the box to find out whether or not the group successfully navigated the city.

I need to go east to the post office.

Treasure Hunt

Using cardinal directions

Imagine searching for treasure at the beach! That's what students do during this pocket chart activity. Color and cut out a copy of the picture cards from page 274. Arrange the star card and eight to 11 picture cards in evenly spaced rows in a pocket chart. (Use a greater number of cards for more advanced students.) Illustrate a small blank card with gold coins and then conceal it behind a picture card other than the star card. Illustrate a craft stick so it resembles a person. Then stand the stick in front of the star.

To lead students to the treasure, use cardinal directions to instruct them to move the craft stick to different cards. When the stick is at the final destination, have a volunteer remove the corresponding card to reveal the coins.

Map Key

lake

picnic table

mountains

river

road

trees

What a Hike!

Making a simple map

After students are familiar with map keys, follow up with this park-themed idea. Write on the board the sights listed to the left. Invite volunteers to suggest and draw corresponding map symbols. Next, have each child illustrate a map key of the sights and glue the key on a larger sheet of paper. Then instruct him to use the symbols to create a park map, reminding him to color the land green and the water blue. If desired, showcase students' completed maps and a large compass rose on a board titled "Pleasing Parks." When students have spare time between activities, direct their attention to chosen maps and ask them questions with cardinal directions.

Adventure Land

Reading a map

What kind of map is sure to be tops among your students? Why, an amusement park map, of course! Gather several identical amusement park maps. Divide students into groups and give each group a map. Read the map key with students. Then ask them to find specific attractions and facilities and describe their locations. **For more advanced students,** instruct each youngster to use cardinal directions to describe a route she would like to take through the amusement park.

Picture Cards

Use with "Treasure Hunt" on page 273.

TEC42037

TEC42037

TEC42037

TEC42037

TEC42037

TEC42037

TEC42037

TEC42037

TEC42037

TEC42037

TEC42037

TEC42037

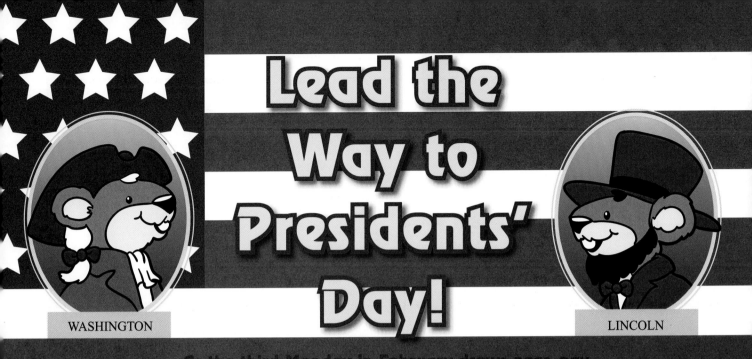

Lead the Way to Presidents' Day!

As the third Monday in February draws near, pay tribute to U.S. presidents with these patriotic ideas!

Letter-Perfect Introduction

Forming words

Here's an intriguing way to introduce the upcoming holiday. Draw a nine-box grid. Then write each letter of the word *president* in a separate box and in random order. Have each child cut apart a copy of the grid. Next, ask him to use the letters to spell the word *it*. After each youngster forms the word, write the word on the board and have students correct their work if necessary. Then instruct each student to form the word *sit*. Confirm the correct spelling. Continue with the words *ten, den,* and *dent* in a similar manner. Then guide students to use all their letters to spell the word *president*. Once each child correctly forms the word, point out that it will soon be Presidents' Day, and tell youngsters about the holiday.

To encourage more word play, give each child an envelope for storing his letters and have him decorate the envelope with a patriotic design. Provide time over a few days for him to practice forming various words. Then invite him to take his envelope home and show his family all the words he can make!

Angie Kutzer, Garrett Elementary, Mebane, NC

Patriotic Puzzle

Geography

To begin this map activity, remind students that the president is the leader of the United States and that the country has 50 states. Then give each child a light-colored copy of page 277. Point out that the states are various sizes and shapes. Help each youngster find the state in which she lives. Then instruct her to glue the map on a sheet of red or blue paper. Ask her to draw lines on the back of her paper to divide it into a desired number of sections and then cut the sections apart to make a puzzle. After she completes the puzzle, ask her to put the puzzle pieces in a personalized resealable plastic bag. Have each youngster complete a classmate's puzzle for more geography fun!

Angie Kutzer

275

Perfect for the Job
Vocabulary

What words describe a great president? That's what students explore with this word-sorting activity! Put a happy face illustration and a sad face illustration in a pocket chart to create two column headings. Write the words shown on separate sentence strips.

Next, ask a volunteer to take a word at random and show it to the group. After you read the word aloud, instruct each youngster to give a thumbs-up or a thumbs-down to signal whether he thinks the word describes a quality a president should have. Invite students to share their reasoning. Then instruct the volunteer to put the card in the appropriate column. Have students sort the remaining cards in the same manner. Afterward, ask each youngster to describe the type of president she would like to be, and have her illustrate her work.

Angie Kutzer, Garrett Elementary, Mebane, NC

That's President Lincoln!
Art and math

Students practice using rulers with this patterning project. To begin, give each child a copy of page 278 and confirm that she knows whose silhouette is shown. Next, instruct each child to use a pencil and a ruler to draw horizontal and vertical lines across the entire pattern. After she finishes drawing the lines, have her color the resulting squares to make a red and blue checkerboard pattern. Then have her cut out the pattern and glue it to a sheet of black paper.

Julie Shields, Canadian Elementary, Canadian, TX

Celebrate!

Since Presidents' Day falls near the birthdays of Presidents Washington and Lincoln, it's a perfect time for a party! Use the ideas below for a fun-filled celebration.

Decorations: Have students make red, white, and blue paper chains. In addition to being fun, it also reinforces patterning and measuring lengths!

Refreshments: Serve strawberry and blueberry Jell-O gelatin with whipped topping.

Activities: Read relevant books, such as *A. Lincoln and Me* by Louise Borden and *George Washington and the General's Dog* by Frank Murphy. Help youngsters create a large Presidents' Day card for the current president. Wrap up the festivities with patriotic songs.

adapted from an idea by Laurie K. Gibbons, Huntsville, AL

The United States of America

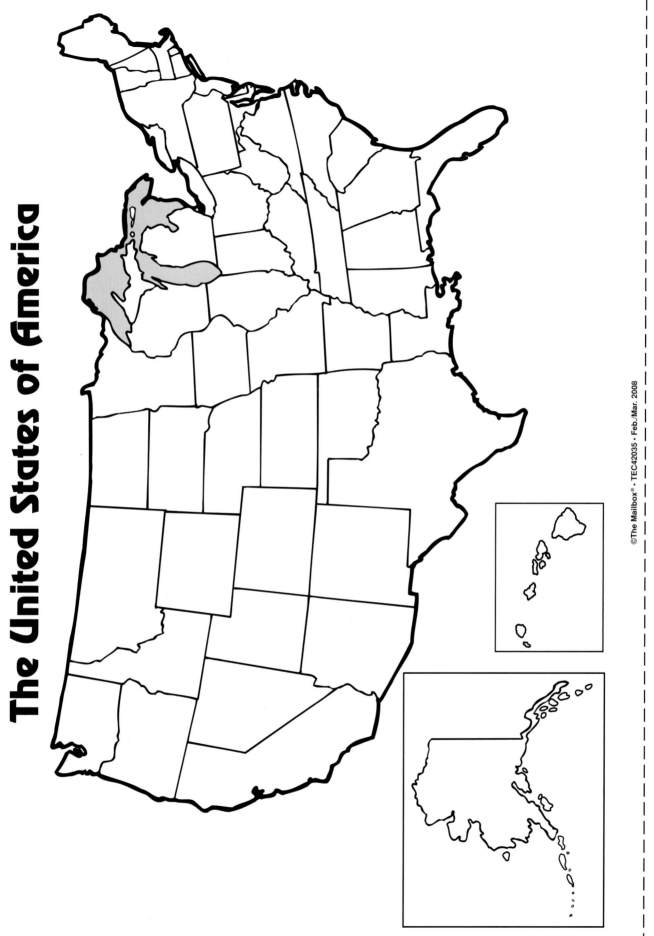

Note to the teacher: Use with "Patriotic Puzzle" on page 275.

277

Lincoln Silhouette Pattern

Use with "That's President Lincoln!" on page 276.

TEC42035

TEACHER RESOURCE UNITS

Favorite Back-to-School Ideas

Use these top-notch ideas from our readers to make the first days of school a success!

This is my dog Daisy.

Meeting the Teacher
Book

Once students get to know you, they're sure to feel more comfortable in your classroom. For a fun introduction, gather several photos that are likely to interest your students, such as photos of yourself at their age and photos of your pets or family. Mount the photos on sheets of paper and add simple captions. Then slide the papers into plastic page protectors and secure them in a three-ring binder. Title the resulting book "[Your name]'s Story." Read the book to students on the first day of school and then place it in your classroom library for youngsters to revisit on their own. Don't be surprised if it's one of your students' favorite reading selections!

Angela Kozeal, Tri-Center Elementary, Neola, IA

A Wonderful Place
School tour

Looking for a creative way to familiarize your students with the school? Begin with this version of "Going on a Bear Hunt." Establish a steady clapping rhythm. Then say the chant, having students echo each line and incorporate motions as appropriate. Add verses as desired.

Later, when students are not in the classroom, remove from your alphabet wall display the initial letter of each location in the chant. (As an alternative, display lettered index cards in alphabetical order and remove the appropriate cards from the sequence.) For example, remove the *o* for *office* and the *m* for *music room*. Place each letter in the actual corresponding school location. When the children return, notice with mock surprise that the letters are missing. Then take students and a camera on a letter search throughout the school. Each time you find a letter, take a photo of the letter and staff at that location. Use the photos as props during later repetitions of the chant.

Laura Pullen, Edmondson Elementary, Brentwood, TN

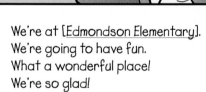

We're at [Edmondson Elementary].
We're going to have fun.
What a wonderful place!
We're so glad!

I see the [office].
What do we do there?
We [call home].
[Ring, ring, ring.]

I see the [music room.]
What do we do there?
We [sing songs].
[La, la, la!]

A New Crop of Students

Great Work!

Way to go!

Maritza

Michael

Allen

Kaili

Latonya

Parker

Watermelon Welcome
Display

This bulletin board is just "ripe" for the beginning of the school year, and with a few changes you can use it throughout the fall! Have each student draw several watermelon seeds on a red construction paper semicircle. Then instruct her to glue the paper to a slightly larger white semicircle to make a watermelon slice. Post each youngster's watermelon with a personalized leaf on a board titled as shown. Arrange green paper spirals as desired to make vines.

To modify the display for later in the year, remove the watermelons but keep the leaves and vines on the board. Have each youngster paint a picture of a pumpkin or use liquid starch to adhere orange tissue paper squares all over a pumpkin cutout. Showcase each pumpkin near the corresponding youngster's leaf. Title the display "Meet Us in the Pumpkin Patch!" and add a decorative scarecrow if desired.

Casey Cooksey, Bruce Elementary, Bruce, MS

Give me a T!

Tyler

In the Spotlight
Literacy

Add pizzazz to the traditional student-of-the-day activity! Invite the honored youngster to stand with you in front of the class. Have him hold up a large card labeled with his name. Then lead students in a call-and-response cheer to spell the name. Next, have students clap once for each syllable as you say the name, and help them determine how many parts (syllables) the name has. Afterward, invite the honored youngster to tell a little about himself, such as his favorite color, food, and animal. Write the information on a sheet of paper and have him illustrate it. Showcase the resulting poster in a designated classroom area, or begin a class book of posters. Repeat the activity to give each youngster a turn in the spotlight.

Cynthia Jamnik
Our Lady Queen of Peace School
Milwaukee, WI

Namely, Writing
Literacy

Classmates' names make this center irresistible to young learners. To introduce the activity, each week show students a letter card or manipulative for a letter that begins the first name of one or more students. Ask students to name the corresponding classmate(s). Write each identified name on a separate sentence strip and mount a photo of the corresponding person beside the name. Display the strip(s) and letter at a center stocked with writing supplies. When a student visits the center, have him practice writing the name or use it in a sentence. No doubt youngsters will be eager to find out whose name will be featured next!

Tammy Lutz, George E. Greene Elementary
Bad Axe, MI

David

Darius

D

Great Work!

Way to go!

(sung to the tune of "Skip to My Lou")

[Jess] likes [soccer]. How about you?
[Jess] likes [soccer]. How about you?
[Jess] likes [soccer]. How about you?
Raise your hand if you do too.

Who Likes It?
Song

Count on this get-acquainted activity to be a hit! Sit with students in a circle. To begin, ask one student to name something that she likes to do. Then lead students in the song shown, inserting the youngster's name and activity. Repeat the song to feature each student. As youngsters learn about one another, they're bound to find out that they have a lot in common!

Suzanne Moore, Irving, TX

Find a Friend!
Literacy

Students put names with faces during this small-group game. Mount each of two identical photos of each student on a separate blank card. Write the student's first name below each photo. Invite students to play as in the traditional game of Go Fish, except have them collect pairs of matching cards and say, "Find a friend!" instead of "Go fish!" **For more advanced students,** instead of using two photos for each pair of cards, program one card with a photo and the name of the student and the other card with just the name.

Sheila Fritz, Mississippi Heights Elementary
Sauk Rapids, MN

I got a match!

Jazmyne

Jazmyne

282

How Sweet!
Following directions
Try this tempting approach to introductions. Give each child a brown paper cookie and one small circle (candy) in each color shown. Instruct each student to program his candies by the code and glue them on his cookie. Collect the completed cookies on a cookie tray and post a large cookie jar cutout. On each of several days, take one or more cookies from the tray. Guide each corresponding youngster to tell the class about his cookie. Then display it on the cookie jar. When all of the cookies are posted, you'll have a sweet look at your class!

Cindy Barber, Fredonia, WI

Code
green — name
red — age
orange — favorite color
yellow — favorite food

Going to School
Math
Transportation is the topic of this song and graphing activity. Post a blank graph with a column for each mode of transportation your students use to get to school. Ask students to sit nearby. Next, lead students in the song shown, modifying the mode of transportation as appropriate and having the designated student(s) stand and cheer. At the end of the song, write on the graph the name of each student who is standing. After everyone is seated again, continue as described with verses for the remaining modes of transportation. Then guide students to read and interpret the graph.

(sung to the tune of "If You're Happy and You Know It")

If you came to school [by car], please stand up.
If you came to school [by car], please stand up.
If that's how you came to school today,
Then stand up and shout, "Hooray!"
If you came to school [by car], please stand up.

Ada Goren, Winston-Salem, NC

Just Alike!
Literacy
Build your classroom community with this class book idea. Take an individual photo of each student. Then make one copy of page 290 for every two students. Mount two photos on each copy. To complete each page, ask the two pictured youngsters to write their names below their photos. Help them determine an appropriate sentence ending, and write it on the blank. Bind the completed pages into a book titled "We Are Alike." It's a perfect read-aloud and discussion starter!

Angie Kutzer
Garrett Elementary
Mebane, NC

Lindsay

Oscar

We are alike because we both like chocolate ice cream.

283

"Toad-ally" Terrific Center Tips

Looking for surefire ways to keep your center time running smoothly? Choose from these teacher-tested ideas!

Choices Made Easy

Prevent overcrowding at centers while allowing students to choose which locations they visit first. Here's how! For each center, label a separate plastic cup with the center's name and the number of students that may visit the center at one time. Secure the cups to a surface within student reach. At center time, give each child a personalized craft stick. To indicate which center he will visit first, have him stand his stick in the corresponding cup. (If the cup already has the designated number of sticks, ask him to choose a different center.) When a child is ready for another center, he simply moves his stick to an appropriate cup.

Adriana Passerini
Saint Joseph's School and Academy
West Orange, NJ

Freddy

Math Center
4

Listening
Center
6

Writing
Center
3

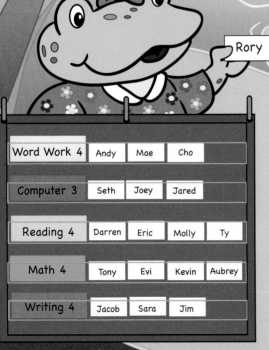

Rory

Word Work 4	Andy	Mae	Cho	
Computer 3	Seth	Joey	Jared	
Reading 4	Darren	Eric	Molly	Ty
Math 4	Tony	Evi	Kevin	Aubrey
Writing 4	Jacob	Sara	Jim	

Pick a Pocket!

This convenient display allows you and your students to see center assignments at a glance. To prepare, write the name of each center on a separate colorful card and write each student's name on a separate white card. Place each colorful card in a different row of a pocket chart. To assign a student to a center, place her name card in the corresponding row. Rotate the name cards to give students an opportunity to visit each center.

For a variation that encourages student choice, write beside the name of each center the number of students that may be at the center at one time. Have each student choose an available center and place her name card in the corresponding row of the chart.

Katie Robinson
Limestone Walters Elementary
Peoria, IL

Super Signs

Don't throw away old compact disc cases. Use them as durable holders for center names or activity instructions! To make a holder, remove any packaging and labels from an empty compact disc case. Size a blank card to fit the case and program it as desired. Secure the card in the front of the case. Use packing tape to tape the case open as shown, with the sticky side of the tape facing outward. (The tape will hold the case to the surface it is placed on.) To use the case for a different center or activity, simply replace the card.

Dianne Young
Seymour Elementary
Ralston, NE

Finish the sentence.

I like _____.

Counting on Captains

Here's a pride-boosting way to promote student independence during center time. For each center, designate a student as the captain. (Establish a rotating schedule for easy management and to ensure that each child gets a turn.) Just before center time, announce the names of the captains with great fanfare and give each captain a construction paper badge to wear. Explain to students that each captain is responsible for reminding the students at her center to work quietly and to clean up the center at the end of the allotted time. The responsibility is sure to be a much-anticipated classroom job!

Michele Galvan
Roosevelt Elementary
McAllen, TX

In the Hoop

If you have limited space for centers, use this idea to designate individual work areas. For each center, place a plastic hoop toy (or a large circle of yarn) on the floor. Place the supplies needed for each center inside the corresponding hoop. Assign students to each center as desired, and ask them to sit around the outside of the appropriate hoop. As students work, have them keep the supplies in and around the hoop. They won't get the supplies for different activities mixed up. Plus, they'll have clearly defined areas to clean at the end of center time!

Sherry Taylor, Maude I. Logan Elementary, Fort Worth, TX

Fun Reading Areas

Motivate students to read with these inviting classroom environments.

A Pleasing Park

Who can resist reading in the park? Place a small bench in a quiet corner of your classroom. To enhance the cozy environment, set out items such as pillows and plants. Create a simple backdrop on a wall or bulletin board and decorate it with cutouts of a tree, a sun, a fence, or similar outdoor sights. (Change the scene with the seasons.) Stock a basket with reading materials and, if desired, set up a nature recording for students to play. No doubt youngsters will be eager to head to the park and read!

Pam Saffle, Jefferson Elementary, Wichita, KS

Reading Hut

Pair one big box with seasonal decorating ideas and you have a special reading corner that's bound to be a hit all year long! Cut a hole in the top of a supersize box to create a skylight and another hole in one side of the box to make a door. Then decorate the box to correspond with the time of year. For example, create a barn in the fall, Santa's workshop in December, Lincoln's log cabin in February, and a rainy-day scene in the spring. Place flashlights and novelty reading glasses in the box if desired. (See "'Fun-glasses'" on page 287.) Set out books related to the theme and other grade-appropriate selections. Periodically update the decorations and reading materials for the seasons. It's guaranteed to spark renewed interest in reading!

Jamie Goehring, Hermes Elementary
La Grange, TX

Teacher, Teacher!

Most students love to play teacher, and this reading zone gives them the opportunity to do just that! To prepare, write a familiar poem or several sentences on a transparency. (For easy management, prepare transparencies for different reading levels with markers of different colors.) Draw a smiley face in the top right-hand corner of the transparency to give students a cue for orienting it. Place the transparency near an overhead projector with decorated pointers and overhead markers. When students visit the area, they're sure to show off their reading skills as they model your teaching strategies!

Sarah Jackson, Meriwether Lewis Elementary
Charlottesville, VA

Fall Leaves ☺
Yellow, orange, red, and brown.
See the leaves tumble down.

Yellow, orange, red, and brown.
See the leaves blow all around!

Pink and Pretty

A Florida Vacation

"Fun-glasses"

Add a dramatic flair to reading with this creative prop. To make one pair of "fun-glasses," poke out the lenses of a pair of children's sunglasses and then secure chosen craft materials to the frame. Place several pairs of "fun-glasses" at an established literacy center to fuel students' excitement for reading!

Kathy Barlow
Southern Elementary
Somerset, KY

Superbird!

Docked for Readers

Use this nautical idea to hook students on a variety of genres. Place a small inflated boat in a chosen classroom area. Decorate the area with water-related items such as a net, fish cutouts, and blue cellophane strips (water). Set out baskets, large sand pails, or similar containers. Stock each container with a different type of reading selection—such as nonfiction books, comic books, and fairy tales—and label the containers accordingly. During independent reading time, invite youngsters to kick off their shoes and relax while they read in the boat.

Emily Ryherd, Helen Baker Elementary, Glencoe, MN

"Tee-rific" Year-End Ideas

Watermelon Countdown

Here's a clever way to keep students' skills sharp right up to the last day of school! Ten school days before the end of the school year, post a jumbo slice of watermelon on a bulletin board. Number ten large seed cutouts from 1 to 10. Write a chosen skill on the back of each seed and then tack the seeds to the melon in descending order.

To begin the countdown, remove from the display the seed with the greatest number. Read aloud the skill on the back of the seed with a great deal of fanfare. Then have students review the skill as desired. On each of the following nine school days, continue the countdown as described. After all the seeds are removed, serve each student a slice of watermelon to celebrate a job well done and a great school year!

Sue Fleischmann, Mary Queen of Saints School
West Allis, WI

Clear the Wall!

When you take down your word wall display, why not reinforce skills at the same time? Remove the word cards from the wall. Then evenly distribute the cards to students. If you plan to reuse the cards, ask the students to remove any adhesive on the back of them. Next, name a letter. Ask the youngsters who have words that begin with the named letter to bring the corresponding cards to the front of the class. Instruct the youngsters to hold up the cards and have their classmates read each word in turn. Then collect the cards and file them for reuse if desired. Continue with the remaining letters in the same manner. Students will get valuable reading practice, and you'll get help organizing your materials!

For a spelling variation, instead of having each youngster hold up his card, have him conceal the word and announce it for the class to spell aloud.

Mandy Bledsoe, Millis Road Elementary, Jamestown, NC

I really liked doing the play!

Thought Bubbles

Take your students outdoors for this entertaining look back! Hold a bottle of bubble solution and a bubble wand as you sit with students in a circle. Tell the group about one of your fondest memories of the school year. Then blow a bubble. Next, pass the bubble solution and wand to the student beside you. Have her share a memory and blow a bubble in the same manner. Continue around the circle as described until each youngster has had a turn. No doubt this activity will become another happy memory!

Randi Austin, Lebanon, MO

Looking Ahead

Kindergarten and first-grade classes pair up for this activity. Plan to collaborate with a teacher at a different grade level (either kindergarten or first grade). Arrange for each kindergarten student to receive a letter from a first grader describing three things he likes about first grade. After the kindergartners talk about the letters with their classmates, schedule a time for them to visit the first-grade classroom. Have the first graders escort the youngsters to their classroom. Ask each first grader to show his visitor his desk or cubby and give a tour of the room. Then serve all the students a snack and lead them in singing familiar songs. It's a surefire way to ease any concerns the kindergartners may feel. Plus, it's guaranteed to boost the first graders' pride!

Katy Hoh, W. C. K. Walls Elementary, Pitman, NJ

Fun Finish

This song is perfect for youngsters to perform during a special end-of-the-year program!

(sung to the tune of "O Susanna")

I'm graduating from [kindergarten].
Aren't you proud of me?
I can read and spell and do some math
And tell a great story.

I'm going on to [the first grade].
I think it will be fun.
But now it is the summertime.
The school year is all done.

I'm so glad now!
Take a look and see.
I'm graduating from [kindergarten].
Aren't you proud of me?

adapted from an idea by Angela Ochoa
E. C. Mason Elementary, Manvel, TX

We are alike because _____

Note to the teacher: Use with "Just Alike!" on page 283.

Thematic Units

Nuts About Squirrels

Home, Sweet Home

What's in this stash of ideas? It's a look at one of autumn's most familiar animals, plus science, literacy, and math reinforcement!

ideas contributed by Laurie K. Gibbons
Huntsville, AL

In a Nutshell

Prior knowledge, reading

Try this fact-filled introduction and follow-up! Cut out a copy of the fact cards on page 294 and place the cards in a container. Tell students that the container holds clues about a secret topic. Then have a youngster draw a card. Read the sentence aloud and ask students to silently guess what it describes. After you share the information on the remaining cards in the same manner, have each youngster tell a neighboring classmate what he thinks the topic is. Then explain that the clues describe squirrels.

To follow up, give each youngster one copy of the fact cards and title card and six copies of the acorn card on page 294. Ask him to color the acorns and cut out the cards. Then have him glue the title and fact cards on separate acorns. Staple the acorn cards with the title card on top to make a booklet. As students review the facts, they'll get valuable reading practice!

All About Squirrels

long tails.

How Sneaky!

Initial or final consonant sounds

To prepare this small-group phonics game, label a paper lunch bag for student reference as shown. Color and cut out a copy of the game cards and mat on page 295. Put the cards in the bag and announce whether the game is for initial or final consonant sounds.

To begin, the players make a pile of 12 brown cubes (acorns). They place the mat and a disposable cup nearby. To take a turn, a player draws a card. If it is not a squirrel card, she names the picture and designated consonant and then puts an acorn in the cup. If it is a squirrel card, she takes an acorn from the cup and puts it on the mat. (If the cup is empty, she takes an acorn from the pile and puts it on the mat.) To conclude her turn, she returns the card. The players take turns until the pile of acorns is gone. Then they count the acorns on the mat and in the cup to determine whether they or Sneaky Squirrel has more!

b
g
n
s
t

Hiding Places

Positional words

In the ground, under leaves, and near their nests—squirrels hide food all over! Invite each youngster to imagine a silly or realistic hiding place for an acorn. Next, have him incorporate a copy of an acorn card from page 296 into an illustration of the hiding place. Then help him use the format shown to write a caption with a positional word. Bind students' work into a book titled "Where Did Squirrel Hide the Acorns?"

Squirrel put one acorn on a table.

Mixed Nuts

Number order or forming words

Squirrels carry nuts in their cheek pouches, but with this idea, students use squirrel pockets instead! For each student, fold up a few inches of a vertical 6" x 9" piece of paper and then staple the sides to make a pocket. Have each youngster write her name on her pocket. Then ask her to draw a squirrel face on a three-inch paper circle and cut out a construction paper copy of the tail pattern on page 296. Instruct her to cut out two ears and paws from scraps. Ask her to glue the ears in place and then glue the head, paws, and tail to the pocket as shown. Then use copies of the acorn cards on page 296 with an option below. Afterward, have each child put her cards in her squirrel pocket for take-home practice.

Number order: Give each student acorn cards programmed with a chosen range of numbers. Then have her arrange the cards in numerical order.

Forming words: Write the letters in *acorn* on separate acorn cards. Ask each child to cut out a copy of the cards and use them to form words such as *an, or, can, car, ran, corn,* and *acorn.*

Mischief!

Characteristics of squirrels

For a look at a squirrel's lively behavior, read aloud *Nuts to You!* by Lois Ehlert. Then arrange for each youngster to do a brown crayon rubbing on the trunk of a tree with a vertical 6" x 9" piece of white paper. Afterward have him illustrate a squirrel on a copy of the tree hole pattern on page 296 and then glue the tree hole to the crayon rubbing. Staple the top of the paper to an equal-size piece of paper. Then ask him to open his project and write about squirrels on the blank paper.

Squirrels have claws.

Fact Cards, Acorn Card, and Title Card

Use with "In a Nutshell" on page 292.

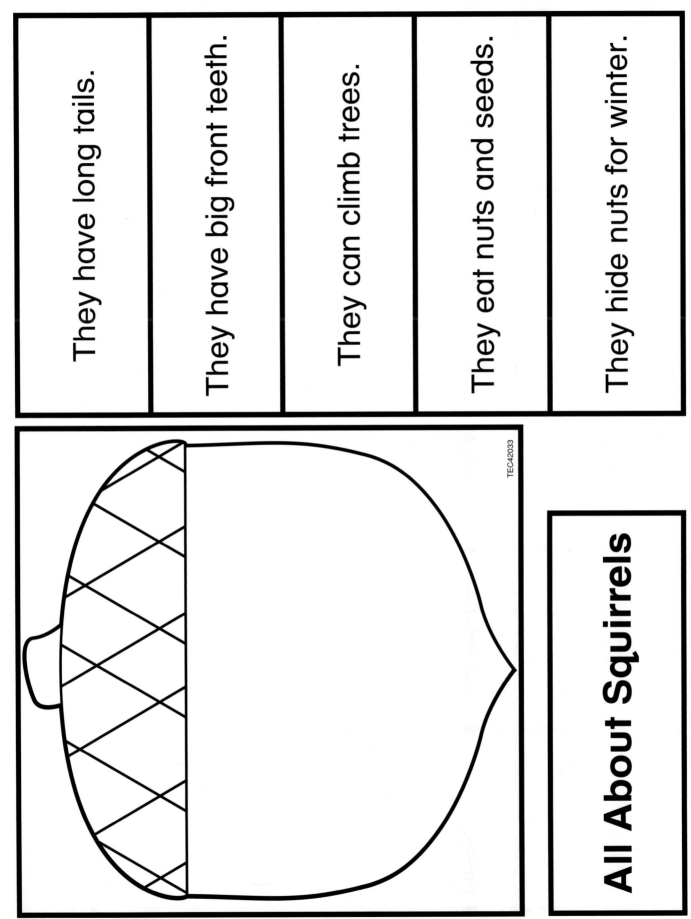

They have long tails.

They have big front teeth.

They can climb trees.

They eat nuts and seeds.

They hide nuts for winter.

TEC42033

All About Squirrels

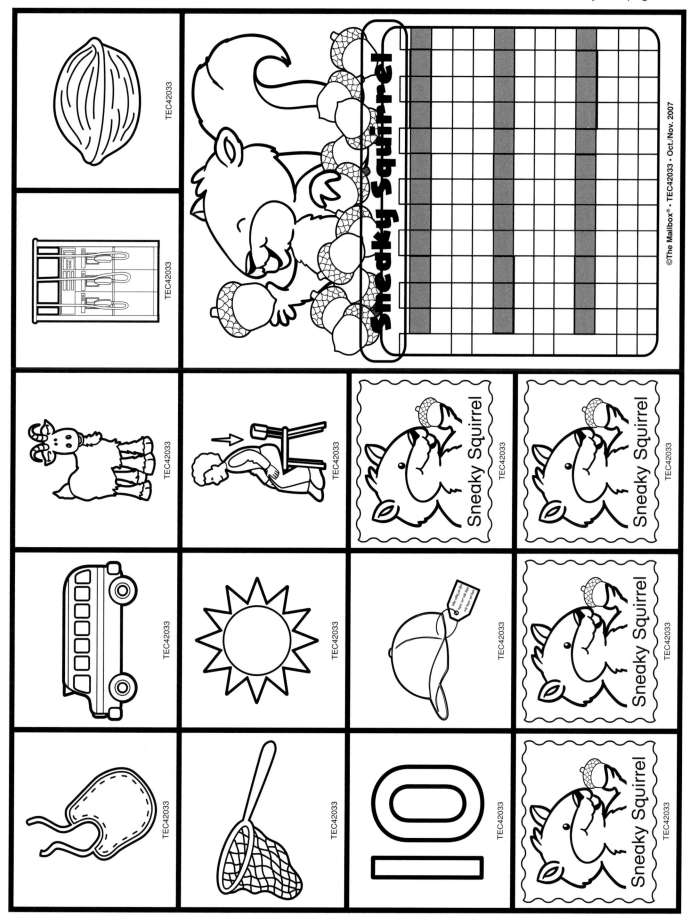

Acorn Cards
Use with "Hiding Places" and "Mixed Nuts" on page 293.

Squirrel Tail Pattern
Use with "Mixed Nuts" on page 293.

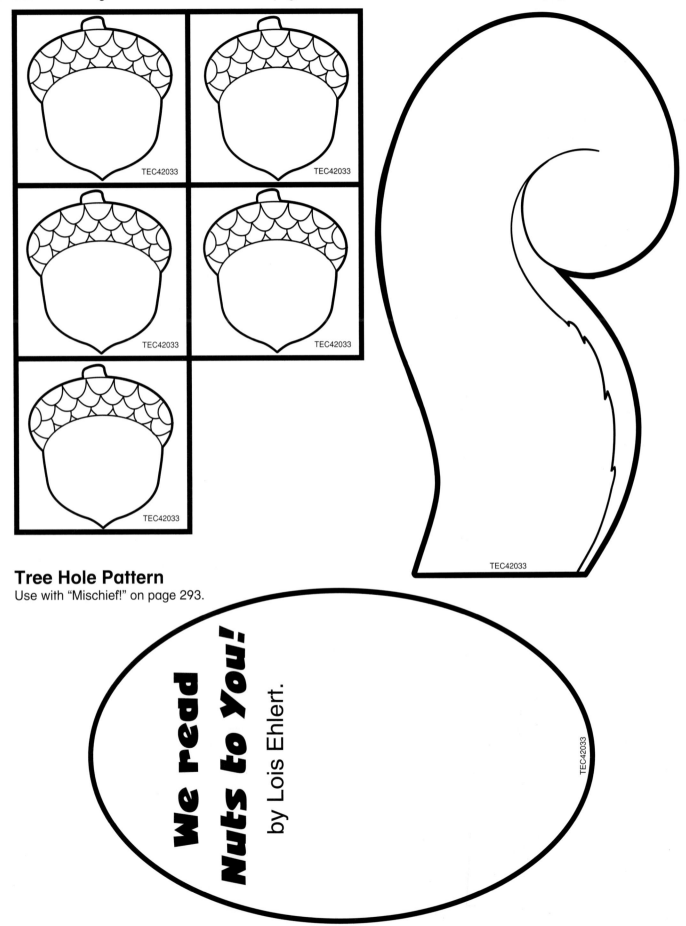

TEC42033

TEC42033

TEC42033

TEC42033

TEC42033

TEC42033

Tree Hole Pattern
Use with "Mischief!" on page 293.

We read Nuts to You!

by Lois Ehlert.

TEC42033

Welcome Winter!

"Sense-ational" Time of Year

Describing the season

Use this language-rich activity to find out what students have observed about winter. Write the word *winter* on a large piece of paper and circle it. Have students name various winter sights. List the sights around the circle and create a web as shown. Then have students describe the sights with sensory words. Use a marker of a different color to write the describing words in the appropriate circles.

Next, give each youngster a large snowflake cutout similar to the one shown or have him make one. Instruct him to refer to the web and write on the snowflake a descriptive sentence and his name. After students complete their work, showcase the snowflakes on a board titled "A Sensational Season."

Laurie K. Gibbons
Huntsville, AL

Frosty Forts

Literacy

Build a variety of skills with this snowy sorting activity. Choose two or more categories of words such as singular and plural nouns or two different word families. Program a supply of white circles (snowballs) with corresponding words, writing one word per snowball. Then scramble the snowballs and stack them facedown. Write the chosen categories on a large sheet of paper to show where students should sort the snowballs.

To complete the activity, youngsters take turns drawing a snowball from the stack, reading the word aloud, and then using a loop of tape to attach the snowball to the appropriate section of the paper. As youngsters attach the snowballs, they arrange them so that each group of snowballs resembles a snow fort. No doubt youngsters will be eager to see which fort is the biggest!

adapted from an idea by Laurie K. Gibbons

Mmmm...Marshmallows!

Math

To give students hands-on skill practice, instruct each child to color a copy of the workmat on page 299. Give him a supply of small white rectangles (marshmallows). Then choose an option below.

Story problems: Have students use the marshmallows to solve relevant story problems, such as "Sarah puts four marshmallows in her hot chocolate. Two marshmallows melt. How many marshmallows are left?"

Odd and even numbers: Ask each youngster to put a designated number of marshmallows on his workmat. Then have him pair them to determine whether the number is odd or even.

Comparing numbers: Pair students and give each twosome several number cards. Each youngster puts a number card on his mug. The student with the greater number puts one marshmallow on his mat and takes the two cards. The youngsters continue with the remaining cards as described.

Laurie K. Gibbons, Huntsville, AL

Mug of Math

Marvelous Mini Marshmallows

Seven is an odd number.

Name Camisha

I lost my mitten!
It is pink. It has stripes. The stripes are purple.

Can you find it?

Lost and Found

Describing words

For this guessing activity, have each youngster decorate a mitten cutout and write her name on the back of it. Then ask her to describe the mitten on a paper similar to the one shown. Collect the papers. Post the decorated mittens on a board titled "Lost Mittens" and letter them for easy reference. Next, read aloud a chosen description and invite students to guess which mitten it describes. After youngsters correctly identify the mitten, reveal who decorated it. Challenge youngsters to identify the remaining mittens in a similar manner.

For an easier version, instead of having students write descriptions, invite each student to secretly choose a mitten, describe it orally, and ask her classmates to identify it.

Ada Goren, Winston-Salem, NC

Bundle Up!

Language

Whether you use this song to transition to recess or to reinforce winter vocabulary for English Language Learners, it's sure to please! Invite youngsters to add motions as they sing along.

(sung to the tune of "Head and Shoulders")

Hats and mittens, scarves and boots, scarves and boots.
Hats and mittens, scarves and boots, scarves and boots.
That's how we dress for the cold and snow.
Hats and mittens, scarves and boots, scarves and boots!

Jackie Lagoni, Children's Campus, Inc., Chicago, IL

Name

Mug of Math

Marvelous
Mini Marshmallows

Note to the teacher: Use with "Mmmm…Marshmallows!" on page 298.

Seasonal Skill Practice
Lions and Lambs

ideas contributed by Ada Goren
Winston-Salem, NC

LANGUAGE
Critter Comparison

Help students understand the well-known saying about March weather with this look at lions and lambs. Color and cut out one copy each of the lion face card and the lamb face card on page 302. Divide a large sheet of paper into two columns. Glue each card at the top of a different column and then post the paper.

To begin, ask students to name words that describe the two animals. Write the words in the appropriate columns. Then explain that people sometimes compare March weather to a lion or a lamb. Guide youngsters to think about how the two types of animals differ, and they're sure to make the connection with wild and mild weather! **For more advanced students,** display the poster throughout March and encourage students to use the words in descriptive sentences. ***Describing words***

loud
scary
roaring
dangerous

soft
nice
quiet
pretty

MATH
Orderly Search

To prepare for this lion hunt, color and cut out one copy of the lion face card and nine copies of the lamb face card on page 302. Back the cards with tagboard. To play one round, scramble the cards and then display them in a row so the back of each card is facing outward. Next, ask a volunteer to use an ordinal number to describe the card he thinks is the lion. Have him point to each card, in turn, from the first card to the named card as his classmates count the cards with ordinal numbers. Then ask him to turn over the named card. If it is a lamb, instruct the volunteer to return to his seat and ask a different student to search for the lion as described. If it is the lion, congratulate the volunteer and invite him to set up the cards for the next round of play. ***Ordinal numbers***

Lion and Lamb Days

On the first school day in March, give each child two small blank cards sized to fit a wall calendar. Have her draw a lion face on one card and a lamb face on the other card. Then ask her to write her initials on the back of each card. Collect the lion and lamb cards in separate containers.

Next, have students determine whether the day's weather is more like a lion or a lamb. Take a card from the corresponding container and instruct the student who illustrated it to post it in the appropriate calendar space. Record the weather as described throughout the month. Then have students compare the number of lion and lamb days and the weather at the beginning and end of the month. ***Recording and describing weather***

LITERACY
Lost Lambs

Use this small-group activity for skills such as word families and vowel sounds. Make a supply of lamb cards (pattern on page 302). Draw a star on each of three cards. On each remaining card, write a word for students to sort. Then put the cards in a container. Write each word-sort category on a separate sheet of green paper (pasture) and illustrate a fence below it as shown.

To begin, the students spread out the pastures. One youngster takes a card at random. If the lamb has a word, he reads it and puts the lamb in the correct pasture. If the lamb has a star, he leads the group in reading any words that are already sorted and then sets the starred lamb aside. Students take turns as described until all the words are sorted. Then they read each group of words. ***Sorting words***

MATH
Paws and Tails

For this partner activity, give each twosome several enlarged lion pawprint cards (patterns on page 302), several cotton balls (lamb tails), and one copy of the recording sheet on page 302 per student. Have the students in each twosome illustrate three chosen classroom objects on their recording sheets. Ask them to measure the length of each object with pawprints and then with lamb tails and record the measurements. After each twosome completes its work, discuss with students why the measurements for the same objects vary. No doubt they'll realize that it takes more small units than large units to measure the same length!
Linear measurement

Lion Face Card and Lamb Face Card

Use with "Critter Comparison" and "Orderly Search" on page 300.

TEC42035

TEC42035

Lamb Card

Use with "Lost Lambs" on page 301.

TEC42035

Lion Pawprint Cards

Use with "Paws and Tails" on page 301.

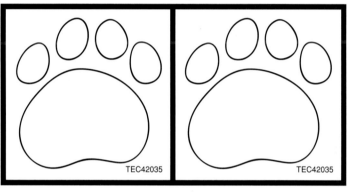

TEC42035

TEC42035

Name _____

How Many?

Lions and Lambs
Recording sheet

Objects			

©The Mailbox® • TEC42035 • Feb./Mar. 2008

Note to the teacher: Use with "Paws and Tails" on page 301.

So Different!

✏️ Write the antonyms.
Use the word bank.

Word Bank

little   dry   girl

stand   down   glad

1. wet _____

2. sad _____

3. big _____

4. boy _____

5. up _____

6. sit _____

Bonus Box: Write sentences about the lion and the lamb on a separate sheet of paper.

Seasonal Skill Practice
Summer

What Happens?

Welcome the warmest season of the year with this simple song! Teach students the verse below. Then lead them in singing it several more times, substituting different phrases for the underlined words. ***Characteristics of summer***

(sung to the tune of "He's Got the Whole World in His Hands")

The [sun shines bright] in the summer.
The [sun shines bright] in the summer.
The [sun shines bright] in the summer.
We're so happy it's summertime!

Suggestions for additional verses:
air is warm, grass grows tall,
crickets chirp, gardens grow

Ada Goren, Winston-Salem, NC

LITERACY

Icy Cold

Use this small-group game to serve up practice with a variety of skills. For each player, tape a paper strip (straw) to a lemonade glass cutout. Set out a supply of white cubes or paper squares (ice cubes). Choose an option below and prepare game cards as described. Put the cards in an opaque container.

To begin, a player takes a card at random. If the card shows a pitcher, she responds as described below and then puts an ice cube on her glass. If the card shows a melting ice cube, she removes one ice cube from her glass. (If her glass is empty, she does nothing.) The players take turns as described for the allotted time, reusing the cards as needed. Then they compare how icy their glasses are!

Beginning sounds and letters: Cut out a colorful copy of the cards on page 306. When a student gets a picture card, she names the picture and the corresponding beginning letter.

Contractions: Color and cut out a copy of the cards on page 307. When a student gets a word card, she reads the contraction and names the two corresponding words.

304

Cool Comparison

Get the scoop on your students' favorite summer pastimes! Write a different summer pastime on each of three ice cream dish cutouts. Post the dishes in a row at the bottom of a bulletin board. Have each student write his name on an ice cream scoop cutout and help him post the scoop above the appropriate dish to indicate which activity he prefers. Then ask students to tell about the display, using words such as *equal, fewer, more,* and *most.* **Data analysis**

adapted from an idea by Ada Goren, Winston-Salem, NC

LITERACY

Dazzling Details

To introduce this sunny booklet, write on chart paper a few sentences about a summer experience, being sure to include descriptive details. After you read the sentences aloud, have students use a yellow highlighter to mark the details. Point out that this information helps readers make pictures in their minds. Next, use the directions below to help each youngster make a sun booklet. Have him include details as he writes in the booklet about a summer experience. Then ask him to mark the details with a yellow highlighter and title the booklet. **Writing with details**

Steps to make one sun booklet:
1. Draw sun rays as shown on an 8½-inch yellow circle.
2. Cut several 7½-inch circles from writing paper.
3. Place a 7½-inch yellow circle atop the writing paper circles. Staple the stack to the illustrated circle as shown.

adapted from an idea by Ada Goren

MATH

The Shade Shop

Give coin counting a stylish twist! Label each of several inexpensive pairs of children's sunglasses with a grade-appropriate price. Place the sunglasses, a mirror, and a supply of imitation coins in a classroom area designated "The Shade Shop." Arrange for a few students to visit the shop at a time. Ask each shopper to choose a pair of glasses to purchase. After she correctly models the corresponding money amount, invite her to wear the glasses for an allotted time before returning them. Then have another group of youngsters visit the shop. **For more advanced students,** ask each student to draw two different sets of coins that equal the designated money amount. **Money**

Ada Goren

305

Beginning Sounds and Letters Game Cards

Use with "Icy Cold" on page 304.

The ice is melting!

The ice is melting!

The ice is melting!

it's	he's	she's	that's
aren't	can't	don't	isn't
haven't	wasn't	hasn't	I'll
I'm	you're	we're	The ice is melting!
The ice is melting!	The ice is melting!	The ice is melting!	The ice is melting!

TEC42037

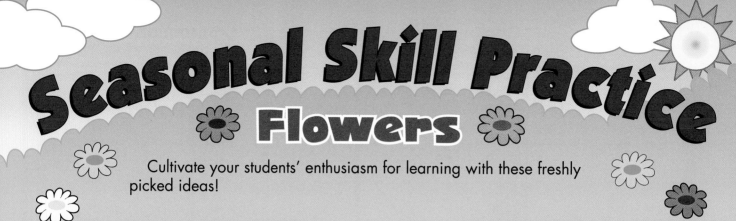

Seasonal Skill Practice
Flowers

Cultivate your students' enthusiasm for learning with these freshly picked ideas!

SCIENCE

Ask and Answer!

To add an entertaining twist to this song, divide students into two groups. Instruct one group to sing the questions and have the other group sing the responses. ***Needs and parts of plants***

(sung to the tune of "Head and Shoulders")

What do all plants need to grow, need to grow?
What do all plants need to grow, need to grow?
Soil and air and light and water,
That's what all plants need to grow, need to grow!

What plant parts do we know, do we know?
What plant parts do we know, do we know?
Roots and stems and leaves and flowers,
They are plant parts that we know, that we know!

adapted from an idea by Telena Hardin, Brilliant Elementary
Brilliant, AL

LITERACY

Super Stems

This sorting activity doubles as a spring display! Label a blossom cutout with a long *e* word and attach a long stem to it. Label another blossom cutout with a short *e* word and attach a short stem to it. Program several leaf cutouts with long *e* and short *e* words, writing one word per leaf. Glue a flowerpot cutout to the free end of each stem. Then gently fold down each flower, concealing its stem behind the blossom.

To begin, have students read the word on one blossom. Then have them say its vowel sound repeatedly as you slowly unfold the flower to make it "grow." Have students identify the word on the other blossom and make that flower grow in the same manner. Post the flowers. Next, invite a student to take a leaf, read the word, and use reusable adhesive to attach it to the appropriate flower's stem. After students sort the remaining leaves as described, have them read each group of words. **For an easier version,** instead of words, use pictures whose names have the featured vowel sounds. ***Long and short*** e

Courtney C. Pate, Burlington, NC

308

Clever Clocks

Give skill practice a kid-pleasing twist with this easy-to-adapt center! Write a different digital time on each of eight cards. (For easy management, program different-colored cards for different skill levels.) Place the cards and student copies of page 310 at a center. When a student visits the center, she takes a card. She reads the time and writes it above the first clock on her paper. Then she draws clock hands to show the time. She continues as described to complete her paper. *Telling time*

Diane L. Tondreau-Flohr, Kent City Elementary, Kent City, MI

READING

Growing Tale

The predictable text of this science booklet is sure to help young readers' skills blossom! For each child, staple five half sheets of white paper (5½" x 8½") between two construction paper covers to make a booklet. To begin, give each child a copy of page 311. Have him write his name in each blank and then cut out the title and sentence strips. Next, instruct him to glue the title strip to the front of his booklet and each sentence strip to the bottom of the correct page. Then have him illustrate the cover as desired and illustrate each page to match its sentence. *Reading sentences with repeated text*

Diane L. Tondreau-Flohr

MATH

All in a Row

For these flower-arranging ideas, give each child a copy of the flowerpot mat and flower cards on page 312. Ask each student to write her name on the flowerpot. Have her color the mat and flowers and cut them out. Then choose an option below.

Beginning subtraction: Make a spinner like the one shown. Then have each youngster put her flowers on her flowerpot. Next, ask a student to spin the spinner and announce the number it lands on. Instruct each youngster to take that many flowers from her flowerpot. Then have students name the number sentence modeled.

Problem solving: Read aloud a Posy Problem (see page 312). Guide students to determine the answer by arranging flowers on their mats as described. Then confirm the correct answer.

adapted from an idea by Jennifer Runkle, Perrysburg, OH

Flo's Flowers

Follow your teacher's directions.

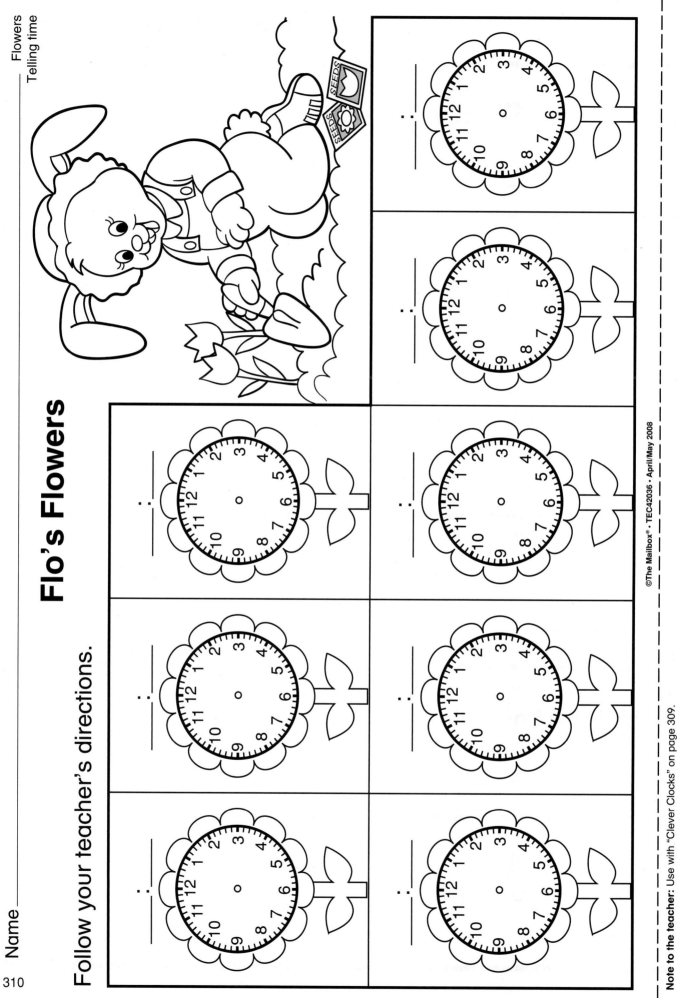

Note to the teacher: Use with "Clever Clocks" on page 309.

The Flower That

Grew

_____

This is the **seed** that _____ planted.

1

This is the **water** that rained on the **seed** that

_____ planted.

2

This is the **sun** that shone on the **seed** that

_____ planted.

3

This is the **flower** that grew from the **seed** that

_____ planted.

4

This is the **flower** that _____ picked!

5

Posy Problem A

All the flowers are in a row.
The orange flower is first.
The yellow flower is last.
The purple flower is not beside
 the orange flower.

In what order are the flowers?
(orange, red, purple, yellow)

TEC42036

Posy Problem B

All the flowers are in a row.
The red flower is first.
The purple flower is before
 the yellow flower.
The orange flower is second.

What flower is last?
(yellow)

TEC42036

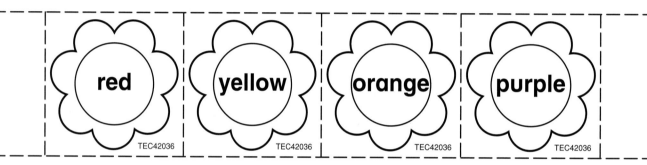

red
TEC42036

yellow
TEC42036

orange
TEC42036

purple
TEC42036

_____'s Pretty Posies

©The Mailbox® • TEC42036 • April/May 2008